JAAP STAM
HEAD TO HEAD

JAAP STAM
HEAD TO HEAD

JAAP STAM
with Jeremy Butler

CollinsWillow

An Imprint of HarperCollins*Publishers*

First published in Great Britain in 2001
by CollinsWillow
an imprint of HarperCollins*Publishers* London

© Jaap Stam 2001

1 3 5 7 9 8 6 4 2

A CIP catalogue record for this book is
available from the British Library

The HarperCollins website address is: www.fire**and**water.com

ISBN 0-00-711708-6

Typeset by Mick Sanders
Printed and bound in Great Britain by Clays Ltd, St Ives plc

Picture acknowledgements
All photographs supplied courtesy of the following:

Actionimages p1 bottom, p4 bottom left, p6 top left and bottom left,
p7 top left and top right, p8 bottom inset; **Allsport** p2 bottom right;
Coloursport p1 top left, p2 bottom left, p5 top and bottom; **Empics**
p2 top left and top right, p3 top, p4 top, p5 middle, p6 bottom right,
p7 bottom, p8 top inset; **John Peters Photography** p1 top right,
p3 bottom left and bottom right, p4 bottom right, p6 top right,
p8 main picture

Career statistics provided courtesy of
Ivan Ponting (Manchester United),
and Jörgen van der Meulen (PSV).

Contents

Acknowledgements

My thanks to the following for their support during my move to United and in the writing of this book: My wife Ellis and my children Lisa and Megan, my parents, Henk Van Ginkel, Tom Van Dalen, Mike Williams and Jeremy Butler.

CHAPTER ONE

PSV'd off

Signing for Manchester United was going to cost me more than one million pounds!

It was a frightening thought which flashed continually through my head as I sat in the warmth of my taxi and gazed out at the hordes of red-shirted supporters making their way into Old Trafford. The pre-match anticipation was building in the air and the chatter of excited voices was drowning out the patter from the hot-dog stands and programme sellers.

But despite the awe-inspiring mass of the Red Army, all looking forward to the clash with Leeds on that May afternoon in 1998, I couldn't take my eyes from a clock attached to the side of Old Trafford's outer wall, with the word 'Munich' etched underneath its white face.

With hands frozen at the time of the tragic plane crash in February 1958, which stole the careers of so many of Matt Busby's famous Babes, the clock and its part in the United dynasty struck a chord with me. How I longed to become part of the legacy that ill-fated team had bequeathed; how I wanted to wear the same badge that had once graced the shirts of Denis Law, George Best and Bobby Charlton.

I was desperate to become a part of the new breed of United heroes, and keen to play a role in pushing United to the next goal on tireless manager Alex Ferguson's list of priorities – that of European triumph.

Already he had moulded a team containing the likes of Eric Cantona, Mark Hughes and Steve Bruce, storming to two domestic League and FA Cup doubles in the process. Now Ferguson was rebuilding. He'd developed a sensational squad of youngsters and saw experienced players like myself as integral to his grand plan.

Such fabulous talents as Ryan Giggs, Roy Keane and David Beckham were heading the effort to make the Red Devils into European Champions for the first time since 1968 and, crucially, they were backed by the mental toughness and exceptional natural ability of Danish keeper Peter Schmeichel. These were exciting times at Old Trafford and I needed to be involved in the glory.

But whether that was going to happen was down to me and my principles. The silverware and kudos that could light up my career and fill my trophy cabinet were now within touching distance. Unfortunately the cost was amounting to a small fortune, due to the hard-nosed commercial practice of PSV Eindhoven.

Alex Ferguson's readiness to pay out nearly £11 million meant that I should have collected a cool £1.65 million, as a clause in my contract guaranteed me 15 per cent of my next transfer fee. PSV wanted more out of the Reds to cover their contractual obligations to me, while United were ready to wash their hands of the deal after refusing to increase their bid.

That meant I was the only person who could save the transfer, but I didn't like having to waive my contractual rights in order to secure my move from PSV. By the time I climbed out of the taxi at Old Trafford on that spring afternoon and strolled into the directors' entrance to watch United play their final home game of the campaign, a deal had been agreed between the two clubs, but it was still possible for me to pull the plug.

In the event, if I'd turned around and headed straight for the airport I would have missed out on one of the greatest footballing fairytales of all time. You see, I wasn't born into the game like many superstars have been in the past.

Unlike some of my current Manchester United team-mates it wasn't a case of having my boots cleaned, meals prepared and days mapped out for me. I guess you could say I learned the hard way. After a spell of national service in the army, I'd come late into the professional game and was an unknown outside my native Holland until my career started to gather impetus as I approached my middle twenties.

Yet within a year of being ushered through the door at Old Trafford as the world's most expensive defender, I was lucky enough to become recognised as a key component of one of the greatest ever club sides.

A European Cup snatched in the most dramatic fashion on an inspirational night in Barcelona in May 1999 remains one of football's most amazing moments and undoubtedly it is the highlight of my career to date. Also, in the space of just 11 rarefied days, I pocketed an FA Cup winner's medal and helped to clinch a Premiership title. It was the stuff of which little boys don't even dare to dream – especially little Dutch boys.

As if that was not enough, the following seasons saw the arrival of the Inter-Continental Cup and another two titles to add to my growing list of honours, all taken as United swaggered around the world playing an exhilarating style of football of which I was proud to be a part.

But all that was still to come. That day back in May 1998 I had to decide whether to take a leap of faith and give up the money in order to ensure that my fantasies had a chance to become reality.

The first time I became aware of Manchester United's interest in me was during my second season at PSV in 1997, when I was 25. Stories started to filter through the football grapevine that the Reds' manager, Alex Ferguson, had taken a shine to me.

In hindsight, clearly, he had been growing concerned about a back problem which was causing his star defender Gary Pallister to miss matches. By that time I was just starting to be noticed in my home country, where I'd been lucky enough to enjoy a meteoric rise after spending the early years of my footballing life with local amateur team DOS Kampen.

I had trained part-time at my hometown club, where my dad had made his mark playing on the right wing. Actually there were better players than me at Kampen and really I thought my chances of playing for a top side had passed me by.

I was known as Little Jaapie until the age of 16 before a growing spurt necessitated a shopping spree by my mother. Then, with my size on my side, things started to look more promising and the more I battled it out with abrasively physical opponents, the more compliments were whispered in my ear.

In 1992, when I was 20, FC Zwolle asked me to turn professional. I accepted eagerly and actually I looked more at home in a higher league where being big and strong was an advantage. My manager at the time, former Dutch international Theo de Jong, moved to Cambuur Leeuwarden in 1993 and I went with him for the modest sum of £100,000 and then followed him to Willem II two years later. I switched from full-back to the heart of the defence and started to justify my latest fee of £400,000. Just six months later PSV came knocking with a £1 million bid which was happily accepted and before too long I was representing my country.

Thus, in the space of four years, I had gone from playing for free to pulling on the famous orange national team jersey and lining up for one of the top clubs in Holland. Naturally, I was loving every minute of it.

As I was on something of a roll, it might have been expected that when Alex Ferguson made his first approach in 1997, I would have been keen to move at once. But I refused his tempting offer and instead pledged my immediate future to PSV.

The thought of playing for United was mouth-watering but I'd signed on at Eindhoven only recently and had much to learn. I was still adapting to life in the often harsh spotlight which goes with playing among the elite in Holland and adjusting to performing at international level.

Though confident about the way my game was improving, I was happier for the moment in my familiar Dutch surroundings than I felt would be possible if I transferred to a massive club like United. Quite simply, I didn't want to uproot at that time and there was also a debt to pay to my employers. They had taken a gamble on signing me and to walk out within months of joining would have compromised my values.

So what if the opportunity might never land on my doormat

again? The bigger concern for me was improving my football education, which was still in its infancy at the highest level. There were plenty of pitfalls just waiting to announce themselves rudely to me when I least needed to look foolish – in the big games.

Confidence is a massive part of a successful player's make-up and while I have a strong self-belief, it could have shattered in the face of a few unfortunate errors while thrust headlong into the limelight.

The decision to snub United was already made when PSV came to me with the offer of a new, improved deal in Eindhoven in late 1997, but I wasn't going to knock back the money. The board promised when I joined that if I produced the kind of performances my international team-mates where posting, there would be a seat for me at the bargaining table.

They were true to their word, although the fact that United were sniffing about must have quickened the offer. I signed an improved deal, tying me to the club until 2003 in return for a rise in wages that put me on level pegging with my Dutch national team colleagues.

Although at the time I was delighted to put pen to paper, it was a contract I regretted signing all too soon. Little did I realise that PSV would quickly turn it into a whip to crack at the first hint of a transfer request.

That came during my second full season at the club, in early 1998, and by then I had become a wanted man. Dutch clubs have a habit of selling off their prize assets, home-grown or otherwise, as a way of keeping the balance sheet looking good. It's a policy which denotes acceptance that they find it difficult to hold on to their better players.

From Johan Cruyff, through Ruud Gullit and Marco van Basten, to Patrick Kluivert and Ronaldo, the raw talent has always been honed before being sold on to the highest bidder. It's a system which keeps the accountants and players happy as the top stars are often keen to leave after proving themselves in the Dutch league.

Soon they realise that the dreams and ambitions every player harbours are simply not fulfillable at that level. While producing some of the world's best players, and not so long after Holland supplied the European club champions – Ajax in 1995 – the industry has moved on at such pace that the game in my homeland, without the big money from TV, has fallen behind that in other European nations.

This wasn't just my view, as PSV team-mates Philip Cocu and Arthur Numan also wanted to move to a bigger stage, as did our coach, Dick Advocaat. But while Advocaat was allowed to finalise his terms with Glasgow Rangers and Cocu was granted a move to Barcelona, my escape route was blocked.

All the more frustrating was the fact that my request to leave was placed much earlier than those of Cocu and Advocaat. I came clean with club officials and let them know I wished to move on, having achieved everything I craved to win in Dutch football by helping to complete a League and Cup double in the same season as being named Player of the Year.

Like all footballers I yearned to lift the top trophies and like other Dutch stars, I knew I had to get out my passport and book some flights if this was to happen. Also I felt I couldn't improve any more at PSV because we didn't have a team that would help me do that.

For Dutch standards our side was outstanding, with talented players like strikers Luc Nilis and Gilles de Bilde, and keeper Ronald Waterreus along with other international stars such as Wim Jonk, Numan and Cocu. But we didn't have a team that would take Europe by storm and challenge for, let alone win, a truly big prize.

By then I had some rather tasty options to consider, with top clubs in England and Italy making me aware that I would be more than welcome if I fancied a change of scenery.

One of them was Chelsea. Now, if you are a Dutch player there is one man you always answer the phone to, and that's Ruud Gullit. He was in charge at Stamford Bridge when my phone jumped to life and he introduced himself.

'Hi Jaap, I was wondering if you'd be interested in meeting with me?' he asked. 'I'm building a team here at Chelsea that I think can go and win the biggest prizes in football and I would love you to be part of that. Are you interested?'

Chelsea and PSV might have been talking for some time for all I knew – a player is always the last to be told in these situations – but a fee certainly hadn't been put in place and Tom van Dalen my agent hadn't been notified when Ruud rang.

The conversation went on at length about how I fitted into his long-term plans for a successful team, and I must admit it all sounded very interesting. Ruud's flattering words certainly captured my imagination.

The Premiership was a league I longed to join and, with Gullit of all people keen to champion my cause, already I was looking forward to the excitement of life in London. I put the phone down and smiled as the prospect of playing for Chelsea started to sink in.

There was no doubting Gullit did an excellent job of selling his club to me and the temptation was there for me to pack my bags straight away. All it needed now was for the two clubs to agree a fee and the wheels would be set in motion, but the second call never came.

I wasn't in tears though. Joining Chelsea was an interesting option, but there was always a preferred choice for me in England, and that was Manchester United.

Getting there, despite the Reds' interest, was not going to be easy. Already I was beginning to suspect that the battle to leave PSV was going to prove lengthy and frustrating. Although PSV had said I could leave the club, a move which would benefit my future, the way negotiations were going made it pretty clear I would not be moving in the near future, if at all.

It was an extremely difficult period for me, one that is still painful and frustrating to talk about. I had such good times in Eindhoven, but PSV's attitude throughout the dealings tainted my feelings for the club.

At first, in March 1998, the president Harry van Raaij was adamant about not selling me. 'Jaap, you've done well here for us. We need you in the defence. You are very important and we don't want to let you go,' he told me.

'But I want to move on and progress my career. Now is a good time to go,' I fired back. 'You're letting a lot of other people move, why not me?'

'You've only just signed a new contract. Why did you sign it if you were about to leave us? Does everything you said when you agreed to sign it mean nothing?'

Now I was fuming. 'I didn't sign it because I wanted to stay here for the rest of my career. I signed it because it gave me a wage that was fair and you know that. That's why you put it in front of me.'

'Well we're not going to let you go and that's the end of it.'

Van Raaij told the press the same. My recently signed contract was raised again and again. I could understand their point of view, but it upset me greatly that it had been used against me when it was meant to be a reward for performing well in the season we had won the Dutch double.

'You want to go only because other guys are going,' the president said. 'It's like rats and a sinking ship.' 'Not quite,' I snapped back. 'It's only since I asked to go that other people have been granted transfers.'

I thought that was it for me. I couldn't see the club changing its mind after being so firm with me, but with a couple of months left in the 1998 season there began to appear the first indications that a move might be on the cards. Out of the blue, Van Raaij went on television and revealed that the club's head had been turned by the money on offer.

Tom told me then that he thought PSV were finally willing to let me go.

Van Dalen said: 'Van Raaij gave a television interview and said that if somebody comes with an offer of 50 million gilders they would have to listen. As soon as you start mentioning figures, that's when the business starts.'

It was a huge relief and a major disappointment at the same time. I knew I could leave at last, but what club was going to pay the equivalent of £15 million for a defender? It didn't put everyone off and Gullit was as good as his word by making an inquiry. There was also interest from Italy with Juventus and

Inter Milan making contact. However, nobody was prepared to put up the money and at that point United hadn't made a move.

I was aware of their interest already, though, thanks to a meeting with Sir Alex Ferguson, or just plain old Alex Ferguson as he was then, a few weeks earlier. The get-together was set up through Van Dalen.

'Some other clubs were showing interest in Jaap and he had not spoken to anyone at United at that time,' Van Dalen explained later. 'I said to Alex: "Jaap wants to hear from you that you want him." I think Alex was in France with his wife for a small holiday and on the flight back to Manchester he stopped in Amsterdam. I arranged a meeting in an apartment near the airport because we didn't want to go to a hotel in case there was even the remotest chance somebody might see us.'

While the meeting may have been technically against the rules, it happens all the time and has become an accepted part of the game, but I had to keep everything under wraps so that PSV didn't find out about the unofficial approach. That morning I was training but was in a rush to get away so I could drive up to Amsterdam. 'Are we going to do something today?' Arthur Numan asked me. 'I can't. I promised my wife we would go and look at some garden furniture,' I lied, hating to trick an old friend.

Soon I was in my car heading north and I don't mind admitting that the nerves were playing up as I waited for the man who could make my dreams come true to enter the room. I tapped my foot nervously and tried not to let the sweat build up on the palm of my hands. The concern about making a disastrous impression weighed heavily on my shoulders. Although I knew it was just an informal chat, I felt I was pitching for the most important job in the world.

Finally he strode in confidently, smiling and ready to make an impact on me. 'Jaap, I want you to play for Manchester United,' he barked. 'I want you to command our backline and help us take that extra step and win the European Cup.

'It's a dream of mine and I'm convinced we can do it. We just need a few extra faces in, a bit more quality and it'll happen. That's where you come in. I know you can adapt to the

Premiership and you've already shown with Holland that you're capable of doing it at the highest level.

'Have confidence in me because I'll do everything to make it happen. Let me sort out the details. All I need to know is: do you want to play for Manchester United?'

He needn't have bothered with the question. My eyes must have told him all he needed to know. Of course I did.

Ferguson's passion was overwhelming and he was even clever enough not to try the hard sell on me. We spent most of our 30 minutes together just talking about what my plans were and how he'd like me to come to Old Trafford. There was no discussion about positional play, contracts or money, I guess he just wanted to meet me and see what kind of guy I was.

I was afraid he might have left the room with the wrong impression, though. At that time my English wasn't very good and understanding his thick Scottish accent proved a problem for me.

I sat and listened intently, just trying to decipher his words behind a creased brow and with a brain that was working overtime. Struggling to take in what he was saying probably helped me get the move though. Ferguson must have been convinced there and then that I wouldn't be a troublemaker in the dressing room. With the way I was listening he must have got on his flight back to Manchester believing I'd hung on his every word!

To be honest, though, if Ferguson walked into the room thinking he needed to persuade me, then he was wrong. My mind was already made up and if we had just sat there, staring at each other blankly for 30 minutes and not saying a single word, then it wouldn't have mattered.

As a kid I had watched the Reds on 'Match of the Day'. I had taken to their style of play and history immediately, even dreaming about running out at Old Trafford to a mighty roar. I was desperate to play for Manchester United and couldn't wait for the nod to pull on the famous red shirt.

'The whole situation was obviously frustrating Jaap,' Ronald Waterreus has since admitted. 'From the day United were rumoured to be interested in him, he said he would like to go and play in Manchester.

'We knew from the first months with us that he was good enough to do that. His first game was against Heerenveen, on an icy pitch. He played at right-back and couldn't keep his feet. Initially we thought the club had made a terrible mistake, because he didn't look a player.

'But within a matter of games you could see the quality in his play and soon the rest of Europe was watching him. What didn't help Jaap a little later was that his close friends like Arthur Numan were being allowed to leave. He felt he should be given the same opportunity.'

If only it was that easy. With PSV finally ready to play ball, the work behind the scenes really started to take off.

Frank Arnesen handled a lot of transfer dealings and contracts at PSV during my time there. Certainly he was busy helping the board to find a new home for me, and a big pot of cash for the club.

It didn't take him long to realise that United's biggest rivals, Liverpool, were willing to pay the most for me as they tried to bring in a central defender to shore up a defence that had received a lot of criticism in the English media. Frank was also keen to tell me about the salary benefits of heading off to Anfield and was disappointed when I had to sit him down and explain money wasn't the key to my move. Success was.

Van Dalen has admitted since that the Merseysiders gave up on their bid to sign me after hearing about my desire to play for United.

'Liverpool were seriously interested,' he said. 'They were prepared to pay Jaap better wages than United as at that time the Manchester club had a limit on what they wanted to pay players.

'When I discussed the financial situation with chief executive Martin Edwards and Ferguson, they were worried that the wage structure might be a problem as regards getting the deal done. But Jaap simply wasn't prepared to talk to other clubs.

'I spoke once or twice with Peter Robinson at Liverpool and he said that after what he had read in the papers there was no point in making an offer because Jaap was so keen to go to United. He told me that Liverpool might be able to pay even better wages than United but as the boy only had United in his mind, there was no point in talking further.'

So I never spoke to Liverpool personally and in the end they found Sami Hyypia to fill the role they had planned for me. He's certainly proved he's worthy of holding one of the key positions at such a big club. Not many people knew about him when he signed from my old club Willem II, and there must have been a few scouts going through their records to find out how they missed him.

Sami's the perfect defender for English football. Big and strong, dominant in the air and quick into tackles, and you only have to look at his brilliant display against Barcelona in the UEFA Cup last season to see he is capable of controlling the best strikers in the world. That day my Dutch team-mate Patrick Kluivert never got a look-in.

But Liverpool were never in my thoughts. In April United entered the race to sign me and I knew where the next stage of my footballing fantasy was going to be played out. All I had to do was sit back and wait, and boy did I wait!

PSV wanted me to talk to a few Italian clubs, but I didn't even ask which ones, as I had no intention of playing in Serie A. The style of the football over there just doesn't interest me. I love following games with goals galore, whereas in Italy it's all about clean sheets punctuated by the odd goal.

Also I didn't fancy spending more time than was necessary away from my family. I'd heard that in Italy a lot of clubs locked their players away in hotels for several days before games. That didn't appeal much and neither did the feedback I got about the lack of everyday privacy from some of the Dutch players plying their trade in Italy.

I preferred England, where the action was. So for me it was United or bust.

CHAPTER TWO

Patience rewarded

Sitting in the dressing room at Eindhoven, jealous pangs hit me as I heard team-mates talking about signing for great clubs like Barcelona and Rangers. There's no-one bigger than United, where Ferguson had made it clear I was wanted, and now I was desperate to make the switch.

While the likes of Cocu and Numan were getting their wishes and walking about with smiles on their faces, I was left waiting for calls from Van Dalen to discover the outcome of his latest meeting with the PSV board. Time after time, his calls didn't bring the news I longed for.

My mental state wasn't helped by the president Harry van Raaij talking to the press on a frequent basis, while I was unable to express my side of the story. I couldn't talk about the deal due to a clause in the contract.

'He's just signed a contract and now he wants to go,' the media were told in no uncertain terms. 'Why did he sign that if he didn't mean to honour it? I don't understand how his mind works.

'We gave Jaap everything he asked for and now he repays us by demanding to go so he can earn even more money. He will get 15 per cent of any transfer fee. We want £15 million for him, it's no wonder he wants to leave. He's being greedy.'

Maybe it slipped the mind of Van Raaij that PSV were, in fact, driven by the gilder at that point. It was amazing how quickly they had changed their mind about making me stay as soon as they saw the number of noughts on the offers ploughing out of the fax machine.

Luckily my relationship with Advocaat didn't change. He was leaving in the summer to take over as manager at Rangers and understood what I was going through. I spoke to him about it a couple of times and he helped ease my concerns by joking with me. 'If I could get you for £5 million I'd buy you myself,' he said.

I've been in contact with him since and he knew it was difficult for me. There was a lot of pressure, but our relationship never changed. The other guys in the dressing room were also fine with me as a lot of them were in the same boat. There was a plethora of players leaving and it would have been rather hypocritical for anyone to get upset.

But although it would be easy to deny it, it's difficult to claim that the transfer talk and the negotiations several senior players were having with new clubs didn't have an effect on our league form and we finished the season poorly by limping into second place.

We didn't play to our potential in the closing stages and when it was time to put in a late spurt to claim the title, we flopped, losing two and drawing one of our final three games.

That brought a mass of criticism from the Dutch media. They didn't need much persuading to blame PSV's collapse on too many players thinking about money and changing clubs. 'PSV would have won the title if no-one was leaving' they reckoned.

But no-one bottled tackles in case it cost them a mega-money move; no-one ducked out of headers or played at half-pace. There was as much desire to win in our dressing room as there had been the previous year when we lifted the double. But just as my game had dipped, it was possible that other players were finding the same problems. At any level, if you don't play to your full potential you get found out – and it's fair to say we were caught out.

While our season was struggling to stay on a winning track, my future was hanging by a thread after United's chairman, Martin Edwards, travelled over to Eindhoven but was given little encouragement to do a deal. He left with little more than a general idea that United would have to pay over the top for my services and it was then just a matter of how far he could exceed his transfer budget.

It was a nightmare time for me as I had hoped that Edwards' arrival would finally end the weeks of uncertainty. I kept telling myself that United must be keen to close the whole messy affair if they were willing to jet in for a face-to-face meeting.

So when my agent rang to tell me talks had broken down I just sat distraught by the phone with my head in my hands. It was tearing me apart with my head in the clouds, my feet firmly on Eindhoven soil, and my whole world in turmoil. I was determined not to let it affect my home life, though. My wife Ellis has always been fantastic in helping keep my life chained down with some sense of normality, and she was a massive support. She isn't football crazy and we rarely talk about the game when I'm at home. We might discuss how I played after a big match, but that's only for a couple of minutes and then we'll discuss our daughters, or what's on television, or even how the dog is!

At that time, having a solid home life was crucial to stop me tearing out what was left of my hair as things just got worse, with United having bid after bid blocked.

Another helping hand came from the frequent phone calls from a certain Alex Ferguson: 'Don't worry, son. We want you and I'll come and sort out this mess,' he told me. 'Be careful, though. Don't go dropping bombshells all over the place. Let us deal with PSV and next season you'll be a United player.'

Ferguson implored me to get in the right the state of mind for the forthcoming World Cup finals. It was typical of him. He knew exactly what I was thinking and could tell that the worry about where I would be playing football the following campaign was preying on my mind.

The situation reached gridlock when my agent phoned once again with a call that left me speechless.

'Jaap, PSV have told me United have upped their bid for the last time but it's still not enough. PSV want more and United are ready to walk away. There's only one thing that can make a difference now – your clause.'

Tom spelt it out. The only person who could save the deal was me, by dropping my rightful claim to 15 per cent of the fee. That clause had been put in my contract only to make up for money PSV couldn't find for wages at the time, so I felt the cash was owed to me. I told Tom I would ring back.

I turned off the television and sat quietly for a minute. I'm a realist and I knew when I put pen to paper on the deal that I was never going to get the full amount, but to be told to drop all that money was a shocker.

In the end I had no choice. It was sacrifice time and I picked up the phone, dialled Tom's number and didn't even bother with the pleasantries before simply uttering: 'Tell them I'm ready to become a Manchester United player'.

This wasn't about the cash; this was what I wanted, a move to a bigger club; and not just any old big club. I was off to Manchester United.

The whole affair left a bitter taste in my mouth. PSV had tarnished my reputation with their continual sniping about how negotiations had been held up because of my greedy demands – and that hurt.

I was entitled to hold out for the cash my contract stated should be mine. After all, I'd worked hard to get to a position where I could go to the negotiating table with some weight behind me, whereas only a few years before Ellis and I had made do with the low wages of second-level football in Holland and been quite happy with our lot.

Now here was a chance to secure the future for my family by planting a huge lump of cash into investments to protect us when I hung up my boots. Here I was, giving up that windfall and being called greedy by a club that was trying to deflect claims of gluttony from its own door.

In the end PSV got everything. They paid £1 million for me and two seasons later they sold me for £10.75 million – a tidy profit boosted by my £1 million-plus contribution from the cash I left behind.

After being given the go-ahead the whole deal was wrapped up in a matter of days. I flew into Manchester on the morning of the Reds' last home game of the season against Leeds and, to my surprise, I was met by Ferguson himself.

Only hours later he had a big game for which to prepare and there must have been a hundred and one other tasks he needed to sort out on a match day. That, to me, was typical of the man.

It didn't take long for me to be impressed with Old Trafford and the amazing atmosphere that grand stadium generated. I'd never seen a game in England and I was blown away by the noise and the passion that spilled from the lungs of United's fervent fans seated around me.

Back home I'd been in games in which 50 per cent of the action was played out to a murmur, with fans only getting worked up when a goal was on the cards.

Buoyed by this immense first impression of the club, I was looking forward to completing the formalities of a medical the next day. All thoughts of turning around and heading for home, which had entered my head fleetingly during that taxi ride to the ground, were now firmly dismissed.

After being a transfer target for the past six months, I knew what my value was and it didn't take long to agree terms. Soon after sailing through the medical I was a United player.

It was a huge relief to finally sign on the dotted line and commit myself to the club I felt would help me reach my true potential. The sense of belonging engulfed me, and it was hard to take in how far I'd come from my amateur days in such a short space of time. The liberation from the months of transfer squabbling made the whole occasion so fulfilling and satisfying for myself and Ellis.

Of course, I wasn't leaving Manchester without another audience with Ferguson, and my new boss arranged for us to meet him for dinner. He is a consummate professional and we spent the evening working out the little things the public don't think about. It wasn't win bonuses we discussed at the table, simply where to find a house and how to settle into life in Manchester, important matters to any family.

I returned home to play in the semi-final of the Dutch national cup against FC Twente. My confidence was high after agreeing my move, and it needed to be with the English press turning up in droves to see how good I really was.

If any of them wanted to an opportunity to start picking holes in my game, I gave them the perfect news copy by knocking in an own goal as we won 2–1. It was a cross from the left side and their striker was on my right shoulder so I dived in to cut out the ball. It crashed off my leg, against the underside of the bar and into the net to leave me wondering what the headlines would be back in England.

The final was even worse for me as PSV were outclassed by Ajax and lost 5–0. The match was played on a roasting hot day, Ajax were at their peak and there was absolutely nothing we could do.

Ironically my relationship with the club was also at its best since the whole transfer episode exploded, and I really enjoyed the meal PSV put on for the players at the end of the season. All the staff and their wives were invited and it was a great way to say goodbye to all the friends I had at the club.

Amazingly, the president pulled up a chair next to me at the dinner and started to make small talk.

'If you struggle at United, you'll always be welcome back here,' he told me.

CHAPTER THREE

Humbling the critics

A lot was said about my first few months in English football –
with very little of it complimentary.

From the outside, my life must have seemed perfect as I
prepared to join up with United for the first time in July 1998.
We were meeting in Norway for a pre-season tour which, for me,
offered a chance to get to know my new team-mates.

But those first few heady and hectic weeks of my United career
made it impossible for me to settle into the kind of routine that's
indispensable if you want to produce your best football.

I was joining up with the Reds just weeks after the heartbreak
of being knocked out of the World Cup on penalties at the semi-
final stage. and before leaving home in Holland there were more
emotional moments for me.

My wife, Ellis, was pregnant with our first baby and if we had
allowed nature to take its course, our daughter, Lisa, would have
been born while I was in Scandinavia. We had some tough
decisions to make. Footballers don't get paternity leave so
something drastic had to be done. I needed to be on that
Norwegian tour to make the right first impressions.

I was so lucky to have an understanding wife in Ellis, and as
we discussed the situation there seemed to be only one way out,
and not a way I would have preferred. But there was an
overwhelming need, so Ellis was induced and little Lisa was born
two weeks early.

Even then I had just five days to share the magical moments
before jetting off to join up with my new team-mates and make

a start on what promised to be the most exciting part of my life. But before I left I treasured each day spent with my new family, trying to take everything in and consign it to memory, so I could recall it at a later, more private date.

As any new father would know, the first few days are chaotic, stressful and absolutely wonderful – I loved every minute of it. So much so that leaving was a massive wrench. I wanted to turn the taxi around and head back home for one more final look at Lisa, but I had to be strong, frustrating as it was, and head to the airport with my mind in tatters.

Leaving Ellis at that time was far more distressing than I would have liked. She needed me with her in those vital first few weeks after the birth, and I felt frustrated at having to fly the nest when I knew my real duties lay at home, comforting my wife and enjoying the thrill of fatherhood for the first time. But, as always, she simply accepted the fact I had to go, making it easier for me to leave when a few sympathy-inducing words would have been enough to tempt me to stay.

The sun in Norway brightened my mood and I went straight to my room when I arrived at our hotel, waiting until dinner before plucking up the courage to say hello to my new workmates. I was lucky that my Dutch international team-mate Jordi Cruyff was at the club, along with another of my countrymen, Raimond van der Gouw. The pair helped introduce me to everyone.

It was a whirlwind time with new names and faces to remember, as well as jokes and puns, firstly to understand and then to laugh at. Jordi must have tired of explaining why things that, to an outsider, seemed bizarre, yet could send a group of grown men into fits of giggles.

There was no grand announcement or a queue of players walking over to shake hands as I sat down to eat in the hotel restaurant for the first time. Conversations would just spark up as people walked by or sat down around me.

Some of the inquisitive guys like Ryan Giggs and Ole Gunnar Solskjaer were keen to find out about me, the World Cup and Dutch football, but I wasn't exactly desperate to hold court. I'm a big guy but it's not in my character to turn up and take over the place with jokes and stories. Don't get me wrong, I'm no shrinking violet, but I'm a lot more comfortable getting on with my own thoughts and tasks rather than being placed in the spotlight and told to entertain.

Luckily, the over-abundance of pranks associated with football dressing rooms was missing – a welcome relief, I might add – and I went to bed with a smile on my face.

Training the following day was carried out in the same relaxed mood, with Brian Kidd taking us for some possession work, then a short game and a bit of shooting practice in the fresh Norwegian air.

It was similar to the training regimes I was used to and that helped ease my fear of making a glaring mistake or giving the ball away too much on my first day. Footballers are great for casting judgements and it's important to impress from the start and get the confidence of your team-mates. Then, once they know you can play a bit, you're easily accepted.

Knowing I had to perform set me on edge as I slipped on my new training kit and listened to the banter in a language with which I was still not 100 per cent comfortable. I'd played in a World Cup but still needed to prove myself here, and I knew it.

We started with a warm-up before starting a few drills, and it was then that I realised the class of the company around me. It wasn't a case of ball-juggling or fancy-dan tricks that really caught my eye, but the simple things. The United players just did them so well, dazzling with their short, sharp passing routines and getting the ball under control with one touch.

Ask anyone in the game and they'll say you need to build a foundation to win a match and that comes from doing the basics correctly. Obviously that had been drilled home by Alex Ferguson. Every pass was accurate and every touch immaculate.

As I have said, at that time my English wasn't the best and I was struggling to follow the instructions as Kidd bellowed them out, but even more tricky was the names of some of the lads.

Spotting the likes of David Beckham, Andy Cole and Ryan Giggs wasn't hard. These players were well known around the world, but when I was put in the same team as a young defender, John Curtis, for a short-sided game I realised I was in trouble. I just didn't know the poor guy's name. Sure, I'd been introduced to everyone the night before, but you try remembering every name when 30 are chucked at you in one go.

So for an embarrassing five minutes I just had to pretend that I didn't want the ball off him, that was until I spotted the back of his boots and saw 'Curt' written on them. I wasn't sure if it was his name, nickname or boot manufacturer, but at least now I could call for a pass.

It turned out that John, who is now with Blackburn Rovers, doesn't have a nickname and was never called 'Curt'. He was magnanimous enough not to raise the point, though, and I was grateful to him for that.

Actually, speaking a bit of English was probably a hindrance in my first days at United. In the heat of a training session the United staff and players forgot I was a dictionary short of words. At one point Kidd tried to set up a new drill and shouted at me to spin off my marker to cover another runner to the near post as a cross came.

It all went horribly wrong as Solskjaer darted in and scored and I was nowhere to be seen. I'd been picking up Andy Cole and, embarrassingly, worked out that I'd got the wrong man. I just looked at Kidd glumly, before admitting: 'I guess you didn't mean Cole then?'

The lads were trying to hold back their laughter as they trooped back to their positions to carry out the drill again. Sniggering aside, the United lads seemed to ease me into their circle quite smoothly; then again, with all their skills on display, maybe they were trying to play tricks on me on the training pitch, with attempted nutmegs and step-overs, without me even realising it!

There were two games on that tour with the first, against Brondby down in Denmark, scheduled for 31 July 1998, the day after I arrived. At such short notice, I was happy to play my part as we collected a clean sheet, cruising to a 6–0 win against the Danish champions.

I thought it was going to be a tough night as I had to keep the Danish Player of the Year, Ebbe Sand, under control and, having not done much stamina work since the World Cup, I was slightly worried about my fitness. But I came through it okay and the game did wonders for my confidence at an important time.

Certainly it was good to get a match as I wanted to settle in and try to win my place for the season as soon as possible. That task was going to be easier with Gary Pallister having left to join Middlesbrough. He had been magnificent for the club and in the match against Leeds, which I had watched towards the end of the previous season, he did a great job alongside David May. The organisation at the back was excellent and I could see his experience shining through.

Everyone thought I was brought in to replace him and that was my hope as well. I felt that with my European experience from my time at PSV I would be capable of stepping into the hole he left, but I was never given a guarantee of first-team football by Ferguson. I had to win my shirt.

My next chance came a couple of days later back in Norway where I found myself lining up against Brann Bergen. Despite many Norwegians traditionally supporting Liverpool, there were plenty of United fans around to welcome me as we cruised to our second win of the tour with four goals and, more importantly for me, another clean sheet as I settled in alongside Ronny Johnsen at the back.

After that match I was allowed home for two days to see my family and made the most of my time by playing the proud father with relatives and friends before the dreaded moment of separation came around once again.

Things are supposed to get easier second time around, but it wasn't the case for me as I sat on the plane to England looking at photos of Lisa, Ellis and me. On doctors' orders, the two of them couldn't board a plane for another three weeks as it wasn't safe for our baby to fly so soon after the birth.

Once in Manchester I checked into the plush hotel surroundings of Mottram Hall in Cheshire, on the outskirts of the city, and for the first few days life was good as I adapted to a fresh schedule and the sights and sounds of a new country. Everything came so fast with a whole new lifestyle to adjust to as people and places slipped from being novel to familiar, but it didn't take long for the boredom factor to creep up and start bugging me.

Initially hotel life is great as you don't have to cook or do the dishes but after a week the dullness crushes your brain. The menu, which once looked so appetising, suddenly felt bland. I could recite the dishes off by heart and, with the diets modern footballers have to stick to, there was not a lot of choice.

Also I was stuck alone for long periods in a small room with nothing to think about apart from what my young family were doing back home. I ran up a huge phone bill as a result.

I would have gone out of my mind if it wasn't for the frequent invitations to dinner at Jordi's house. That got me out and about and stopped those dreaded four walls closing in on me and bringing on a severe bout of depression. I spent a lot of the week at his house and he was almost my crutch as I tried to adapt to everything life was throwing at me.

Even driving was proving difficult. I'd not grown use to keeping the car on the left side of the road at that time, and there must be some drivers in Cheshire still living with the nightmare of a near head-on collision with a mad Dutchman. I didn't get out much though; even if I had felt capable in the car I didn't know the city well enough to enjoy a day out.

United were good to me when I needed them at this point. I wasn't left constantly to stew in the hotel and if I needed a lift anywhere I just called the club. I'm an independent character, though, and felt capable of getting myself around most of the time.

I kept myself going by counting down the days until Ellis and Lisa joined me. Every morning I woke up was a night I could chalk off my calendar until, finally, I was at Manchester airport waiting at the arrivals gate with an excited look in my eyes.

It's hard to put into words how much their arrival brightened up my life. But, like me, Ellis soon became frustrated with hotel life, especially as it is not the best place to be when you have a very young child. We wasted no time in contacting estate agents so that we could begin looking for a new home, thus relieving the boredom of sitting in our suite watching television in a strange language. Unfortunately, without going into tiresome detail, it took three months before we could move in.

By that time, I had grown to like Manchester despite worrying about the culture change of moving from my house in a small Dutch town to a big industrial city. I had been told it was a grim place, with grey buildings, where days without rain were rare, but when I turned up the sun was always out and the city was a thriving place to be. There's a lot of green areas around Manchester, too, so don't let the cynics and the stereotypes fool you.

Even if the place had looked like something from my worst nightmares, it wouldn't have put me off signing for United. They are the biggest and best club in the world and if you really want to make it to the top in football there are few better places to be.

I've heard of players refusing to come to England unless a London club wants them. They wanted to soak up the cosmopolitan lifestyle and enjoy the trappings of life in a capital city, and I'll admit to being surprised at players with that kind of attitude. They're cutting out the opportunity to win things – and that's why most people start out in the game.

Manchester may not be as big or fashionable as London but there are few clubs you could join that afford so many chances to add a bit of silver to your trophy cabinet. And anyone visiting the city will probably be surprised by the sophisticated feel it has acquired in the past few years. Designer shops and chic bars have set up home in the heart of the city as money was pumped in to revitalise the area ahead of the 2002 Commonwealth Games. The cash is being spent well and Manchester is emphasising its stature one of the top spots in the north of England for a day or a night out.

To me, just as important as the regeneration is the fervent way football is followed by people in the area. It's amazing to realise that the clubs here are so close together. Liverpool and Leeds are only 30 miles along the motorway and lower division sides like

Stockport, Bury and Bolton are minutes away from the centre of town.

The one thing about Manchester that did surprise me was the condition of United's ageing training ground, The Cliff. We've since moved to a state-of-the-art complex at Carrington, but when I first arrived and slipped my car between the red-brick walls in Salford it was a massive shock.

For a club of United's finances and stature to train at a facility with one grass pitch and use weathered buildings which suggested the architecturally arid 1960s came as a real surprise. Certainly, the feel of the place was touching on the archaic. What I had left behind at PSV was space-age in comparison, and I could not quite believe United had turned out so many fantastic teams from this primitive base.

But I'm not a particularly flash person so it didn't bother me, and in a way the old wood in the changing rooms had a lot of character. I knew when I changed that legends of the calibre of George Best and Denis Law had sat in the same seats and shared jokes while hanging up their shirts on the same pegs. And certainly I didn't hear any of the other players complaining.

What did astonish me was the one pitch. In the summer it was fine and firm, but once the rain came you'd have a better chance of making the ball run smoothly over a ploughed field. There was nothing the groundstaff could do as we worked on it day in, day out, and churned up the mud to such an extent that in the middle of winter it was a case of playing 'spot the grass' rather than 'spot the ball'.

I'm not moaning, though. Really, it didn't bother me. I spent my amateur days in Holland playing on similar surfaces and learned when not to dive in and slide from the penalty spot to the dead ball line. But when I thought about modern training techniques and how high the standards have been set, it was amazing that United could not only keep pace with other clubs, but also top the pile.

It astonished me to think that legends like Bobby Charlton and Ryan Giggs had been able to hone their talents on that kind of surface, and the fact that they did was a testament to the coaching advice they received in their formative footballing years.

There was an indoor facility at The Cliff but the playing surface was more like a Subbuteo pitch with a concrete underbelly rather than the stud-taking lush surfaces we enjoy now at Carrington. To make sure we did not pick up injuries it was used only for gentle games on a Monday after a match, or the odd spot of running.

But even the best training facilities in the world couldn't have killed off the thought that all the disruption to my life over the past few months meant it was going to be hard to start my United career in peak form.

I needed time to adapt to my surroundings, the English game, my new team-mates and the thousand other things that were going on. But time was something I accepted would not be on my side. Already I had fallen victim to the English media's habit of knocking players down simply because there was a big fee involved in the move.

While I was helping the Dutch side to a semi-final place in the World Cup, and a position as one of the best four teams in the world, my game was being picked apart by papers and pundits alike, with many giving the thumbs-down verdict.

Spurs' director of football, David Pleat, said I looked like 'Bambi on skates' during his analysis of the World Cup. Well, I'm sorry if you didn't think too much about me, Mr Pleat, but to be honest I didn't even know who you were until someone told me about your comments. Even now I wouldn't be able to point you out if you were stood in an empty room, admiring my treble-winning medals.

I guess Pleat was judging me on one game at that point, and you can't form a firm opinion on just a single match. When he was a manager, would he have bought a player after just seeing him just the once? I don't think so.

The money from doing media work must be good, though, as it seems everyone is at it at the moment. Alan Hansen made a living out of moaning about poor defending on BBC's 'Match of the Day' and is now proclaimed as one of the best pundits.

However, his opinions don't hold much sway in the United dressing room. The game has moved on so much from when he was playing, and I doubt whether he'd enjoy the same reputation as a superstar if he was 28 again tomorrow and told to pull on a pair of boots.

He was superb in his day and he has a decent amount of medals to prove he could play, but everything is quicker in the modern game. You don't have the time to think any more.

At the speed we play now, getting our timing right to catch players offside is much harder, and delivering the perfect pass is tricky as space is closed down within seconds.

Obviously he enjoys what he's doing, but even when I've retired I would never slaughter another player. It's too easy and cheap to do that.

I didn't help build a defence against the pundits when Nicolas Anelka scored in my first competitive game for United in England, the Charity Shield meeting with Arsenal on 9 August 1998.

You could say, literally, that I got off on the wrong foot as the French striker raced outside me to score. Maybe I could have stopped it. I was running with him and I didn't stick my leg in to halt his charge, but I wasn't in a position to do it. I would have had to go left leg first and that would have given him a chance to skip past me.

The game finished 3–0 and, apart from that one moment, I walked off feeling I hadn't done that badly on my first match on that massive Wembley pitch. But picking up the papers the next day I soon realised that the rest of the country would not be allowed to perceive my performance in the same way.

Opinion columns and match reports were picking my performance to bits and claiming I wasn't worth the money. I was never simply Jaap Stam. I was the £10 million defender and soon it became apparent that in the media's eyes someone of my value shouldn't be making any mistakes at all.

At times it felt like I was being hung by the price tag even though the fee had nothing to do with me. I always saw the figure as a sum of money to get me over here, not a valuation on my true ability.

Even now I think it's a crazy price for a club to pay for a footballer. We are not worth that kind of that cash, but that is something I have no control over. I didn't say United had to pay that money. PSV did, and I wouldn't have cared if I'd been on a free transfer.

Unfortunately, the infamous fee was being used as a tool by the media to try and pull me apart. The press didn't know what I could do or how I could play and, rather than waiting to find out, the journalists jumped straight in and highlighted the things I wasn't doing well. Once headlines like that started hitting the streets it was impossible for the fans not to believe some of it was true.

Of course, English fans didn't know me or my game and were totally unaware of my strengths and capabilities; they just read the views of the experts and feared the worst. I'd been through all this before in Holland; it happens whenever you join a new club and need to prove yourself. But the Dutch press didn't bare their teeth as ferociously, and showing my talents under this weight of expectation was a new experience for me.

Luckily I have a strong character and that's a massive advantage when dealing with situations like that. Just imagine going to work and reading about your supposed faults in the company newsletter and listening to people snipe behind your back. The most obvious thing to do is to ignore the criticism but, when the attacks are sustained, it's hard to put it out of your mind. Deep down I knew the tide would turn, though. I had faith in my ability and so did those closest to me at Old Trafford.

Why would they have spent that huge sum on me if Alex Ferguson was not convinced I could become a bedrock of the United defence? Of course there were times when I needed to hear something positive so I did speak to people at the club, like Brian Kidd and Alex Ferguson, men whose opinion I valued.

'Don't worry,' Ferguson reassured me. 'I wouldn't have spent all that money on you if I thought you were crap. Just get on with your own game and do the things you've always done. That's why I brought you here. Those vultures in the papers will get on your back, but stick with it. You'll soon have them eating out of your hand.'

My new team-mates were also a massive help without ever realising it – by leaving me to my own devices. There was never a posse set up to try and boost my game by being over-complimentary, and even though some of them must have had doubts, no-one criticised me.

The contact between us was exactly the same from day one. I guess they had seen it all before and knew I needed time to take the giant leap that playing for United entails. I've been told great players have failed to find their feet once the pressure of running out at Old Trafford and the demand for success kicked in. Also, I've heard Ferguson talk about players who had arrived at the club in the past and just couldn't deal with the pressure.

I was determined not to fall into that category and, meaning no disrespect to those guys, they hadn't gone through the experience of playing in a World Cup for their country. That had already given me the confidence that I could perform on any stage.

One of the reasons I had such a strong conviction that everything would fall into place was the fact there wasn't that much wrong with my game at that point. It was true that I needed to adjust myself to the speed of the play and the high tempo during a match, plus the game was a lot more physical than I was used to in Holland. There was also the factor of playing against better players week in, week out.

But I did change one thing – when I was in possession I figured out my options quicker. At home I was used to having the time to cradle the ball with my foot while looking around for the next pass.

It didn't take long to realise that in the Premiership I wasn't going to be able to enjoy that luxury. The game here is so fast that you need to know where your next pass is going before the ball comes to you. If you hang on to it for too long you'll be under pressure with strikers diving in from all angles and chasing what, in Holland, would be considered a lost cause.

One option I didn't consider as a way to improve was watching old video tapes of my game. It's something I've never done. I hate seeing myself on telly, even if it's just a quick after-match interview.

When I was playing at PSV, my dad would always tape my games even if he was planning to watch the match live at the stadium. When I went home he'd want to see the game and I'd have to insist we turned the video off. He couldn't grasp the fact that I didn't want to watch it all over again, despite hearing me constantly rolling out the old line of 'I was there, I played the game and know how it went.'

Still, I have to say my parents have been an enormous help throughout my career and I'm glad they didn't see the strain I was under after my move to England. Their grip of the English language was not brilliant and, I am thankful to say, they were unable to read what was being written about me. Even if my parents had seen it, I know exactly what advice they'd have given me. The same solid logic has been passed on throughout my career and it has worked well.

'Just do the best you can, that's all you can do.' It had been drummed into me constantly from the day football became important to me. It was a great policy and was one that flicked through my mind as I looked in the mirror the day after my lowest point in those early moments – another 3–0 defeat by Arsenal, at Highbury this time, in September.

The game was shown live on Sky. It was my first League outing in front of the cameras and I knew I hadn't played as well as I could. The critics were bound to have a field day, but in that match I'd worked hard and could tell my reflection in the mirror that I'd given it my all.

In the week around that Arsenal game I felt the settling-in period was pretty much over and that the only thing affecting my play was the pressure I put on myself to try and prove so many people wrong.

Once my first two months had passed, in which time there were eight games, including a defeat of Liverpool and a draw with Barcelona, I started to play with real confidence and my abilities began to shine through.

Before long the papers changed their tune and this one-time flop was winning the odd man-of-the-match award and finding some kinder words in ink. That gave me a colossal sense of satisfaction as I sat back and read those same erstwhile detractors admit, no doubt through gritted teeth, that I was actually doing well.

Unlike them, I never had any doubts. I knew the facts and I was confident things would change. It was just going to be a matter of time.

CHAPTER FOUR

Make mine a treble

When you step into a dressing room where the likes of David Beckham, Ryan Giggs and Roy Keane are chatting casually before a game, you know there is a fantastic chance of taking three points. And if you have that feeling before every game, it's a fair assumption that the odd trophy could be winging your way come May.

So, after joining up with my new team-mates, I felt my first season in English football could hold some successful times for me, but I never dreamed I would finish the year celebrating a treble.

When I put down my knife and fork after my first pre-match lunch of the season before the Charity Shield, I decided to set some goals for the coming year, and for me the main prize was the League. You want to win that in every country in which you play.

A title is proof that you picked the right club and were good enough to play in the best team in your new country. I felt that getting such an achievement behind me in my first season would ensure that any doubters would be put in their place.

It wasn't going to be easy. Arsenal had taken the title the previous season with a brilliant late run which caught United by surprise. They managed to pick up momentum while other teams were struggling to keep pace and the accomplishment of Arsene Wenger's team was not to be sniffed at.

We needed to match their spirit, and we did. We grew in belief as each game passed, with close shaves turning into something of a regular occurrence. But whereas teams which are destined to fall short tend to struggle to grab that crucial goal, or perhaps lose that game which they shouldn't, we always seemed to come up trumps. Even when things didn't go our way, often we managed to get back into the game and grab an equaliser or a winner. Upsetting teams at the death started to become our forte.

David Beckham struck in the third minute of injury time to earn a 2–2 draw with Leicester City on the opening day of the League season to set the trend. And there was only a minute left when Dwight Yorke's header secured victory at Charlton, helping him on his way to a remarkable tally of 29 senior goals.

In addition, there was a remarkable defeat of Liverpool in the fourth round of the FA Cup. They led through Michael Owen's strike just 180 seconds into the match and our treble dream was dying until first Yorke, and then Ole Gunnar Solskjaer, scored at the end to snatch an amazing win.

That kind of defiant play bred confidence in our game, which transferred itself on to the biggest club stage of them all in the Champions League. It's a superb competition where you face the top teams in the world and test yourself at the highest level.

There are a lot of mind-games to overcome as well, but we were lucky at United. Where some teams would have been crushed by reputations before walking out on to the park, we were strong in body and mind.

That was down to the mentality of the players Alex Ferguson had amassed rather than stirring, Braveheart-style team talks. Of course the gaffer strolls purposefully into the dressing room before a game and makes his point, urging us to remember tactics and look out for runners. But by then Gary Neville and Roy Keane will have been on our backs anyway, making sure everyone is desperate to win. The fact that we might lose is never mentioned.

'C'mon boys, this is it now,' Neville will yell. 'We can't let this bunch of tossers turn us over. Have you seen what they've been saying about us in the papers? Let's dick 'em.'

The teams we faced in Europe were made up of football's most inspirational and talented souls, but I felt we had one of the strongest line-ups in the world, too. It boiled down to a matter of working hard for each other and enjoying the fruits of our labour.

The Champions League group games went well for us and even though we came second behind our eventual final opponents, Bayern Munich, we didn't lose a game and finished as top scorers in the competition at that stage, with 20 strikes in six games.

We opened with a comfortable qualifying round defeat of Polish side LKS Lodz before being drawn in a tricky group alongside Barcelona, Bayern Munich and Danish side Brondby, a team I had faced in my first game for United during pre-season. Poor Brondby must have been sick of us as we thrashed them 6–2 at their ground and then stuck five past them at Old Trafford. Still, they did enjoy a creditable win over the Germans with two goals in the last three minutes to seal a 2–1 win before bowing out.

Our group games began with a remarkable 3–3 draw against Barcelona at Old Trafford. We got the perfect start when goals from Ryan Giggs and Paul Scholes put us 2–0 up, but Sonny Anderson pulled one back before Rivaldo tumbled at my feet, despite the fact that I didn't touch him. I did stick my foot out for the ball but never caught him. I was sickened by the way he went down to cheat the referee. To my utter amazement the official was fooled and Giovanni scored. Beckham's free-kick got us back in front but another spot-kick was awarded, after Nicky Butt handled and was sent off. Luis Enrique converted that one to earn Barcelona a valuable draw.

'The referee was a shocker,' Alex Ferguson claimed later. He was dead right.

Then Munich were lucky to nick a point off us in the Olympic Stadium on September 30. We had gone one behind before goals from Yorke and Scholes set us up for a superb win at a venue where the Germans are rarely beaten, but then Peter Schmeichel made a terrible error and handed them a point. The game was in the last minute when they won a long throw-in and as it was chucked towards the near post I got ready to leap and head clear.

Before I could get airborne I felt someone diving on my neck and I guessed Peter had come to collect the ball. He made up the ground okay but missed his punch and the ball sailed over us. Teddy Sheringham's desperate attempt to clear under pressure from Elber succeeded only in sending the ball into our net.

We were so deflated when the final whistle went. We were so close to a win that would have allowed us to ease into the next stage of the competition and had seen it snatched away. Everyone, including Peter, knew he was at fault, but we don't start pointing fingers over mistakes like that. He hadn't done it on purpose and the fact that he was so unusually quiet after the game was proof enough that he felt bad about it. It would have achieved nothing to give such an experienced man a verbal hammering. We knew we could still get through – it would just be harder.

Dwight Yorke and Andy Cole really came of age as a partnership as we drew 3–3 in the Nou Camp in November. The pair nabbed all three goals, and we finished second in the group after being held to a 1–1 draw by stage winners Munich at Old Trafford in our last game. Barcelona were out, a major boost for us.

A 2–0 win in the first leg of our quarter-final against Internazionale of Milan was earned on one of David Beckham's best nights for us in his wide role. Astoundingly the Italians left him in space time and again near the right touchline to whip in his radar-guided crosses and twice Dwight Yorke cashed in with coolly taken headers.

The result looked good but the win didn't come easily. We were under tremendous pressure at the end and Schmeichel produced a wonder save to deny Ivan Zamorano before Henning Berg cleared Francesco Colonnese's shot off the line in a dramatic finale.

That meant the hard work was already done when Paul Scholes' late goal levelled in the San Siro to send us into the semis. Inter had even brought back Ronaldo for that game but he wasn't fully fit and faded well before the end after adding some early sparkle to their play.

Javier Zanetti hit the post before Nicola Ventola scored in the 63rd minute, but we held out until Scholes struck with two minutes left to kill the tie.

It was after beating Juventus in the semis that we really believed we would win the Champions League. It wasn't just the fact that we knocked out one the world's most famous sides, it was the way that we did it.

After all, Juve were in the driving seat after drawing 1–1 at Old Trafford in the first leg. That night they had taken the lead through Antonio Conte's early goal at the Stretford End and enjoyed a huge slice of luck when Teddy Sheringham's diving header was ruled out when a linesman flagged very late.

Unlike the previous occasion when the two clubs had met at Old Trafford, this time United were mainly in charge and we gave ourselves a lifeline in stoppage time when Ryan Giggs rammed a drive into the roof of the net.

Still, when the Italians took an early two-goal lead in the Stadio Delle Alpi on April 21, we had to produce the impossible and score at least twice without conceding again.

Through sheer grit and a refusal to give up on our dreams, we achieved a miracle in sealing a sensational result at one of football's most famous fortresses. It was made all the sweeter for me by the fact that we had managed to deny Italian international Filippo Inzaghi his moment of glory after he had netted twice after a mere 11 minutes.

I simply can't stand the way the guy cheats his way through a game and the circumstance that I was marking him at the time when he scored his pair did not help. Admittedly I wasn't picking him up when he scored with a far-post header for the first, but his second was a fluky effort that spun up off my leg and looped over Peter Schmeichel.

In the event, the fact that they struck so early was an advantage to us as we always felt there was enough time to come back. If they had scored their second after an hour it might have been a different story.

We had been in tricky situations so many times before, so when I looked up and saw there were 70 minutes to go I was still calm. There was no sense of panic in my brain, and as I tried to rally my team-mates I could tell they felt the same way. Our mental strength had an effect on the Italians, I'm sure of it. They are used to sides coming to their ground and rolling over after going 2–0 down; most teams would shut up shop, concede possession and hope to avoid a hammering. Not us. Everyone in a red shirt still wanted the ball, we all wanted to get forward and no-one was hiding.

Beckham was still trying to find the space to curl in a dangerous cross, Giggs was striving to charge down the left flank, while Keane, Yorke and Cole were chasing every ball to hustle black-and-white-shirted men into mistakes. I could see the sense of purpose in our play and I think that unnerved Juventus. Our attitude spelt out to them our conviction: 'If you can score two, so can we!' That was the self-belief we had.

Certainly the timing of our goals helped, with our captain, Roy Keane, getting us back into the game with a storming header after 24 minutes. Keane had been booked earlier, a caution which ensured he would miss the final, but the setback served only to spur him on to play one of his best games for the club.

It was an amazing insight into the strength of his character. Others might have gone to pieces with thoughts of missing the biggest match of their lives reverberating around their heads.

I can remember Paul Gascoigne being reduced to tears during the 1990 World Cup semi-final against Germany in similar circumstances. But Keane just stepped up a gear to make sure his team-mates still had something to look forward to. His actions that night highlighted vividly the camaraderie that existed, and still exists, in our dressing room. It is one of the key factors to the success United enjoy.

Yorke really set the cat among the pigeons by adding a second ten minutes later and we knew that if the scoreline stayed at 2–2 then we were through. For most teams that would have meant sitting back and soaking up the pressure by filling our box with bodies. That's not Manchester United's style, though, and as the home crowd whipped itself up into a frenzy of intimidation, we went for a third.

It was a strategy Ferguson backed at half-time.

'This game is yours if you want it,' he barked. 'You've got the upper hand now and although they're still dangerous, only you can lose it. Make sure we keep it tight at the back. Jaap, don't allow Inzaghi to run freely, and if we do have to play offside, make sure it's perfect. If in doubt, stay with the runner.

'But just as importantly, keep going at them. They're not used to it and don't like it. You can see they're unsettled by Cole and Yorke and if you stick at it another goal will come,' he urged.

The tactics worked a treat as Juventus could not get into their attacking stride and were fearful of the damage our strikers could do if given a bit too much space. Their worries were well founded as Dwight and Andy combined with only six minutes left to send Cole racing in for the remarkable winner.

At that point the Italian side seemed to lose their heads as they realised the game was over and the Champions League was once again a distant dream for them. You could see the little kicks off the ball, the sly shirt-pulls and skin-pinching, and one of the worst offenders was my international team-mate Edgar Davids.

The midfielder is a born winner. I know from experience just how much he hates losing – especially when his side is 2–0 up and expecting to coast to a final. Just like the rest of the Juventus players, he had been vocal in telling us exactly what he thought as the game petered out.

We were even subjected to a snub at the final whistle as several of our opponents refused to shake hands as they wandered off the pitch. The worst of it was to happen away from the sight of the cameras, though, in the tunnel.

Davids chased after Beckham and got right into his face before firing an angry volley of abuse at him. David kept his head and pushed the Dutchman away as other United players jumped in to try and calm the situation down and get Davids away from Beckham. All we wanted to do was celebrate and as soon as we got Becks into the dressing room the door was slammed shut and the Italians' anger was firmly locked outside.

I guess the whole event took Beckham by surprise as he didn't react. Perhaps, also, it was the start of the new-found maturity which emanated from him during that season. The campaign had started with so-called supporters burning effigies of him outside West Ham's ground, as what seemed like the whole of England wanted him beheaded for his kick at Diego Simeone in the World Cup quarter-final against Argentina. As if being sent off and having to watch the national team go out on penalties wasn't enough, he took some disgraceful abuse from the stands.

David just ignored it. It couldn't have been easy and there were times when I really felt for the guy. But if there had been a problem with his reaction before, it certainly didn't resurface on that magical night in Turin.

People have said it was an amazing game to watch and I can reveal that it was just as much fun to play in. Winning through to the final in such an unexpected manner was a superb achievement.

Getting the result in Milan in the previous round was probably just as professional a performance, but the stakes this time were so much higher and that was what made it so special.

Ferguson told us afterwards that we had given him the best performance of his career in management. Anyone who stepped into the dressing room could have worked out how much it meant. The walls were soaked in champagne and the cheers echoed throughout the empty corridors in the underbelly of the stadium. At that point we didn't care how our celebrations were rubbing up the Italians the wrong way, considering their appalling lack of sportsmanship after we took the lead in the match.

It wasn't just the Juventus players; their fans were just as bad and it's always like that in Italy. We were warned before the Milan game that supporters would provoke us in an attempt to upset us so their beloved team could get a result. We knew they would throw coins and oranges at us when we took throw-ins, and we discussed how to deal with it.

'There's no point in reacting,' Ferguson advised us. 'If they see one sign of weakness they'll jump on you. That will be a lot worse than having a hundred oranges smack you in the back.'

Personally, I feel that people need to try a lot harder than lobbing coins, oranges, even plastic bottles of piss in my direction if they want to provoke me. I tend to block it all out and just concentrate on the game.

At times I just have to chuckle at it, especially on the way to the ground. I always have a laugh when I see 40-year-old supporters foaming at the mouth, giving me a 'wanker' sign as I look out of the coach window. It's comical to think that a grown man still believes it's going to make any difference to me.

That kind of thing happens quite a bit in England, and when we go to Leeds and Liverpool the fans start giving us stick the moment we step off the coach, but it's a lot worse in Italy. Coin-throwing isn't normally a problem in England, where I think people respect their opponents a lot more, but in Italy it's common and something we have to live with.

The problem is how to stop it. If you searched everyone that came into the ground and took all their coins away you could probably buy Ronaldo at the end of the season!

It's not just an Italian dilemma, though. I've played in Turkey with Holland and that's a hostile atmosphere, for sure. It's mad over there and they'll throw anything at you. A friend of mine coached in Turkey for a while and said if there was an elephant on the terraces then the Turks would throw that.

Back on the pitch, the win over Juventus and the remarkable defeat of Arsenal in the FA Cup semi-final replay on April 14, when my Dutch team-mate Dennis Bergkamp had a penalty saved by Schmeichel and Giggs scored a wonder goal, set us up for a thrilling end to the season.

Our FA Cup run that year had been just as dramatic as our European adventures. After seeing off Middlesbrough in the third round, we were drawn against our old foes, Liverpool, in the fourth. They took the lead almost immediately with Michael Owen being left unmarked in the box to head home what for a long time looked like being the winner.

But we didn't give up, despite struggling to get to grips with

Gerard Houllier's side, and it paid dividends in the final moments. First Dwight slid home an equaliser with two minutes to go, and just as most people in the ground had settled for a draw, Ole popped up off the bench to score the winner.

'You're a bloody marvel, Ole,' I screamed as I joined the chase around the Old Trafford pitch to congratulate him. 'A bloody marvel.'

He's come off the bench so many times to save our skins that there seems to be a touch of magic about Ole. When we see him trot on, tucking his shirt in his shorts, we get a lift, so God knows what emotions his timely appearance brings to a worn-out defender desperate for the final whistle.

I know I would have hated being Carlton Palmer when the Norwegian strode on to the pitch at the City Ground on February 6 and smashed home four goals in ten minutes to seal an 8–1 rout.

That unbelievable scoring spurt may have come as a surprise to the rest of the League, but it didn't to us. Ole does it in training all the time; If you give him space in the box he'll kill you.

Ole must have taken my lead, as three games previously I had at last found the net for my new team in the 6–2 defeat of Leicester at Filbert Street – and it was a poacher's strike of which Solskjaer could have been proud!

The game was ticking into its final minute when I wandered upfield for a corner and stayed there when the ball was cleared. Astoundingly, Leicester's defence failed to spot me and there wasn't a blue shirt near me when Beckham delivered the perfect cross to the back post.

I took it first time and sidefooted my volley past a startled Kasey Keller before setting off on a crazy celebration. I hadn't thought up a plan for such a momentous occasion and just set off running, then darting away from my team-mates as they tried to catch me, with a massive smile on my face. It looked mad and possibly daft, but I loved every second of it. It's just a pity I haven't scored since.

Kevin Keegan's Fulham were next up in the FA Cup and although they kept it tight at Old Trafford, we proved too strong for what, despite the media hype, was still a First Division team. Cole's goal in the 26th minute was all we needed.

We were drawn against Chelsea in the quarter-final, the glamour tie of the round, although it didn't turn out that way at Old Trafford. Referee Paul Durkin had an afternoon to forget, going card-crazy and sending off Roberto Di Matteo and Scholes. Both decisions were harsh with Paul particularly unlucky as he barely made contact in the challenges that brought first a yellow, and then a red card.

The game was an uninspiring battle with the only exciting moment arriving when Gary Neville made a shock foray into the Blues' penalty area and saw a header come back off the post. The replay at Stamford Bridge proved to be a magical night for Dwight Yorke, though.

Since joining United during the previous August, the former Aston Villa man had added an extra dimension to our attacking play. A willing worker, Dwight formed an excellent partnership with Andy Cole which appeared to stem from a close friendship both on and off the pitch.

They bonded almost instantly, like brothers, and that closeness helped them develop into the best strike partnership in Europe that season as they snatched 53 goals between them. Yorke was happy to drop deeper than Cole and would chase down defenders. That allowed Andy to push on to the last man, often terrorising defenders with his pace.

The pair's link play was marvellous to watch and never more evident than in Barcelona, where they combined for a sensational goal. Yorke dummied and then collected Cole's pass before feeding Andy to score. The passing and intuition was fabulous and totally bamboozled the Spaniards' defence. It was the kind of stuff only Brazilians dream of playing.

His deeper role didn't deter Dwight from finding the net, either, and his tally of 29 goals for the season demonstrates that when the ball drops in the box, he knows exactly where to put it. I wasn't the only one impressed with his performances that term as Yorke won the Premiership Managers' Player of the Season award.

On that night at Stamford Bridge, Dwight delivered a high-quality volley for the opener and a stunning chip for the second that left Dutch keeper Ed de Goey in no-man's land.

If ever evidence was needed of a striker in form, that second goal was it. Cole made the chance with a tackle to win possession and Yorke strolled in to clip the ball home from 25 yards. Fantastic.

Dwight's double set up a tasty semi-final tie with our title challengers Arsenal. The Gunners had started mounting a serious push in the League and probably this game would have made the perfect final, but fate intervened.

Referee David Elleray had a brainstorm in the first match, which ended in a 0–0 draw, by ruling out Roy Keane's volley thanks to an extremely debatable offside decision. Ryan Giggs, out by the touchline, had strayed behind the last defender after whipping the ball in and was somehow judged to be interfering with play. God knows how!

It wasn't to be Roy's tie. He was to be sent off in the replay and was forced to watch the climax of a stunning match from the sidelines rather than controlling it from the centre of midfield. David Beckham scored the opener, then Dennis Bergkamp levelled before Phil Neville's foul on Ray Parlour handed the Gunners an injury-time penalty and, as appeared likely, a place in the final.

But Schmeichel guessed right, went left, and saved the spot-kick to give us another chance. Boy, did we take it! Giggs came off the bench to collect a misplaced Patrick Vieira pass just inside our half and set off to score one of the best goals I've ever seen.

Quite literally, he danced past four tired defenders, sending them one way and then other with his close control and body-swerves, before shooting high into the roof of the net. What a goal. It still sends shivers down my spine thinking about it now.

The scenes at the end were fantastic, with fans surging on the pitch to mob us as we dashed to each other to celebrate a tremendous win after more than four hours of unstinting football during the two games. You couldn't move on the pitch for supporters, but there was no ugly stuff, no riot. Like the players, those supporters were buzzing off the adrenaline rush and wanted to express their emotions.

Always looking for an angle, the media called for the FA not to punish the fans for breaking the rules about entering the field of play, and for once they were right. The FA had no choice but to let the whole situation go and allow us all to glow in the reflected glory of such a stunning match.

It was not until the dust had settled that the relevance of the win dawned on me. The result had set up had a remarkable 11 days in which United would finish the season either as champs or chumps!

We were on a run of 30 unbeaten games as we prepared for a tricky final Premiership clash with Spurs, where only victory would make sure of the title; then it was Newcastle in the FA Cup Final and, finally, we had Bayern Munich standing between us and the European Cup.

That fabulous run had started following an Old Trafford reverse against Middlesbrough, after which Ferguson brought the roof down with his tongue-lashing. It was our only home defeat of the season, but the manner in which we'd let Boro – who were managed by Ferguson's former United skipper, Bryan Robson – dictate the game had angered our gaffer.

He had missed the match through a family bereavement but when he returned, and watched the video, he raged at us. 'Shut up and listen,' he stormed. 'I can't believe what I've just witnessed. Your concentration was gone and you were unforgivably sloppy. The goals we've given away were a joke. There's nothing wrong with the quality of your game or the effort you're putting in. So from here on in, let's get the show on the road.'

We certainly did, and our subsequent undefeated sequence had taken us to the final-game showdown against Spurs at Old Trafford. For everyone connected with the club, the period was one of expectancy and nervousness, but for me it was a time of sheer frustration.

My Achilles tendon had been getting more painful as the

season pressed on, with the hard pitches causing it to flare up during and after games.

The only real solution was rest but after spending the last nine months battling against the pain, I didn't want to sit it out when all the glory, and the fun that entailed, was about to be enjoyed.

In the end I didn't have much of a choice. The club's medical staff had let Ferguson know the pain I was enduring to get through games and he came to me with his concerns.

'Listen, I know how keen you are to play every game,' he started as my heart began to drop in anticipation of what was about to come. 'But I want you to be 110 per cent fit for the European Cup Final, and if that means missing both the League decider and the FA Cup final, then so be it.'

It was a bombshell for me. I was desperate to play against Spurs. All season I had worked towards this moment and now it might be snatched away from me. Frustratingly there was nothing I could do. It was like the PSV situation all over again.

I tried to think long-term and reasoned that I could live with the pain of having to watch the exciting finale to the domestic season from the sidelines if it gave me a good shot of playing in the Champions League Final.

It was small consolation, and as I walked away from Ferguson I was clenching my fists. In the back of my mind, I hoped people would understand that the League is won over a season and not just in one game.

Although the decision to skip the title decider was taken a couple of days before the match, it was still hard to deal with. I made a point of going into the dressing room before the game and listening to the team talk before wishing the guys well.

I wanted to feel as close to playing as I possibly could and I also wanted to savour the atmosphere on a day that could lead to the momentous arrival of my first trophy in England.

After the players ran out to receive the tremendous greeting we always get at Old Trafford, I strode purposefully down the sideline and sat on the bench in my suit.

With my large frame and lack of hair, I know it's hard to miss me, and the fans were great in shouting out messages of support and letting me know they realised how I had helped the club that season. It meant a lot to me.

I'm not a great watcher and that afternoon was a nightmare as the tension built up during the game. I thought we were about to take the lead when Ian Walker whacked a clearance against Yorke and the ball flew towards the goal. Agonisingly it smacked against the post and ricocheted into Walker's arms.

Lady luck was clearly on Spurs side, and when Les Ferdinand scored in the 24th minute, totally against the run of play, we began to wonder if it was going to be our day.

Arsenal were eminently capable of beating Villa at Highbury, and if that happened, a defeat for us would leave our bid to take the Premiership back from the Gunners floundering at the final hurdle. At the moment Ferdinand scored, Arsene Wenger's men were drawing, and even though they had lost their previous match against Leeds in the dying minutes to end a 19-game unbeaten run, we were sure they would see off the Midlanders.

As chances came and were missed, with Yorke shooting wide when well placed and a linesman's flag ruining Scholes' bid to score, the anxiety on the bench kept twitching up a notch. I actually started to doubt that we would do it and struggled to keep the fear out of my head that a massive disappointment was right around the corner.

The media, in their normal cynical fashion, reckoned Spurs would lie down and die in front of us, ensuring that their local London rivals Arsenal would be denied the title. The conspiracy theories were given more alleged credence by the fact that George Graham was now in charge at Spurs and was still fuming at the way he was dumped by the Gunners over the infamous 'bung' scandal. But it was obvious to all who watched the white-shirted Spurs players chasing down every ball that such talk was rubbish.

Unfortunately, there was little I could do from the sidelines except shout and encourage and listen to the cheers from fans around the ground tuning in to radios. It seemed that every supporter either had an earpiece in or was stood next to someone who was listening for the score from London.

The wind-up merchants in the crowd were having a field day passing on false messages of doom and gloom for a joke. I can tell you it was no joking matter on the touchline, with the manager as tense as I've ever seen him as he tried to orchestrate a couple of goals to claim the title.

We did have someone in front of us with a radio to keep me in touch with what was happening elsewhere, and I tried to focus on what the lads were doing on the pitch while waiting for his factual broadcasts.

Then, just before half-time it happened. It was David Beckham – who else? – who scored with a dynamite drive and the whole red half of Manchester seemed to let out a collective sigh of relief. I was so pleased for David. He had endured hell from fans and media alike for the past ten months and had the strength of character to come back and enjoy his best season to date.

It was fitting that he was the man to bring us on level terms. For so long he'd inspired the team with moments of magic when they were most needed, stamping his class on matches that had threatened to slip away, and once again, against Spurs, he produced when it mattered.

Soon after the break our super-sub for the day, Andy Cole, came off the bench and produced a typically individualistic finish to lift the tension and put us in front. Andy had been severely disappointed to be left out on the day of the game and felt that he had a point to prove. Before he went on I told him I reckoned he could notch the winner and he claims we agreed a special celebration if he did. So after his characteristically classy finish he made his way to the bench for a party with me.

He's since told me he had expected me to race down and grab him. Only I didn't know what he had in mind and stayed put to leave him looking a little bit silly, before he was saved by the lads who threw him to the floor and dived on top.

Still, Arsenal kept the heat on with Kanu scoring the eventual winner at Highbury. That meant we couldn't afford to draw and, from that point to the final whistle, the time seemed to creep by. I've never seen so many anxious faces in a dugout.

We had plenty of cause for concern, too, as Spurs kept going at us and were even denied a penalty. Steffen Iversen's shot smashed against David May's arm, I held my breath, then gasped in relief as the referee waved play on.

Finally we were put out of our misery as the referee blew for time and I jumped to my feet as nine months of hard slog, frustration and ultimate joy enveloped my senses. I was so excited I didn't even take in who I was hugging in celebration. All I wanted to do was get out on the pitch and I remember applauding until my hands hurt while the lads went mad.

Within minutes the guys on the bench and the other players not in the squad were ushered away down the tunnel to the changing room, where our kit had been hung up. We threw off our jackets and shirts like schoolkids going for a dip in a pool on a sizzling hot day, and slipped on our United tops. Then it was a race to join up with the other guys and soak up the plaudits from the frenzied fans as we collected our medals, cracked open the champagne and walked round on a lap of honour.

Holding that first trophy in my hands was a wonderful feeling and I felt wholly rewarded for all the heartache that went into making the decision to quit PSV. Although Arsenal made us fight all the way to the wire, I felt an immense sense of satisfaction as the crowd roared their approval.

Once the fireworks on the pitch subsided, the feeling of success continued with more champagne in the dressing room. The banter was flying and although most of the other lads already knew the special feeling that winning the title brings, I was just loving being part of it for the first time.

Gary Neville was leading the singsongs with Nicky Butt and Ryan Giggs chuckling away at anything and everything, and making sure everyone was soaked by a jet of bubbly. 'Glory, glory Man United' was still ringing in my ears as Gary and Phil bellowed yet another chorus, before stopping mid-sentence to scream out more rubbish.

Schmeichel, who had announced already that he was leaving Old Trafford in the summer, was just as excited as he sat down beside me and whispered: 'Jaap, this was my last game at the

Theatre of Dreams, and we've won the League. It's absolutely fantastic. I'm going to treasure this for the rest of my life. But let's make it just the start. We'll let our hair down tonight, and then we'll win the fucking treble.'

Despite the fact that we were only a week away from our next big date with destiny, the gaffer was wise enough to allow us to celebrate with a party that night in a local hotel – after he had given us a pep talk, of course.

'What a season!' he smiled. 'Well done. You've played with the quality we expect of Manchester United, but most of all you've played with the spirit of Manchester United. That's the important thing. Now when we go to Barcelona and Wembley, we'll enjoy ourselves.'

The party was strictly for players, backroom boys and their wives or partners only. The drinks flowed, the music blared out and we broke off for a spot of that favourite footballers' ritual of karaoke.

First up to the microphone was our disco duo, Ryan Giggs and Nicky Butt, to provide us all with a giggle as they showed off their best Elvis impressions. Then Jim Curran, who does our massages, got up and did a turn to impress the boys with his moves. Although Ferguson is portrayed as a disciplinarian there were no drinking curfews and the party went on through the night.

The next few days were dramatically different from the time I won the League with PSV. Ferguson told us to take Sunday off and report back on Monday morning to get ready for the next two games.

At PSV we didn't have any other games after the title win so we kept on drinking. We didn't plan the relentless and thoroughly enjoyable bouts of celebrations, but the PSV supporters clubs and sponsors seemed to throw a party or a dinner every night and we were all out on the town for days afterwards.

Unfortunately for the United camp, our early preparations for the FA Cup Final were disrupted by an unfortunate incident involving Roy Keane. Our skipper got into a bar-room fracas after some Sunday drinking, and although the police decided not to follow up the episode, the press did. That led to us keeping our heads down for a day or two, and in a way Roy did us all a favour as most of the lads' heads were still banging from the hangovers.

We were together for pretty much the whole 11 days after driving down to our hotel in Windsor and the time spent in each other's company did wonders for team spirit. There are rarely any fall-outs at United, but there is nothing like winning big games to bring people even closer together.

As I know from my early days with the Reds, being in a hotel can drag on, so it needed all the lads to muck in to keep each other entertained. In the evenings there was always a game of pool or table tennis and the card games were up and running. If you felt like being unsociable for the night and wanted some rest, you just drifted off to your room to watch television.

Scholes, Butt and some of the younger players turned into demons on the table tennis front, although I'm proud to say I kept the Dutch end up with the odd decent display when I ventured down from my stint as a movie buff with my roomie, Ole.

He's fantastic to get on with. He's not too busy around the room and tends to chill out rather than fidget, possessing the most important attribute you look for in a room-mate – he doesn't snore. He makes the occasional phone call but he's not always on the phone like a previous roomie of mine, Jordi Cruyff.

Jordi grew up in Spain where, despite the fact that it's only an hour or two away in a jet, they seem to live in a different time zone. He could be on the phone until two in the morning, driving me mad by chattering away in Spanish as I tried to get some kip before an important game.

I think Ole shared with him as well, so he must have been happy to see me, as I like a good nap, although I'm a nightmare in the snoring stakes when I've got a cold.

Usually, when we go away for a week or so, I ask for my own room, but if it's only overnights I tend to share as we are only in the rooms briefly. I don't mind a few hours but when we're away for a week I want a little more privacy and space to relax in.

Some of the lads like to be own on their own even if it's just a day trip. Beckham, Cole and Yorke are always first to jump in if there's a single room on offer. I tend to be on my own quite a lot as well, certainly more frequently than in my first season. Maybe there's something the lads aren't telling me, although I prefer to think it's down to how many rooms the hotel has available at the time!

We trained hard in the week building up to the FA Cup Final cup and nobody pushed themselves harder than me as I tried to shake off the Achilles problem. I was up before the other guys in order to see the physio for the first of my two daily treatment sessions.

I would hop on to the table and let Jim get to work on the tender tendon before running out to join the lads in the fitness and ball drills. As they traipsed off for a shower I was back on that damned table having the Achilles manipulated and cajoled until the pain subsided. It was hard work but something I wanted to push myself through. 'Who knows if the chance to play in an FA Cup Final at Wembley will ever come again for me?' I thought as the frequent pain shot up my leg to remind me that all was not well.

Even though I'm Dutch, I know all about the tradition of the FA Cup and the magic of running out at Wembley to play in front of a worldwide television audience. Now here I was, with the final I had dreamed of just days away, and the determination not to be robbed of a chance to enjoy the event was driving me on to prove my fitness.

The hard work seemed to be paying off. As the week wore on I was ever more hopeful that I could pull off the comeback of the season and pronounce myself fit. I was helped by a relaxed mood in the camp, at odds with the way the world's media was dissecting our every move.

You couldn't open the sports pages of any newspaper without opinions, comment and space-filling tittle-tattle on how United would fare in our chase for the treble.

Many claimed we wouldn't mind losing the FA Cup if that meant Champions League glory, while others reckoned we should go all out for the Cup as the clash with Bayern Munich was a game too far. Naturally, the regular worms also crawled out of the woodwork to claim the whole team was getting too arrogant and were on the verge of getting their come-uppance.

But while the frenzy was being whipped up outside our temporary new hotel home, inside it was just another week in the single-minded life of Manchester United.

My team-mates had been through so much before and, although they were excited about the prospect of achieving something unique in football, there were no get-togethers after meals to discuss the issue. The only difference was that the lads worked even harder in training, no doubt hoping that an eye-catching session or two on the training ground would help push their case for inclusion in the starting line-up.

With the Champions League Final just a few days after the Wembley date, there was a feeling that some of the guys who had played hard all season might be rested for the Wembley game, and that meant opportunities for players who did not consider themselves to be automatic choices.

All my time was being spent concentrating on getting the troublesome Achilles right. On the Friday, with the chance of a starring role sitting atop my wish list, the game kept popping into my head.

I was pleased with myself for managing to get a good night's sleep on that Friday, probably helped by the conviction in my mind that I was going to be playing. The manager had said nothing to me during the week and I felt the treatment was working. With my Achilles comfortable when taking my weight, surely I would be in.

I woke up on the morning of the match and the Achilles seemed to be in perfect shape as I snapped out of bed with a contented smile on my face. It felt like all the hard work I'd put into the past two weeks, all the long hours on the treatment table, were going to pay off.

I got up early and rolled down for breakfast. Some players prefer to lie in and are allowed to do so. There are no hard-and-fast rules about that kind of thing at United, but I always haul myself out of bed and nip down for some food. If I don't, and stay in bed dozing, I don't feel awake enough when the game starts.

Once I had finished my cereal I walked straight into a corridor meeting with the manager, who obviously had asked the backroom staff about the state of my injury. He must have known from the smile on my face that I was about to give him the thumbs-up when asked about my condition, but unfortunately the conversation didn't get that far.

'It's a big game, this,' he probed.

'I know, but I feel much better and I reckon the Achilles can stand up to it,' I was quick to reply.

'But what if something goes wrong and there is a setback? I need you to be in perfect shape for the Bayern game, Jaap,' he explained.

'I think I will be. I've worked really hard this week and I can't see it being a problem,' I replied as I tried to change his mind.

'I know,' he said. 'But I don't want to risk it. How about I start you on the bench at Wembley and if the game goes well, we'll put you on?'

I badly wanted to say: 'No way boss, just fucking play me,' but it wouldn't have made a blind bit of difference.

Ferguson had already decided, so I just nodded and tried not to show my obvious disappointment. I'd already missed out on the final Premiership game and to have done so much work during the year and then sit out the crucial games was starting to get to me. It was my first season in England and I wanted to experience everything, rather than see the high points of the season float by from the bench.

Also I was conscious of the number of Dutch players who had actually won the FA Cup. It's not exactly a list that takes much reading. Marc Overmars with Arsenal and Arnie Muhren during his time at United had already achieved the feat. But before them, the names don't exactly trip off the tongue, do they?

In Holland we can pick up the BBC so I grew up watching 'Match of the Day' and the FA Cup final was always live on TV as well. I used to love watching the cameras following the team for the whole day from breakfast, through getting on to the coach and then driving down Wembley Way. It made the day so unusual and one of best in world football.

I shuffled back to my room, picked up the phone and told Ellis the grim news. She could tell how frustrated I was and tried her hardest to brighten my mood – an impossible task, I told her.

After lunch the gaffer started his team talk by announcing the team and, as I heard all the names being rattled out, once again I felt sick to the pit of my stomach.

It was something I tried not to show and soon after I wiped it from my mind because I began dreaming about coming on as a substitute and playing my part.

Because I wasn't starting, there wasn't a lot else for me to take from the team talk. I listened to the tactics in case I made a fleeting appearance, but really they didn't involve me. Basically it was the same routine we have heard time and time again, a simple, but effective message from Ferguson urging us to concentrate and enjoy the occasion.

The coach trip to Wembley was enjoyably slow with a sea of red-garbed fans waving us on and banging on the side of the bus to show their unstinting support. We had an eternity of time to kill before kick-off, so once we got bored by the dressing room, we decided to go for the obligatory pre-match amble on to the pitch in our swanky new suits.

Everyone had told me about walking out on that famous Wembley pitch and they were right. It gave me goosebumps from head to toe. I stood in the centre of the pitch and had a glance around at the famous old stadium.

There were a few diehard supporters already parked in their seats and they tried their best to make some noise before I went back in to get changed. I needed to be in early so I could have yet more massages on my calves.

From that point it was just a matter of waiting for the time to come to take that famous walk in single file, and hear that deafening Wembley roar, before getting out a ball and warming up. As usual, Dwight Yorke was a bundle of energy, walking around the room with a ball at his beck and call. No matter how big the occasion he doesn't seem to feel any tension before a match. That trademark grin just creeps across his face once again and you know that he's ready for action.

Most of the guys in our changing room had seen it all before, so although the nerves were jangling, no-one was throwing up or chattering away in an anxious fashion. There are a few who can't sit still, with Nicky Butt noticeably roaming around, but even among the most relaxed lads, no-one can quite touch Dwight's class for being laid back. As kick-off got nearer I tried to keep the same routine I use when I'm playing – standing up and stretching my legs and grabbing a ball to play a little one-touch against the wall.

Certainly it was a different atmosphere from the one we enjoy at Old Trafford. We have never been a team that needs the ghetto-blasters pumping out tunes to get us in the right mood. We don't need gimmicks like that.

In fact, the tension before a big game in our home dressing room is normally interrupted only by a television tuned into BBC's Grandstand. It seems odd that while other teams are limbering up to the latest thumping dance tune, we'll be sat around watching a bit of water-skiing or horse-racing.

Maybe that's an indication of just how well the players Ferguson has assembled manage to motivate themselves. Of course, the television is turned off before the gaffer makes his final rousing speech and we all line up before going out.

The Wembley roar lived up to all expectations and the tingle that ran down my spine as we strolled onto the pitch will stay with me forever. I'd been to the home of English football before with Holland in Euro '96, and while the noise the home fans made on that occasion was fantastic, this was different. That day the supporters were all pretty much against us, while here the United fans made it feel almost as if it was a home game with the red-and-white out in force.

The Geordie supporters were just as fanatical, with their half of the stadium resembling one giant barcode as they bounced up and down in unison in their famous black-and-white strips. I waved at family and friends as we marched out to parade in front of the royal box and waited for the guest of honour to come out.

I didn't have a clue who it would be before Prince Charles emerged from the dark and was led on to the pitch to shake hands with the players. To be honest, although it's great to be involved in the tradition that surrounds the FA Cup Final, meeting royalty didn't do too much for me. Don't forget I'm Dutch, so meeting England's future king is not a moment that will change my life forever.

As he made his way down the two lines of players, I was in my own world, hoping we would get off to a flyer and grab some early goals. It's a common thought among substitutes around the world, from Sunday football to the very top of the profession.

No-one wants their team-mates getting injured just so they can have a game, but the earlier your team is in the ascendancy, the earlier you can strip off and grab a piece of the action.

The match didn't start well for us with Roy Keane limping off after a few minutes following a strong challenge from Gary Speed which caught his bad ankle. I felt for our skipper as suspension had already ruled him out of the Champions League Final, and now this. Like me, his season certainly wasn't ending up the way he'd planned and I could sense his disappointment more acutely from being in a similar situation.

Roy's exit brought Teddy Sheringham into the fray and immediately he made his mark as we changed our tactics to adapt to the loss of Keane. Beckham took a central role but it was Scholes who fed the precision ball through for Sheringham to net just 96 seconds after coming onto the pitch.

It would prove to be a magical time for Teddy after a season of frustration spent mainly on the bench while Cole and Yorke stole the limelight. Before long his intelligent running and neat passing was dragging a disappointing Newcastle side all over the place, and it was his clever pass that set up Paul Scholes for the clincher.

Even the most ardent of United fans would have struggled to match the joyful emotion those strikes brought me, as I had an added incentive for willing the team to win – my own chance to get on.

The call finally came with about a quarter of the match left, when the manager told me to warm up. I was like a greyhound out of the traps as I left the bench and made sure my Achilles felt supple enough.

Luckily I was able to warm up right in front of the United fans and as they spotted me the 'Jip-Jaap' song was filling my ears. It's a song the United fans have devised for me and although I don't agree totally with the sentiments, it's impossible to put into words the lift it gives me every time it rings out from the Reds' supporters.

Hearing a ground as famous as Wembley booming to that chant gave me the perfect reception as I stretched and eased my muscles. Before long I gave the bench a nod to let them know I was ready for action and, with my heart racing, I jogged on to replace Scholes. I was on a massive high as I out-jumped Alan Shearer to get in a couple of headers and made swift tracks across the Wembley turf to power into some early tackles.

It felt like I'd hardly broken sweat when the referee blew the final whistle and I clenched my fists in satisfaction at celebrating a double in my first season. Now I was ready to enjoy all the trimmings of an FA Cup Final.

Although meeting Prince Charles didn't have that big an impact on me, I was really excited about another Wembley tradition – walking up those 39 steps to pick up the trophy.

I couldn't wait to get in line and was almost barging my team-mates out of the way as we started the walk. I grabbed scarves and shook hands as I almost floated up the walkway.

It was a sensation I wished could have gone on forever, and the moment Keane lifted the cup high in the air caused reverberations that rose through my body and will stay in-grained in my mind.

We did the customary lap of honour with the trophy and I felt a bigger part of the scene this time, having got my kit dirty on the big day. I made sure I got an early touch of the silverware and thrust it above my head to the cheers of the crowd. Now this was something I was beginning to get used to!

But all the celebrations on the pitch seemed to fly by and we left that pulsating cauldron of excitement and returned to the dressing room where I sat next to Ole.

'That was brilliant,' I told him. 'Miles better than I expected.'

'You can't beat the feeling of winning here,' he admitted.

'It's odd though, Ole,' I continued. 'I'm from Holland, you're from Norway, and here we are feeling on top of the world about winning a trophy in England.'

Ole laughed: 'It's strange, all right, but then how many countries have the FA Cup?'

The champagne corks were popping like mad again as the chatter about the game – and the fact it was United's third League and FA Cuo double in six years – reached fever pitch. As the players prepared to plunge into deep baths the manager went round, one by one to each player, and offered some words of congratulation. There was no big speech in the dressing room and I wonder whether he was overwhelmed a little by what his carefully constructed team had achieved.

His gruff Scottish voice was back that night, though, as we had our second party in a week. It had taken us a while to drag everyone on to the coach after the game, what with press interviews and champagne bubble-baths to take care of.

But we all got our best suits on and headed to a London hotel where the wives and girlfriends were waiting to join in what had been a magnificent day for me.

The gaffer took the microphone and resurrected the oratory skills learned on the shop-floors in Glasgow to summon up the right words for the occasion. Then we headed to the bar, where we enjoyed ourselves, in moderation of course.

Ferguson had not laid down any drinking laws but the lads are not dumb. In just four days we would be playing in one of the most important games in our careers. Everyone drunk a couple of beers and then switched to the fruit juice.

There was no point in being bladdered. We had a date with destiny in Barcelona that needed our full attention.

CHAPTER FIVE

Barcelona

We flew out to Spain on Concorde and after being made to feel kings of the air we settled into our hotel in the beautiful seaside resort of Sitges and began concentrating on our aim of becoming kings of Europe.

It was hard to imagine I was preparing for the biggest game of my life as I sat on the terrace sipping coffee and watching the inviting sea slip over the rocks below us.

If the idea was to take our minds off the task in hand it certainly seemed to work as the mood of the camp was one of total relaxation. We almost forgot the fact that just days ago we had completed a double.

'This is perfect,' I told Teddy Sheringham, who was next to me with his top off, soaking in the sun. 'It's going to be hard to get nervous about the game too early with all this to take our minds off football.'

We did train, of course, and it was a lengthier affair for me than the rest of the squad because of my need to warm-up the Achilles tendon before joining in. Although the fears of breaking down had been eased by that confidence- boosting run-out at Wembley, still I wasn't going to take any risks. The European Cup Final isn't a game you mess around with, so I took every precaution possible.

As the days passed, I realised that the precautions had paid off and I'd be fit to pull on a shirt for what would prove to be the biggest game of my life. We had a team meeting the day before the game when we watched a video of Bayern, but the biggest question on our lips was not answered. Who would replace the suspended Keane and Scholes?

Having the heart of our midfield ripped out against a side bidding for their own treble was not the best preparation. There was talk of pushing Ronny Johnsen forward from defence to fill the gap. He had played there against Inter Milan in the San Siro, helping to stop Roberto Baggio and Ronaldo dropping deep to pick up the ball, and he looked accomplished in the holding role.

Not many people can get past Ronny in the tackle and he's mobile for a big guy, but just as importantly he can get the ball down and pass it. We're not talking about hitting 60-yard bombs on to a sixpence – that's not his game – but Ronny can get it and give it to the likes of Beckham and Giggs, who'll do the real damage.

There were several other options which meant a bigger reshaping of the team, but by the way we trained leading up to the game, we had all come to the same conclusion before Alex Ferguson cleared his throat on the morning of the final and announced the line-up.

Beckham went to the middle alongside Nicky Butt, with Giggs swapping to the right flank and Jesper Blomqvist coming in on the left. That meant losing some of the balance we had enjoyed during the season as Ryan wouldn't be able to deliver such damaging balls on the run with his right foot as he could manage with his left.

But at least he could cut inside and cause mayhem, a side of his game Ferguson was keen to encourage, and Jesper would be comfortable in his natural position on the left.

With all the shuffling in our pack, we expected to ask some questions of a Bayern side that weren't a new proposition to us. We'd played them before in the group games and done reasonably well against them. Like all German teams, they were physically strong, with players like Mario Basler and Lothar Matthaus adding some extra flair to the work ethic.

We had a certain edge, knowing they had held us to a 2–2 draw at their place only through a rare error from our keeper, Peter

Schmeichel. Now the most famous Dane in the world game had a chance to make amends in his last appearance for the club.

He had been a tremendous servant to United and shocked even the players when he announced, earlier in the season, that he was to quit in the spring. Now, after tucking two legs of a fantastic potential treble in the bag, he was awarded the accolade of being skipper in the absence of Keane. If Ferguson wanted someone to inspire and cajole in equal amounts he picked exactly the right man.

The game kicked off at the unusually late hour of 8.45pm, meaning a long day for the players to sit and stew. I ditched my normal early breakfast and laid in until nearly midday before going for a 20-minute walk along the scenic cliff-tops with a few of my team-mates.

'I can't wait for the game,' Ryan Giggs said.

'I just wish it was sooner, I replied. 'I'm going to be bored rigid all day. If there was something else to concentrate on it would be okay, but all I can think about is this game.'

We headed back for the team talk. I wasn't suffering from nerves but there was a genuine sense of relief after finally being named in the starting line-up in a half-hour meeting before lunch.

It would have been a major shock to me if I'd been left out after the gaffer had spent so long demanding I didn't take risks in the previous ten days to make sure I was fit, but there's always that little doubt tucked away in the back of your mind. Ferguson killed it off when he announced I would step in alongside Johnsen, with David May having to make way after starting at Wembley.

I didn't have to say anything to David about grabbing my shirt back. I know he was disappointed, but not devastated. He had actually enjoyed some unexpected glory in the past few days after resigning himself to being third choice behind myself and Ronny Johnsen towards the end of the season.

Because of my injury problems, he was able to nip in and sample two memorable occasions, lifting the Premiership title in the win over Spurs and then starting in an FA Cup Final. Both must have felt like massive bonuses to him.

As the day progressed and the butterflies started their pre-match flutter, I read John Grisham's latest thriller and flicked through magazines without the words really sinking in. As hard as I tried, my mind drifted off into a world of anticipation as I thought about my battle with their massive striker, Carsten Jancker, and how I was going to combat him.

After letting a spot of lunch go down, like most of the players I slipped back between the sheets for a couple of hours of extra kip. It's a ritual which not only helps to pass the dragging time but also ensures you save all your energy for the big night ahead.

When the alarm bell rang at 4pm I jumped out of bed like a kid on Christmas morning and threw on my tracksuit for the pre-match meal. Nobody really felt like eating. We were more interested in the task ahead, but my body needed fuel to power it through the evening's exertions and this was the last chance to make sure I would be at my physical peak.

European Cup Finals tend to be won by the smallest of degrees. A missed tackle, a misplaced pass, a slip when going to jump for a header, any of them can cost a team dear, and all of those situations are more likely to occur when you're tired. So I was keen to fill my tank and make sure I wasn't going to be the one to be caught out.

After eating, I changed into my official United grey three-piece suit and once again opened my book as I waited for the hands on the clock to haul themselves lazily towards leaving time.

Everyone thinks footballers enjoy a fantastically exciting lifestyle with glamour trips to the world's top destinations. It's not quite like that. I wish people could understand the reality, which frequently involves sitting in a hotel room watching television programmes in the host nation's language, longing for time to slip past. It's so boring for just a day, but I seem to spend most of my life cooped up in a room or on a plane when I would rather be sat at home with my family, playing with Lisa or listening to the gurgling sounds coming from Megan's carry-cot.

That night in Barcelona the frustration got so bad that I was down in the lobby well before the meeting time for the coach, and I wasn't the only one. Players were buzzing around, trying to find an interesting topic to discuss as the nerves started to build.

The journey into the Nou Camp was enjoyable as we started to re-enter the real world after the surreal few days spent on the waterfront. Having endured so many dreary city-centre hotels it had been a shock to the system to be in a place so picturesque just hours before kick-off.

Somehow it was only when we started to see the mass of United fans making their way to the game that reality jerked us into our familiar pattern of approaching a match. It was hard to believe that so many of our supporters had got tickets as every street-bar and cafe was packed with red shirts. Officially there were only 30,000 Reds there, but as we wove between the hordes under police escort, that figure seemed impossibly low.

Our arrival seemed to spark a spontaneous bout of United songs and rounds of applause from lager-swilling, bare-chested men displaying a nice line in beer bellies. The unusual welcoming parties cheered us on until the coach pulled up outside the imposing structure of the Nou Camp, a footballing pantheon, and a venue I hoped would play host to one of my finest moments in the game.

As soon as we arrived I made my way up a flight of steep steps to check out the pitch and get an early taste of the atmosphere. Already there were masses of fans inside and the cheering almost taunted the stadium's sound system.

In contrast, the dressing room was painfully quiet as I walked back in to spot the guys flicking through the programme and strapping on the shin-pads.

'Come on then,' I urged. 'This is what this season has been about, winning a treble. Now we're 90 minutes away from it. Let's go and do it.'

'That's right,' Schmeichel added in his captain's role. 'I've dreamed of this day for far too long to let it slip now.'

The sight of so many Reds already in the stands during my excursion to check out the pitch had begun to instil in me a sense of the historical importance that was attached to this match.

It wasn't a case of the proverbial: 'We'll treat it just like another game'. It was a contest that would go down in the record books and a night when heroes might write their name into folklore. I was aware from the atmosphere in the dressing room that I wasn't the only one thinking along those lines.

Even the jokers like Butt and Giggs were in a serene state, with the play-acting and normal pre-match pranks failing to materalise. The sense of occasion had started to kick in and now we were here, we had to win. We all knew it. United is too big a club to be happy with second best.

That meant pressure; and the pressure was starting to take a grip among the players. We might never get to this stage again, never have another chance to say to our children: 'Daddy won the European Cup'. We had to take this one.

As more players got into their kit, I carried out my recently acquired procedure of getting a massage before jogging out on to the pitch for a warm-up, partly to loosen my muscles, partly to escape the tension that was building in our dressing room, but mostly to enjoy the atmosphere.

I had played in a World Cup semi-final ten months previously and knew what the big occasion was all about, but this one was starting to throw me a little bit and I wasn't alone in that. It wasn't just the relative youngsters in the side, like Nicky Butt and David Beckham, but also some of the older hands such as Andy Cole. I could sense they were having trouble in keeping to their relatively care-free pre-match routine. Even that bundle of jokes and toothy smiles, Dwight Yorke, was a little more subdued than normal.

'This is our night,' Gary Neville screamed, in his key role as chief rabble-rouser in the absence of Keane. 'We can do it this,' chipped in David Beckham, while Dwight went into his familiar trick of keeping the ball up along with Nicky Butt.

There was no one key speech from any of the lads, nobody would have listened anyway. All the yelling and screaming was simply to lift the lid and let off a bit of steam.

We needed to get out on the pitch and the manager knew it. Alex Ferguson kept his team-talk short. We all knew our roles, they had been covered before and he could tell that now was not the time for information retention.

'Get out there and come back with the cup,' he implored as we stood in unison, shook hands with each other and wished everyone good luck.

As we walked towards the tunnel we saw the Germans for the first time, oddly separated from us by a wire-mesh fence. That ruled out any chance of shaking hands and there wasn't even any vocal contact. We knew they were there, but we weren't going to acknowledge them. The war of nerves had begun.

We simply got on with the leg shakes and quick flicks of the head to ensure that muscles were loose before making our way up the sharp run of steps to pitch level. A Champions League Final is a game you play possibly only once in a lifetime and I could see from my team-mates' eyes that everyone was totally focused.

Despite the high concentration levels, I wasn't the only one stunned by the huge roar that greeted us as we walked on to the pitch. All I could see was layer after layer of red and I wondered if there were any Bayern fans in the place.

It was a thrilling moment as the cacophony of noise swept down the terraces on to the pitch and made the hairs on the back of my neck stand to attention. It's a moment that will live with me forever.

Time flew as we lined-up for the Champions League anthem. It's a stirring tune that is now firmly ensconced in my personal top five after the events of that night in Barcelona. I tried to look straight ahead as that annoying camera came down the line of players standing almost to attention. You know it's going to send a close-up of you to the world and there is nothing more disconcerting than having a lens inches from your nose.

The sound level just didn't drop and we were almost shell-shocked as we got ready for the kick-off. I've never known such an electric start to a game. The early moments were cagey as we expected and although I've since read in press reports that myself and Johnsen were having trouble handling Jancker, it didn't seem that way on the pitch.

It depended on where he headed as to who was going to pick him up. Jancker can be a difficult proposition for some defenders as he's very strong, ensuring that it's almost impossible to get in front of him and pick off passes laid into his feet. Also he's powerful in the air and a great outlet for a team looking to relieve pressure, but having played against him twice earlier in the season, I felt comfortable taking him on.

Unfortunately it was a foul on the bald-headed hitman that handed the Germans their goal in the sixth minute. A ball slid off David Beckham's boot in their half and I managed to get in a challenge on Jancker, knocking the ball away in the process. However, my momentum took me to ground and he turned to run into space through the middle.

The ball quickly found its way to him and as I recovered my feet, Johnsen, who had been pulled across to cover Alexander Zickler, dashed back to cut out the danger. As the pair reached the edge of our box they collided and the Italian referee, Pierluigi Collina, awarded a debatable free-kick.

At the time it was a concern, but although Basler is good in dead-ball situations, we had a solid wall and behind that was the best keeper in the world. I was convinced that nothing would come of it.

But the Germans managed to push a hole in the side of the wall with Markus Babbel charging into Butt while I was pulled away from my close attendance by the run of Jancker. Although Basler's shot wasn't well struck, it found the gap and the ball slipped past an unsighted Schmeichel into the corner of the net.

'Shit, how are we going to pull this back?' I thought. Bayern are so well organised and play with such team spirit that it's almost impossible to find a way through when they drop into two ranks of four and defend like demons.

I know Peter has been blamed for the goal in some quarters, but I'm not so sure he was at fault. It was hard for him to see the ball as it came round the wall and if he caught sight of it only at the last moment it is hardly surprising that it fllew past him.

As the clock ticked on it became more and more evident that our task was bordering on the impossible. On our day I would back us to grab goals against any side. But this didn't look like being our day. We weren't playing well as a team and the chances we normally carve out, seemingly without breaking sweat, simply weren't coming along. Usually even if someone is having a rare off-day, there are enough strong shoulders to carry the burden, but at this point, when we needed someone to drive us on, we were found wanting.

Nobody stood out and the realisation that the masterplan was going horribly wrong was starting to meddle with our thoughts. Until that night everything had gone our way that season, but unlike in Turin against Juventus or in the FA Cup semi-final replay, when Giggs had scored such a sensational winner, that spark appeared to be missing. Thus we crashed into our dressing room at the interval feeling bitterly disappointed by our performance.

It was time for one of those inspirational speeches that turn fearful men into world-beaters and the gaffer delivered in some style.

'You've come this far and now you're letting yourselves and the club down,' he growled. 'We can play far better than this. It's not the tactics and it's not a lack of skill. You've got to go out there and work twice as hard, be twice as tough in the tackle and, most importantly, want to win twice as much as they do.

'You might never get within touching distance of this trophy again and at the moment you seem prepared to blow it without really giving it your best shot. I want you to be able to look in the mirror, even if we lose, and tell your reflection: "I did everything in my power to try and win the game."'

The go-get-em attitude spread through the team. There was no arguing with the sentiments or the delivery when the gaffer turned to certain players and urged them to do better. I was among the men singled out for some extra advice, with Ferguson demanding I became more aggressive against their strikers, and get in quicker. He wanted the ball won back as quickly as possible.

There was no arguing among the players, either, even though our disappointing display was starting to get people worried. We knew there were 45 minutes to go and that was more than enough time to craft the opportunities needed to win the game.

But, regardless of the stirring words, nothing changed. We couldn't impose ourselves on the game, couldn't find a way through their defence, and instead of us fashioning chances, it was the Germans who looked most likely to score.

They exploited the gaps left in our defence as we pushed for the leveller and how we managed to avoid conceding a killer second is probably still a mystery to Bayern even now.

The Germans certainly had the chances. At one point Basler carried the ball from deep inside his own half and fed substitute Mehmet Scholl, who chipped Peter for what looked certain to be the clincher.

As the ball arced up in the air and over the despairing dive of Schmeichel, it was almost like slow motion in my head. I was convinced the ball was flying into the net and my heart sank, distraught at the fact that it was all over. But for the first, and not the last time on that night, we had luck on our side and his shot clattered against the post and away to safety.

Soon after that we failed to clear a corner and Jancker, who was almost sat down at the time, launched a well-executed overhead kick that crashed back off the bar.

Those misses lifted the United fans and the early roars that had made it almost impossible to hear calls for the ball on the pitch started again. It was an incredible cauldron in which to play out a match, a real piece of life-theatre. But while I was enjoying the surroundings and what they were adding to the occasion, I was fuming at the arrogance of our German opponents.

Bayern's pompous players felt they had the game sewn up way before the final whistle and when Basler took Bayern's corners he was an absolute disgrace. He was posing and milking the applause, believing he was the man of the moment, having scored what he thought was the winning goal.

I was livid. I wanted to run over to the side of the pitch and smack him across the head. Losing was bad enough, but having to watch that sod conduct his own private celebration when the game was not even over infuriated me.

'I'm going to hit the arrogant wanker if he carries on,' I told Ronny Johnsen as we prepared to defend a corner. 'You'd have to get in line,' came a shout from somewhere behind me.

My frustration increased when Basler and Matthaus were both substituted before the end of the game and they left the pitch as though they had just collected Oscars. It was disgraceful and arrogant, and I'm delighted to say that it worked against Bayern Munich.

After watching those tossers proclaim themselves as winners I was even more determined to find that extra bit of energy in my cramping legs. I wanted to beat them more than any other opponent I'd faced.

We launched attack after attack only to be denied by a wall of Bayern shirts defending stoutly on the edge of their area. Despite the fact that we were controlling possession, the final ball just wouldn't reach the feet of our front men.

Ferguson threw on Teddy Sheringham and Ole Gunnar Solksjaer as the desperation mounted. It showed the intent and the desire was certainly there but still the goals weren't coming. With just two minutes left I looked at the stadium clock and thought the game was up. Still I was hopeful of finding an equaliser, but now it was merely a hope rather than a conviction.

We'd pulled ourselves out of trouble before late on in games, the defeat of Liverpool in the FA Cup earlier in the season being a case in point. In that match we had been creating chances, though. Here we weren't.

'It's not too late,' Gary Neville cried out as the fourth official stuck up his board to show there were three minutes of added time. 'We've won at the death before and we can do it again.'

As we poured forward in waves, the noise level was so loud we couldn't hear any instructions from the bench. So as I surged up for an injury-time corner and saw Schmeichel race past me, I guessed he must have taken it on his own shoulders to try and save the day.

But you know him, if there was a chance he could cause some mayhem he was up for it – and this time it paid off handsomely. Between us we managed to cause enough confusion to ensure the defensive clearance was too weak and the ball dropped to Giggs on the edge of the box.

Ryan's not known for his deadliness in front of goal and his scuffed shot was never going to trouble the Bayern defence until it struggled through a pack of players and landed at the feet of Teddy Sheringham. His reaction was purely instinctive, as he swung a leg at the ball and managed to roll it just inside the post.

Normally I'm a calm man but at that moment I went crazy. Once again United had pulled something stunning, astounding and wonderful out of the bag. I raced after Teddy as he made off towards the United fans and jumped on top of a mob of red shirts, screaming like a banshee and letting that lovely feeling of satisfaction creep all over my body.

We must have been deep into added time as we went back to our places for the re-start and you could see that the Germans were deflated. As our emotions had risen, theirs had sunk in comparable amounts and they were on their knees, there for the taking. Within seconds we had won the ball off them and worked our way upfield to force another corner.

Now was our chance. It was clear that the Germans were dazed and still kicking themselves about conceding the equaliser. Now came the opportunity to deliver the knock-out blow.

As the corner came in they weren't concentrating, their marking was all at sea, and after Sheringham rose brilliantly at the near post to flick on Beckham's immaculate delivery, all it needed was someone to touch it into the net.

The ball was arrowing in my direction at the far post and I started stepping in to guide the ball home. Already I could see my name up in lights and was just about to start glowing in the kudos of snatching the match-winner when Ole nipped ahead of me to deflect the ball high into the top of the net and claim the glory.

If my room-mate had missed the ball, I would have been the hero but I didn't care! The adrenaline levels were so high I didn't know what to do. I just ran to him and grabbed him and started kissing him. That's not like me but what else could I do in a situation like that? It took me time to get to him, though, as poor Ole was surrounded by the lads, the subs and the backroom team.

Just as good was the sight of the deflated Germans. Samuel Kuffour was on the floor banging the turf in frustration and had to be hauled to his feet so we could go through the formalities of the final seconds of the game. As between the English and the Germans, there is always an extra rivalry between Holland and Germany, so to see them down and out after we had won in such a German way helped to make the moment all the more sweet. They always seem to find that bit extra to steal a game deep into added time, or sneak through on penalties. For once it was their turn to suffer.

I know the myth surrounding that game says that United were lucky but also it can be stressed that it was bad defending by Bayern which cost them so dearly. They were undone by Schmeichel's presence in their box and let their heads wander rather than quickly organising themselves to snuff out any threat. He may be a big guy, but Peter is just another player to mark.

The few extra seconds of play after our second goal served only to interrupt the celebrations, and as the Bayern players collapsed around us in despair, everyone ran to each other, celebrating and congratulating.

We charged towards the United fans who had shared the incredible experience with us and I could pick out people crying tears of joy as the relief busted out of their system and rolled down their cheeks.

UEFA had immediately constructed a little white stage on the centre of the pitch and we managed to regain our composure for the ceremonies and feigned interest as the Germans went to pick up their losers' medals. Their body movements and bowed heads showed how pissed off they were. The odd Bayern player looked at the cup as they wandered past. 'Great,' I thought, 'have a good look but don't touch. It doesn't belong to you.'

Finally it was our turn. One by one we climbed up to collect our treasured medals and gathered round the trophy like it was a campfire. I positioned myself a couple of metres from the cup and gave it a quick stroke while we waited for the rest of the players to have the winning ribbons draped over their necks.

Also, we were waiting on Ferguson. This was the trophy he coveted, this was the cup he had set his heart on winning when first taking over at United in November 1986. Now, after more than 12 years of hard work, his dreams had been realised. The United players knew he should be there, wanted him there even, lifting the cup.

Finally Fergie was in front of us, and along with Peter he picked up the cup and held it towards the heavens. Then the party really began.

We did a lap of honour and everyone in the stands was either screaming or crying their eyes out. I'm happy to say I can remember it all. I was desperate to cram my head with every sight possible and soak it all up, so I could replay it all in my mind whenever I felt like it.

As we jogged around I picked up a dodgy red, white and black wig and posed for the hundreds of photographers who buzzed around among us trying to get the best picture. A group of Dutch photographers grabbed my attention by shouting to me in my native tongue and I happily modelled the cup for them.

Then David May came into his own as master of ceremonies. Already he had managed to ensure himself a spot in history by picking the best spot to get in all the photographs when the cup was lifted. Somehow he got into frame for every picture taken that night, even though he didn't play.

It wasn't just us who noticed. A few months later an English magazine did a mock-up of the most important pictures in history and stuck David's head in every shot. It was hilarious and we made sure he saw it.

On that night, though, he was in top form. We had lined up for a group photo in front of our fans when Peter lifted the cup high again and brought a cheer. May stepped in quickly and through a combination of waving his hands and putting his finger to his lips he managed to get the whole crowd to go quiet for an instant. Peter flung the cup into the warm night air and the cheers drowned out all other sounds again.

Within seconds the rest of us decided that we wanted a piece of the action. Dwight Yorke did a little calypso dance, Andy Cole a run from side to side, while Nicky Butt wriggled his hips like Elvis before lifting the cup to a thunderous reception. I stuck out a hand and clasped it, thrust the heavy trophy forward and the Jip-Jaap song filled my ears again. What a breathtaking moment!

It wasn't just the guys on the pitch that night who were appreciated. The United supporters sang the names of Keane and Scholes, who both missed the match through suspension. Because they didn't play, neither of lads wanted to come on to the pitch and take the plaudits, but the eagerness of the Reds' fans soon put an end to their reluctance.

It must have hurt like hell to have had the opportunity to play in the biggest game they'd ever known plucked from them by a referee with a penchant for handing out yellow cards, although Roy might not have made it anyway following his injury in the FA Cup Final.

After the game they were quiet. They handled it pretty well on the outside but inside the frustration and emotional turmoil they suffered must have been awful. Keane still says to this day that he doesn't feel like he won the cup because he missed the Bayern game. Don't fool yourself, Roy. Without you we wouldn't have been there.

We stayed on the pitch for close to an hour as nobody seemed to want to end the party until, one by one, the lads filtered back into the dressing room, singing 'We're by the far the greatest team, the world has ever seen.' Then the drinking started. We all jumped into the baths and jacuzzis with a bottle of bubbly and still I have a picture of me sat there in palatial splendour hugging the oversized cup.

'You lucky sod,' joked Ole Gunnar Solskjaer, spotting me lording it up. 'You've been here five minutes and picked up a treble.'

I must admit I couldn't have timed it better.

Ferguson managed to force a minute of peace among the mayhem to thank everyone for helping him achieve the best night of his life. We knew after reading what he had said in the build-up to the match how important this prize was to him and some papers claimed we won it for him. Of course we wanted him to be happy, but we did it for ourselves as well.

Once he finished, the chaos continued and I chatted to Ronny Johnsen and Steve McClaren as a video camera recorded the events.

'I didn't think we were going to do it,' I admitted. 'You weren't the only one,' Johnsen replied. 'I kept having the nightmare thought that my foul was going to cost us the cup.'

'It nearly did,' laughed McClaren. 'But maybe for once we got lucky.' Ferguson joined in: 'It was written in the stars, boys. It was fate.'

While we chatted the party went on all around us with Schmeichel in the thick of everything. It was his last game and I could see the emotion affecting him as he tried to take in what he had achieved, and the fact that he would never sample this again.

There was a disco lined-up for us at a local hotel but we didn't get there until two in the morning. First we had to wait for the slowcoaches among us to finish their drinks and get dressed, and then there was the world's press to take care of.

For once nobody was unhappy about taking time to share our views, although after the amount of drink some of the lads had put away, there must have been an awful lot of rubbish talked. Finally we got to the hotel, dumped our bags, turned tail and hotfooted it to the party. A massive room had been set aside for us and it was full of tables filled with the smiling faces of families and friends.

The trophy went round the room and we took pictures for the family albums. I had invited my former PSV team-mate Arthur Numan to join me and, just like him, he spent the whole night worrying needlessly about whether the United players would want him ejected for being an unwelcome stranger.

The drinking that went on that night was awesome, but I was so tired I needed to see my bed at five. Not everyone followed my example – some of the lads managed to keep going through the night and the plane trip home. The stewardesses on the flight worked overtime to keep the supply of alcohol flowing as we switched back into party mood once again.

Any hangovers were being drunk away, but the effect of the beer wore off when we got home to a remarkable reception in Manchester. As soon as we stepped off the plane the applause started and it rang in my ears for several hours as we were ushered on to an open-top bus to tour the city.

That journey was unbelievable, it seemed the whole of the city had come out to cheer us. The streets were packed and all we could see for miles were hands, waving at us. It took me completely by surprise, but provided the perfect end to 11 days that will live in my memory forever.

The formalities were completed when we walked on to a massive stage in the Nynex Arena and enjoyed a standing ovation from the massed ranks of our loyal supporters. It was like a mini-Nou Camp. The manager and a couple of players said a few words. Then that was it. I didn't see the guys again until after the holidays.

CHAPTER SIX

When a title is not enough

I just couldn't shake off the Germans. In truth most of the Bayern Munich fans I met on my holiday in Tenerife, weeks after winning the European Cup, were good-natured. They simply wanted to talk about the game and, even though their side had lost, they seemed interested in hearing all about the defeat.

I had jetted out to a quiet part of the holiday isle with Ellis and Lisa, along with another family of close friends. I'm not the type of guy who likes to go night-clubbing so we spent the days lazing by the pool and the evenings tucking into local dishes. Trying to forget all about football, in fact.

I was just glad to have a break. The previous summer I'd had only ten days between the World Cup and starting life with United, and all of that was taken up by the drama of Lisa's birth.

Also, there was United's pre-season tour to the Far East coming up and once again I would be far away from my family. I wanted to make the most of our time together.

Unfortunately, as every school kids knows, even though we had five weeks off, it slipped by far too quickly and before long I was driving my car through the gates of The Cliff to start that dreaded spell of pre-season training.

I'm not a bad runner, but I hate the monotony of timed sprints and then long-distance races. Certainly I wasn't looking forward to the first day back and once the trainers were on, the stopwatches came out.

'Why can't we get a ball out?' I moaned. 'Can't we run with the ball or something?' 'That will come later,' Steve McClaren answered back, knowing I didn't seriously expect a quick five-a-side and a shower before being allowed to go home again.

It was going to be hard work, the kind of lung-busting, muscle-aching torture that makes you hate being a footballer, but I tried to concentrate on the emotions that flood my body once it's all over.

Once the sickening sensation quits your stomach, you feel cleansed with every sinew jumping for joy at being tested to the limits and passing that test. Psychologically I felt a massive a sense of pride that the mountain had been climbed.

Unfortunately, we did the same on the next day, and then for a more than a week it was like Groundhog Day. But once the sickness-to-sweetness cycle was over, we were sat in an airport lounge once again, with Australia the first port of call on a money-spinning two-week tour.

We were to play games against Australia's national team in Melbourne and Sydney before short stops in Hong Kong and Shanghai, where the training would be broken up by a further two games.

Now, I know these trips are great for boosting United's corporate brand overseas and increasing revenue streams that are needed to pay our wages. But to the poor guys being dragged round the world to meaningless showpiece games, they are a real ball-ache. I would rather stay close to England and tour somewhere like Holland, Germany or Norway, where we can get the same fitness work done but without the added hassle of being ambassadors for the club.

I'm not daft. I realise the way football is going, and that money is the force driving it. When someone offers a large cheque for our services, and at the same time we can further boost the coffers by increasing the overseas merchandising markets, we have to go.

But I would prefer to get in, smile, wave at the crowd, play a bit of ball and then skip town. The two weeks we spent on the road Down Under was far too long, and I wonder whether it was actually beneficial to our preparations for the season ahead.

To make matters worse for me, I hate flying. It's not as bad as in the case of my Dutch team-mate, Dennis Bergkamp, who simply refuses to board a plane, but I wouldn't suggest shaking my hand after take-off unless you want a palm full of sweat. I can handle short flights, an hour or so in the air, but when we start talking long-haul the palpitations begin.

It's both ends of the journey I really can't stand; the judder as the plane reaches its take-off speed on the runaway, and that horrible sensation of falling slightly backwards as the front wheels lift off the ground. Just as bad is the descent and waiting for the impact of touching the ground, wondering if the landing gear will hold out, and then being sucked back into the seat hoping the brakes are good enough.

My fear of flying wasn't helped by being a passenger on a Concorde flight from Paris to New York just one week before an Air France jet crashed into a hotel seconds after taking off from Charles De Gaulle Airport. It wasn't exactly a confidence-booster watching the television pictures of that terrible tragedy.

After nearly 24 torturous hours in the air, we landed in Australia for the first, and most enjoyable, leg of the tour, which was enlivened by a party on the yacht of the man who had financed the expedition.

Now this guy had some money and liked people to notice the fact. His yacht was massive, with all the trimmings. There was even a helicopter on deck and a jacuzzi tucked away for those long days at sea.

But what caught my eye was the number of flash cars he had parked on the quayside as we arrived. I've got a fondness for cars – the bigger the better – and I think that was relayed to this gentleman.

We had some time off the following morning and one of his staff turned up at the hotel asking for me, so I slipped downstairs to be confronted by this monster of a motor from America.

The Yokohama, as it's known, is a huge powerful Jeep, the

kind only America would think about making, and within seconds I was behind the wheel with the intrigued Raimond van der Gouw and Jesper Blomqvist along for the ride.

It felt like driving a tank, it was so wide, and I needed to drive on the white lines in the middle of the lane to ensure no pedestrians were hospitalised. That didn't bother drivers coming the other way. They must have seen me from two blocks away and were in no position to argue as I put my foot down.

It was a great morning, driving around feeling like a king, and although I haven't got plans for adding a Yokohama to my car collection, I can't wait to get my hands on one again.

I'm not sure if its owner made a huge sum for his efforts in bringing United to Australia. Over there our game is a poor relation to Aussie Rules football, Rugby League and cricket, but it's growing. Certainly there were plenty of people who knew all about United and watched our late, late show in winning the European Cup – even though it didn't start until 4am Down Under.

The licensing laws are more relaxed in Australia. I was told the bars stayed open all night and fans enjoyed a marathon drinking session and were still up for work the following morning, talking about our exploits to the unconverted.

We didn't take a full squad on the tour, but despite David Beckham and Roy Keane remaining at home, the two games were well supported with fans cramming into stadia to watch us beat a national team which was only slightly below full strength.

Certainly Andy Cole was there and soon he was embroiled in controversy over a tackle on one of the Aussie defenders, Simon Collisimo, that left the youngster needing surgery. Andy dived in to win the ball but caught the lad's leg, and at the time we didn't think too much of it. No pro likes to see a fellow player leave a game injured, but at the final whistle the whole incident had slipped from my thoughts.

But by the next day it was all over the papers with Cole accused of being a bully and trying to ruin the young fellow's career. His club claimed he was soon to be shipped off to Europe for a decent fee and that Andy's tackle had devastated his chance of making it big in the game.

Now that's not Cole's style. He would never single out a player and decide it was time to put him in hospital but, of course, the hullabaloo followed us all across Australia and even continued at home with talk of legal action that, I'm happy to say, came to nothing.

After the driving delights of Oz, we flew to Shanghai and as soon as we landed I knew I was going to hate the place. We were popular in Australia but I just could not believe the amount of people waiting at the airport to get a look at us, and worse, follow our every step when we landed in China.

As our coach raced through the airport gates, hundreds of manic locals on mopeds and pushbikes set their wheels in motion to begin the chase. When we got to the hotel the day took another nosedive as the security guards' feeble attempts at making a protective tunnel for us left myself and the rest of the lads in danger of being ripped apart. In their desperation to get an autograph or photo with a United player, those crazed supporters pulled and tugged at our clothes.

'It's like Indiana Jones,' I screamed at Nicky Butt as we ran the gauntlet to what we thought would be the safety of the hotel's revolving doors. Once inside it was even worse, with the hotel staff just as keen to get a piece of us, so I made for my room and stayed put.

Our trips to the training ground were like the Wacky Races with bikes, cars and all sorts of contraptions in tow. The whole scene was played out against a backdrop of depressing grey buildings which gave the impression that the whole place was filthy. It didn't get much better when finally we found sanctuary behind the closed gates at our training facilities. This time it wasn't fans causing annoyance; it was flies, big ones. We played one game and left and I, for one, won't be going back.

Our short spell in Hong Kong was just as humid, and by that time we just wanted to go home. All the travelling and the 'pop star' reaction we received from the locals were starting to take their toll. When finally we boarded the flight home, I didn't even care about my adverse reaction to flying. I just wanted to get back to my family.

We opened our season in England with a Charity Shield defeat by Arsenal, having spent only a few days getting the jet-lag out of the system. It was another trip to Wembley, but for me the glory of the place had already worn off. People in England used to think it was a foreigner's dream to appear on the hallowed turf whenever they could, but in my case they were mistaken.

It retained an aura of being a magnificent stadium, steeped in history, but the past is where it belongs. I'm glad I got to play there so often before it was closed, but when I looked at the Stade de France it was obvious to me that England needed a new national home. Wembley was looking old and tattered and its facilities had been surpassed by many of the new club stadia.

Despite my reservations about Wembley – and don't get me wrong, the atmosphere for our FA Cup win was tremendous – now I was just concerned about lasting 90 minutes on that big pitch so soon after the Far East tour. Indeed, I didn't make it to the whistle. David May come on for me as we lost 2–1 after leading through Dwight Yorke's goal.

We opened the League season at Everton in early August, with Yorke scoring again, as we cruised towards what we expected to be a comfortable win. In fact, we should have had two or three as we dominated the game, only for the ball not to fall kindly for us.

Then, with a couple of minutes left, Nick Barmby nodded across goal and as a reflex reaction I attempted to head clear. To my horror, I didn't get the connection I wanted and it skimmed off me and into the net. I felt terrible. I played really well that day, keeping Kevin Campbell quiet, and all I would be remembered for was the scabby own goal.

At the time the lads left me alone, but the snipes started in training with Ryan Giggs and Nicky Butt cracking away at me. 'I'm going to cross this one in,' Ryan joked. 'Be careful where you head it, ten-bob head!' I didn't react, I wanted to forget about it.

Soon enough, it was history as we beat Sheffield Wednesday 4–0 and Leeds 2–0 before heading to Highbury and another clash with Arsenal. I love playing against the Gunners; for me it's the biggest game of the season. The tension in the build-up lifts me and I can't wait to get out and put in some flying tackles.

There are a lot of talented and determined players on both sides and Arsenal are one of the few teams that can stand toe-to-toe with us and slug it out. We have kept the title between us for the past few years and now it's more than just getting three points. Pride is very much at stake.

This time around we came back from 1–0 down with Roy Keane scoring twice and rubbing salt into the wounds of his marker, Patrick Vieira. When these guys meet, the earth shakes. Neither man is intimidated and backing down just isn't an option. Add to that volatile mixture a short fuse on either side and tempers that might make Alex Ferguson blush, and it's quite an experience to be on the same pitch as them.

Patrick is a truly great player, with strength on the ball and in the tackle, and a technique that's surprisingly good for someone of his stature, but in my view he ruins his game by picking up too many cards for stupid things.

There's always an elbow here or a sly kick there, and when you look at him it's easy to tell when the red mist is about to descend. I know Arsene Wenger has moaned that opposing players are always out to wind up him, but hey, that's football! You just get on and deal with it. In the modern game each team knows who is capable of losing it and getting red-carded, so they go for the weak spot.

Of course, Keane is no angel himself, but he gets just as much devilment from opponents like Vieira as he dispenses, and these days he is not dismissed too often. He's so focused on winning and even in training he hates decisions going against him.

He's always going to clatter into people and if someone tries to take liberties they may find themselves waking up aching all over. He's no madman, though. Roy has worked hard on holding his frustration in check and the flashpoints involving him have become fewer.

Ironically, in that game it wasn't Keane or Vieira who grabbed most of the headlines, but Martin Keown, after he booted our keeper, Raimond van der Gouw, in the mouth in the dying seconds. We were under pressure and it needed a brave act from someone to sort out the pinball game going on in our box. Rai doesn't bottle it. He got a nasty cut for his trouble, though, after flinging himself on the ball.

In came Keown and launched a foot at man and ball, catching Rai full in the face with a sickening thud. Instantly the claret was running and once again it started a flare-up between the two sides. I know Raimond refused to make a big thing out of it, but in my eyes the kick was late and should not have been delivered.

At least a bloodied and bruised Rai could smile. Those two goals from Roy Keane had given us a 2–1 win and inflicted Arsenal's first home League defeat since December 1997.

That clash began a hard week that left us suffering a frustrating reverse at the hands of Lazio in the European Super Cup. We played Arsenal, had three days before facing and beating Coventry 2–1, and then jetted out to meet the Italian giants two days later.

To say we were leg-weary would be a massive understatement. There was no zing and zap in our play and we petered out after a promising start to end up losing the game to a solitary goal from Marcelo Salas.

Obviously Lazio had not been told of the workload we'd been saddled with before the match, as their celebrations at the final whistle were a joke. They were posing with their medals like they'd just won the European Cup Final rather than some concocted game that, although we wanted to win, was not too high on our list of priorities that season.

One man who will not forget the occasion is their striker Simone Inzaghi, brother of one of my least favourite players in this glorious game, Filippo. In a freak accident, I managed to spread his nose halfway across his face as we both chased the ball. It was out on the touchline and I got ahead of him in the race for possession, forcing him to try and squeeze past me.

At that moment my elbow smashed into his face and split his nose wide open with a cracking sound that I heard clearly above the roar of the crowd. It wasn't intentional, my arm was certainly not raised. I was just in my normal running motion and

I'm not proud of it but, typical of his family, the man felt cheated.

The blood was spurting down his face and, as he realised how bad the damage was, the threats started to pump out as fast of the red stuff. I couldn't understand the words, but the body language was pretty clear. 'I'll slit your throat and break your legs,' he might as well have shouted.

Normally I'm not a man to go looking for trouble but certainly I'm not going to back down when it finds me. In this case though, I would have felt more threatened by a Teletubby. Did he search me out later to follow through his threats? What do you think?

It wasn't long before I had another voice bawling away at me, and this time I did take notice as the angry Scotsman laid into the whole team. It was early October, we'd just been beaten 5–0 at Chelsea and I could see in Ferguson's eyes how much it hurt him.

Quite simply, we hadn't played well and were caught out by our own change in tactics which didn't go to plan. Phil Neville was handed a man-marking job on their marvellously tricky Gianfranco Zola. The Italian soon cottoned on and pulled Phil all over the pitch, leaving a gaping hole on our left flank.

Albert Ferrer realised that and stepped into the space with the gratefulness of a man handed the freedom of his favourite bordello. Quickly we were made to pay for our generosity as poor Denis Irwin was left with two men to mark, and cross after cross came bombing in.

It didn't help that Massimo Taibi, playing in the last game of his ill-fated spell at Old Trafford, made a hash of coming to collect and let Gus Poyet nod a first-minute opener. Then Chris Sutton headed a second and the floodgates opened.

'What the fuck is that shite you just served up out there?' Ferguson blazed at us as we shuffled back into the dressing room.

'You may have won a European Cup, but if you do that again I'll get rid of the lot of you. Not one person today can say they were fit enough to wear the shirt. Not one.'

To a man the team was just as angry about losing, but there's no point letting your blood boil over and confront Ferguson.

You just have to sit there and take it. It was a blip and we decided to treat it like that.

Luckily we didn't have one of those blips in the first stage of our defence of the Champions League. We were drawn in a group which hardly set the pulses racing, despite containing teams capable of causing an upset if we let our guard slip.

In the end only Marseille embarrassed us by snatching a close-run 1–0 win at their place thanks to a William Gallas goal. On that night their supporters gave them a tremendous lift by filling the air with patriotic songs which must have made the French players feel ten feet high.

Unfortunately it was not the same for us at Old Trafford where the fans seem to need a goal to get them excited against some of the supposed lesser teams in Europe. Keane made the point in his own vernacular style with his 'prawn sandwich' attack last season after another disappointingly quiet night, but he was only saying what a lot of us were thinking.

Far too often the crowd at home is muted until we spark them into life with a goal or a touch of magic from the likes of Giggs or Beckham, and it gets beyond a joke when they actually get on players' backs as happened in the win over Dynamo Kiev.

Mikael Silvestre had come on as a substitute and his first touch wasn't the best. To my amazement, instantly the fans were giving him stick. It was disgraceful and led Roy Keane to claim that some of the fans 'couldn't even spell football, let alone understand it'.

He added: 'We knew it was going to be hard at Old Trafford but they want us to win these games by three or four goals. They want fantasy football and they should stay in the real world.'

He was right. Just because Sturm Graz and Anderlecht haven't got the same prestigious names or glorious history as, say, Juventus or Barcelona, it doesn't mean that these teams are easy to beat. Our supporters seem to think we should be stuffing them by five goals, but in truth even the minnows of Europe are employing top coaches and adopting techniques which make them supremely difficult to break down.

A look at recent seasons will confirm that sides like those I've mentioned are starting to top their groups. Maybe their football is not as nice, but it can be effective. When United face such opponents, then support from the stands is of paramount importance to boost the players.

Back in 1999, the second phase of the competition hardly got off on the best footing as mistakes by Keane and Henning Berg allowed Gabriel Batistuta and Abel Balbo to score in Florence, giving Fiorentina a 2–0 win.

Soon after that we faced another dreaded long-haul flight as we set off for Japan to play Palmeiras in the Toyota Inter-Continental Cup on November 30. This one-game competition is designed to see which is the best club side in the world with the European Cup winners pitted against the best from South America.

The Brazilians checked in a week before the game, three days ahead of us, and our late arrival, forced on us by our usual heavy League schedule, certainly took its toll. We did not have enough time to adapt. No-one could sleep at night and during training sessions we could just about drag ourselves around the pitch.

On the day of the game I feared the worst and I was not wrong. As we started to warm up my legs felt so stiff and sore it was as though I had played a game already.

I said to my defensive partner, Gary Neville: 'Gaz, I don't know about you, but I haven't got an ounce of energy. I just hope they don't make us chase the ball as I'll pass out before the end.'

How we managed to battle through and win the match is still beyond me. I was exhausted by half-time and I could tell I wasn't the only one feeling the effects of the trip. Roy Keane scored the winner and, thanks to some marvellous saves from Mark Bosnich, we clung on.

Surprisingly Mark wasn't handed the keys to the Toyota on offer for the man-of-the-match, though. That prize went to Ryan Giggs, although no-one was particularly jealous as the car was hardly free. He had to pay all the tax on it when it was shipped back to England. I think his brother drives it now.

Giggs was not the only one to come home with a souvenir; Bosnich used our sole shopping expedition to buy a massive samurai sword. God knows why! We all tried to work out why he would want it and the only thing we could come up with was that it might be handy as a burglar deterrent.

I guess if he kept it in the bedroom he could jump out on anyone attempting to break into his home. A mad-looking Bozzie with that thing in his hands would be enough to scare off the most hardened of criminals.

Mark was the only one to find something to take home. We had all been ushered out to a mall that turned out to be one long street with every kind of electronic device I could think of. The gadgets, mostly mobile phones, wouldn't work in England so the whole evening seemed to be a waste of time.

Instead we went back to the hotel and sank back into our post-dinner routine of splitting into teams of players and staff for the sports quiz. I must admit, I tend to sneak off once the questions start flowing as the quiz nights are not the most exciting for a foreign player. All the questions are about English football history and, not being a student of the game over here, I struggle to come close to the answers. So I go off and get treatment on the latest niggle I've picked up or stick my head in a good book.

Book tokens proved indispensable for the trip to Brazil, which I have covered in another chapter, but there was little time to read once we returned from Rio as our bid for the Champions League and the English title started to reach full pace.

The only problem was that while we had been refreshed by the warm Brazilian sun, our own troublesome pitch was as bad as ever. Any sliding tackles brought up grass divots that would have embarrassed the world's worst golfer and we had to stop trying to dribble the ball out from the back because the bobbles were so bad.

Although we didn't necessarily change our style, I tried to pass the ball quicker and not take any risks. Fans or TV cameras don't always pick up the little bobbles a ball can take just as you're about to kick it, and that can make you look an awful player as the ball sails into touch via a massive slice off the outside of your boot. So safety first was the best method, a case of 'if in doubt, get rid of it'.

While we were away in Brazil the news from England was good, with Leeds and Arsenal dropping points and wasting the chance to open a decent gap at the top. But the way it was portrayed in the papers just made us laugh. It was as if they had handed us the title on the plate. It was never going to be that easy.

Leeds were pushing us hard, and after the Christmas programme we were still a point behind them. Although our challengers had played more matches than us, still we had to play catch-up and if we didn't win the games in hand all the talk would mean nothing.

As if to emphasise that point, we drew disappointingly with Arsenal on January 24 after creating enough chances to finish them off. However, finally we did put a smile back on the manager's face by picking up nine points in a row, including a tough 1–0 win at Sheffield Wednesday.

On the journey back to Manchester from that game we had the radio tuned in to one of the talk shows that have become popular in recent years, and we chuckled all the way home. Caller after caller laid into us, claiming our ten-day 'break' had allowed us to wallow in the sunshine and recharge our batteries. What those same people seemed to forget is that we have to play so many extra games in Europe every season.

It's been a long time since United have gone through a campaign that's allowed us to have seven-day gaps between games to rest aching limbs. While many of our Premiership rivals spend the week working on new training tactics or sitting on a treatment table, we're walking through customs at three in the morning after playing 90 minutes against some of the best teams in Europe.

We've done that ever since I've been at United and still managed to pick up the title in each of my three seasons. When we won the treble we were playing midweek matches right up to the end of the season. Yes, we went away, and the sun was good, but still we played three games, and had jet-lag to shake out of the system.

There isn't a harder-working team in the Premiership than Manchester United and Brazil was certainly no holiday. So to suggest everything is made easy for us is a joke, especially when stupid people with no knowledge of the game start shooting off at the mouth.

It may surprise people but often we have the radio tuned in to phone-ins on the coach after games. Most of the time we just laugh about the opinions and the lads are forever shaking their heads at some of the daft things people say. A lot of people seem to think they know everything that's going on, but don't understand professional football at all – and that goes for the presenters as well.

Our mini-run of three successive wins came to an abrupt halt on February 12 at Newcastle. Roy Keane had one of those days and saw red as we tried to haul back a 1–0 deficit and eventually we crashed 3–0. I didn't even feel we should have been behind as Newcastle hardly caused us a problem. Even their opening goal had a large chunk of luck involved in it.

While it may have looked good on the telly, Duncan Ferguson's strike was nothing more than a case of hit and hope. There wasn't any time for him to see where he was aiming. He just swung a leg and it flew in. Don't misunderstand me, I think Ferguson is a good player, with his formidable ability in the air and a decent touch, but he's not the type of forward who causes me many problems. So to see that one fly in was annoying for me.

Roy's red card was the turning point, though, as Alan Shearer twice caught us on the break as we pushed for an equaliser. Keane wasn't happy with the decision to send him off for two yellow cards, but you have to walk and it's certainly hard in the Premiership to succeed with ten men.

That result made the trip to Leeds nine days later a massively important game for us. David O'Leary's men had been the surprise package of the season, and with their confidence high from some superb results in Europe, Leeds were proving a match for any team.

We knew if we won at Elland Road it would be impossible for them to catch us, and knocking one of our rivals out of the title race in February would be an enormous boost to our chances of winning the Premiership again.

To do that we needed to be at full strength and on the ball and that's what made the lead-up to the game all the more surprising. We woke up to astonishing news that David Beckham had been dropped for the Sunday morning kick-off after a bust-up with Alex Ferguson. It was a shock to the team.

I'd seen the papers that morning but took little heed of the tale that Beckham would be left out after being sent home from training for missing a session earlier in the week. I managed to escape the drama as I was away with the Dutch national team, but had been filled in with a few scant details later.

Despite the back-page headlines, I expected Beckham to play as he had travelled with the squad and that's always a sign a player of his quality is going to be involved. The jokes were flying about over breakfast with Beckham the main topic, although the man himself was a little bit sheepish.

'You might as well have this seat,' Dwight Yorke smiled at me as I looked for somewhere to eat my cereal. 'I think it was Beckham's but he's not going to turn up.'

David didn't say anything and must have been expecting the worst. Certainly we weren't. That's why there were a few mystified faces once the ritual of the team meeting began with Ferguson reading out a line-up that didn't include David.

There wasn't a stunned silence in the room but it wasn't far off. Although he must have been gutted by the news, David handled it well and went round the room wishing everyone good luck before disappearing to let us concentrate on the game.

It was a bold move by the manager in an era when big-name players seem capable of running clubs, and it sent a message out to the rest of us in big block capitals. Ferguson was telling us: 'Don't mess with me'. The point wasn't lost on us.

With the gaffer, it doesn't matter if you are a star name or a youngster coming through the ranks, the same rules apply. I know other coaches who would have been afraid to leave a superstar like Beckham in the stands for a game as crucial as this, but that's Ferguson for you.

The move paid off as David watched a clinical performance from us, with Andy Cole scoring a great individual goal to ensure a 1–0 win which was vital to our championship bid. Just as important as Andy's goal were some stunning saves from Mark Bosnich and a terrible miss by Leeds midfielder Lee Bowyer, when he swept his effort over the target instead of planting it into an empty net.

That win proved the point that when it comes to big games there are few teams as good as United at putting on a performance. I guess it comes from all the experience we have in the side. So many players are internationals and are used to the nerves and the drama which tense matches carry with them.

The ability to handle pressure was just as evident as we went down to London for what used to be the least enjoyable fixture of the season, the meeting with Wimbledon. With both the Dons and Crystal Palace plying their trade at Selhurst Park, the over-used pitch is a nightmare, bumpy and with little grass. Add to that the way tackles fly in with a frequency and ferocity rarely seen elsewhere, and it's easy to understand why it's a fixture to which I have never looked forward.

This time, to be fair, the Dons started superbly against us and were 1–0 up after 60 seconds through a Jason Euell goal, but we drew level twice, with Andy Cole's 80th-minute equaliser ensuring a point from a horrible game.

Soon came two matches in complete contrast, as we kicked back into Champions League mode with a comfortable win over Bordeaux at home and a slightly trickier three points in France.

Things looked to be going well at Stade Lescure when one of their lads was sent off for kicking out at Beckham in a bid to wind him up. David gets targeted as a weak link when it comes to discipline after revealing a short fuse earlier in his career.

These days he has learned to deal with the attention and does his talking with his boots. The crosses he bombs into the box can kill off any team and when someone starts winding him up, he knows that just one point at the scoreboard is enough to keep his tormentors quiet.

With the home side down to ten men it was going to be a case of breaking down their resistance by passing the ball well and tiring them out, but our game plan suffered a blow when Raimond van der Gouw let a poor shot slip through his hands.

It was one of those moments that haunt keepers and, unfortunately for Rai, the error came at a time when he was enjoying a great run between the posts with some strong performances.

He redeemed himself a little later after Roy Keane had once again produced a European rescue act with the equaliser. Rai's long kick landed at the feet of Solskjaer and, as per normal, Ole's finish was immaculate.

The Champions League run continued with a sense of sweet revenge as we recovered from a shaky start and a Batistuta goal to win 3–1 against Fiorentina at Old Trafford and then confirmed our place in the quarter-finals by holding Valencia 0–0 at the Mestalla.

At the time I had little reason to suspect that the Spaniards would make it through to that year's final. They are always a threat with Gaizka Mendieta's clever running from midfield and Claudio Lopez's pace on to through-balls. If you leave a lot of space behind you they love to run into it, but we decided that when they got the ball and had time in midfield, we would drop off to neutralise Lopez's space. That limited their chances and we took four points from them.

We didn't have real problems with Valencia, but they got the bit of luck needed to go all the way to the final before they lost to Real Madrid. Mind you, if there were any doubts about their quality, a glance at the scoreline in Rome – when they beat Lazio 5–2 in the quarter-finals – offered proof that they could play.

Our draw in Valencia left us with a tasty quarter-final tie against Real Madrid and we could not have enjoyed a better preparation for the first leg in Spain.

On successive Saturdays we beat Bradford City 4–0 at Valley Parade, with Paul Scholes scoring a stunning volley, then crushed West Ham 7–1 at home after going behind to an early Paulo Wanchope strike. Scholes continued filling his boots with a hat-trick and we were frightening that day; the passing combinations were flying about and everything was easy.

It wasn't so rosy in Spain on the following Wednesday despite our air of calm. Real Madrid may be one of the biggest names in football but when our name was pulled out next to theirs there had been little concern at Old Trafford.

We had an amazing sense of self-belief that comes with being the reigning champions, and the Spaniards' results in the competition up until then were hardly of an order to leave us shuddering in trepidation. Madrid weren't playing their best football, had been beaten twice by Bayern Munich in the group stages, and had conceded four goals each time.

We weren't going to underestimate them but there was a feeling around the squad that the draw could have been a lot trickier. Bayern, Barcelona and Lazio were all still in the hat, don't forget.

We had to travel to Spain first and coming away from the Bernabeu with a 0–0 draw was an excellent result, although Andy Cole came close to nicking a vital away goal with a header which flew over the bar.

But running out at Old Trafford for the crucial second leg, with eight goals in our previous two League wins over north-east clubs Sunderland and Middlesbrough to boost pour confidence still further, it was hard to anticipate the pain we would suffer later that night.

We were used to steamrollering teams in the opening quarter of the game and even if the vital early goal didn't materialise, that meant our opponents were on the back foot. Unfortunately our whole game-plan was thrown into disarray by a freak own goal from Keane. He slid in at the near post to cut out a cross, only to divert the ball into our net with our keeper, Rai, standing helplessly behind him ready to sweep up the danger.

It was a shock to the system, prompting us to throw caution to the winds and go for the Spaniards' jugular to get back into the game. We knew two goals were needed and felt, following our exploits in Turin the previous season, that we could get them.

There is nothing to beat experience. We had been there before and pulled ourselves out of the mire in style. Something similar was needed this time around and we battered away at them, but the ball wouldn't drop in the right place and Madrid clung on far too comfortably for my liking.

Then, in the space of two second-half minutes, our dream fell apart in the most disastrous way as Raul stole the show. Our midfield pushed up when the Spaniards' play-maker, Redondo, found space down our left in the 50th minute. As Henning Berg went out to the touchline with the Argentinian to close down the danger, Redondo pulled off a sensational little trick by back-heeling the ball past Henning and turning him. That left me isolated, and as I tried to block off one angle of Redondo's attack, he threaded the ball to the feet of Raul for a simple finish at the far post.

From Real's point of view, the goal would have looked fantastic, but from mine it was awful. Sure, Redondo showed a little bit of magic, but a turn like that is something you just can't allow to happen at that level. He found it far too easy and as a defender you know you shouldn't let players beat you as simply as that.

Soon afterwards, Raul ended a sweeping move with a cool finish and we were right up against it. Now we needed four strikes, taking account of the away-goals rule, and certainly we gave it a go. Casillas pulled off some superb saves before David Beckham skipped past three defenders as if they weren't there and rifled a shot into the top corner.

There was still time, but we couldn't find a way through despite chucking everything at them. Paul Scholes added an 88th-minute penalty after Steve McManaman brought down Keane, but by then we knew the game was over.

The frantic last ten minutes had been as exciting and tense as any in my time at United, and in contrast the dressing room after the final whistle was as quiet as I'd known it.

Losing to Real was a body blow. We'd become so used to winning the big matches that we couldn't register what had just happened out there on our own turf. I felt like a boxer staggering around the ring after being knocked out. My mind refused to concentrate on the fact that we would not be in the final again.

We had been turned over 3–2 and it stuck in the throat, especially as I didn't even believe Madrid were the best team in Europe that season.

Everyone sat quietly in their places and undressed slowly. Even Ferguson spared us an ear-bashing this time as the events of the evening took their time to sink in. In fact, it took a couple of days to get over.

'Have we really lost to them?' Gary Neville questioned. 'I can't believe we've been knocked out.'

He wasn't the only one. There was widespread disbelief in the dressing room and people were walking round like zombies. It was so hard to stomach. We never expected it, hadn't really seen it coming and the shock was sickening.

We had a chance to clinch the League three days later at Southampton, but even the excitement that should have generated failed to lift the blues in training. Each session was carried out without the normal sparkle and jokes that had peppered my United career up to that point.

We tried to talk about it to alleviate some of the pain but I simply couldn't understand how we had conceded three goals at home in a European tie. United just didn't do that. The gaffer tried to lift us with talk about winning the title, but I could tell from his voice that he couldn't let the Madrid game go.

'I want to play it again,' I told Ole Gunnar Solskjaer as we changed for training. 'I know if we played it again we'd win. I'm sure of it.'

The 'what ifs' became a refrain around the club until finally we jetted down to Southampton on the Friday for the game. It was just what we needed, a match to snap us out of the doldrums and a prize to put a smile back on our faces.

But first Liverpool needed to slip up to leave the title dangling within our immediate grasp. They had to beat their Merseyside rivals, Everton, in a televised Friday night game to keep themselves in the race.

After dinner at the De Vere Hotel in the heart of Southampton, I went up to my room and watched the match. My room-mate

Ole joined me in cheering on Everton and our efforts paid off as Gerard Houllier's side were held to a 0–0 draw.

Now it was up to us! But winning at The Dell is never an easy task and in recent seasons the Reds had been embarrassed by three painful defeats, including a 6–3 hammering.

Luckily, it was nowhere near as difficult as we expected. The roar of the crammed-in crowd at the Saints' tiny ground along with a sense of anticipated success kick-started the United spirit.

We cruised into a two-goal lead by the break, helped by some ineffective tactical changes Glenn Hoddle had made to the Southampton side. It was like a stroll for me at the back and that made the whole occasion seem weird. We weren't being tested at all and the lack of action seemed to make the match drag on for an eternity after we got a third goal to seal the points.

Marian Pahars cut in from touchline to pull one back for Southampton, but by that time I had already started to clock-watch, willing the big hand to move on around to 4.45pm so the party could start.

The agonising wait finally ended and we all made for the pocket of Reds fans in the corner of the old ground to celebrate. A massive 'Champions' banner was brought out and as the champagne corks popped on the pitch I made sure I got right in the middle of the celebrations.

My tender Achilles meant I had missed out on the fun during the previous season, so to play in the game when the title was actually secured meant so much to me and I intended to enjoy it.

We didn't spend too long out on the pitch, despite the insistent fans urging us to stay and share the champagne. After some more bubbly in the dressing room and on the coach, we were safely belted in on our plane home, full of high spirits.

However, that's where the party ended for the time being. We had a game against Chelsea two days later, so despite being crowned as champions, the bulk of the champagne was put on ice for a week.

Then we had a real party at a Manchester hotel with friends and family all invited. This bash was worth waiting for, especially for me as my domestic season was over. With the title in the bag, and my Achilles playing up again, the gaffer left me out of the remaining four games. That allowed me to save my energy and rest my weary bones ahead of Euro 2000.

CHAPTER SEVEN

The Rio fiasco

Doubtlessly Manchester United will go down in history as the club that started the decline of the FA Cup.

In 1999 we became the first holders to pull out of the competition, under pressure from the Football Association, and headed off to Brazil to play in the inaugural Club World Championship instead.

But if the FA Cup is suffering a malaise, that's not just down to us. Clubs seem more interested in a Champions League place these days, as Liverpool manager Gerard Houllier admitted frequently during 2000/2001. His team were chasing three trophies, including the FA Cup, and yet he claimed that winning a unique treble would still be considered failure in his eyes, unless Liverpool booked a Champions League place.

Personally I love the famous old competition, the history, the glamour and driving up to Wembley on the big day knowing that the focus of the world is on you. Who wouldn't?

So the depressing news reports claiming that my club had betrayed football by pulling out were painful, especially as I never had a say in the decision. United were placed in an impossible position once our chief executive, Martin Edwards, and Alex Ferguson were instructed by the FA to participate in the FIFA Club World Championship to boost the bid to bring the 2006 World Cup to England. What could they do?

It meant we weren't in the country when the FA Cup fourth round was taking place. The proposal of playing a reserve team was thrown out as soon as it was suggested, and ties could not be suspended until we got back from Brazil. There was no solution. United's hands were tied and despite all the vitriolic rhetoric hurled at us, we had no choice but to board a plane.

The *Daily Mirror* launched a campaign to stop us from pulling out – that failed – and the rest of the media pilloried the club for the decision to head off to a 'joke' tournament which, we were told, was concerned largely with expanding the club's merchandising market.

It was declared that we were 'killing the FA Cup' and the words hurt. It's a wonderful competition to play in and as holders we nursed a strong desire to defend our crown. But the death knell for our cup hopes came in a meeting with the manager in November.

We were all called into a room at The Cliff and sat down to face a glum-looking Ferguson. Clearly he found it difficult to break the news, as he must have known how keen we were to retain the FA Cup.

'I'm sorry guys,' he opened, and we knew the rest. 'It's just not possible to do both and if we snubbed the offer to go to Brazil it would make things really tricky for us. So we've had to bite the bullet and pull out of the FA Cup. I know how much the cup means to all of us, but there's nothing we can do.'

He didn't need to spell out the facts to us. It was impossible for us to play in both competitions, and as the FA had all but put a PR gun to United's head, we were off to Brazil.

There was no players' revolt and talk of secret, behind-the-scenes discussions among us was utter rubbish. To a man we wanted to stay and play in the FA Cup but the board made a decision and that was it. Whether we liked it or not we had to be professional and get on with the fixtures. So, shortly after Christmas 2000, we jetted off to the sunshine of Brazil and yet more controversy.

United couldn't win. We were portrayed as the greedy boys from up north who cared little for football but passionately for our bank accounts. It was claimed that at the first whiff of a new market, the club had set off to exploit it like a money-grabbing ogre. But make no mistake: this was no publicity stunt to drum up more shirt sales. Once the decision was made there was only one thing on the minds of the players – we wanted to win the world championship.

It would be crazy to suggest that a team of players which possesses the hunger to lift a treble would then go into a professional tournament concerned only about getting the sun on their backs and enjoying a mid-season break. The only reason we're at United is our unquestionable desire to win, and that flows through every member of the squad. The desire to win every match, every tackle, every header and every game of cards.

You don't make it at United unless you are a winner, and as we queued to check in at Manchester Airport there was a steely determination that we would be returning as champions of the world.

That wasn't quite how the rest of the world saw it. As the FA Cup storm raged, it seemed like open season on the club, and the idea prevailed that the holders were sunning themselves on a beach while the rest of the Premiership teams were slogging away back home in the rain.

Once we landed in Brazil, the cameras were out and the papers' desire to portray the expedition as a Club 18-30 trip began in earnest. Back home it would have been hard not to be conned as sun, sea and sand just happen to be the major features of Rio.

We were prepared for the worst and the mass of photographers didn't disappoint in conjuring up a picture to fool the readers in England. We couldn't believe it when we caught a glance at the back pages of the English papers on sale at our hotel. Splashed across them, under headlines such as 'Life's a Beach', photographs had been cropped so it looked like we were on a holiday in Ayia Napa.

Dwight Yorke was pictured lying face down in the sand, while some of the guys sat in the pool in the background. Frustratingly for us it looked bloody convincing. It was the perfect illustration of the 'relaxing' time we were having.

But here are the facts which the reports omitted to mention. We were using Flamengo's training ground, the exotically named Fla-varra, and which boasts a stunning backdrop of mountains. But despite training in the morning when the mist was sweeping through the air and keeping the temperatures the right side side of bearable, it was still red hot by the time the sessions finished.

To combat this Flamengo had built showers and a swimming pool next to the training pitches for their own players to cool off, and next to the pool was a sand pit housing two beach volleyball courts.

After several hours in the searing heat we were desperate to cool down and the pool was the perfect place to wash away the sweat and bring our body temperatures under control before racing for the shade.

But while most of the players, myself included, dived into the pool, some of the guys who wanted to work on their touch played a bit of volleyball using their heads and feet. The paparazzi loved this, of course, and we could hear the camera shutters clicking away in the distance. Foolishly we thought nothing more of it at the time.

'Can you believe this?' Teddy Sheringham piped up after seeing the papers. 'I would like to see them do a training session in this heat, then ignore the presence of a pool and just walk off.'

'What do you expect, though?' Nicky Butt interrupted. 'We are Manchester United and we are in the sun. We are just going to have to ignore it, as always.'

The one thing the press didn't get a picture of was the swimming race we held after training one day, although I wish they had as I won it. Mark Bosnich had been instrumental in setting the whole thing up after boasting constantly about his ability in the pool. As the last Olympics proved, the Aussies love their swimming and Bosnich was convinced he could outstrip us all.

'Come on and get in the water,' he challenged every day. 'I'll show you how good we Aussies are.'

In the end we gave in, and with Mark winning the first leg, I just touched home first in the second to set up a two-man race-off. Ferguson was at the far end of the pool ready to judge and it was close as we both powered through the water. So close, in fact, that the gaffer originally gave the decision to Mark before the lads forced a change of thinking.

'I think you've got it wrong there, Boss,' Nicky Butt said. 'I thought it was clearly Jaap that got in first.'

'He's right,' chipped in Ryan Giggs. 'Jaap by a nose on that one.'

I pulled myself out of the pool with a big smile on my face. I didn't win much in Brazil but that one little moment was certainly satisfying. As Mark knows now, the Dutch aren't bad in the swimming stakes, either.

With the sun beating down, that little bit of fun came in a rare moment when we were allowed out of the shade. The club's doctors gave us permission to walk around the tourist spots the day before a game but we weren't given the nod to crash out on the beach in our bathers. Even the hotel pool was out of bounds unless it was for a quick dip followed by a short spell on the sun loungers. Afternoons round the pool drinking cocktails were definitely off the agenda.

I have to admit, it wasn't all work, work, work, though. It would have been stupid to spend every waking hour working out to impress the media and leaving ourselves too tired for the games in the process. We did have a couple of afternoons off and on one occasion a few of the guys came a cropper in a game against some bare-footed local kids on the beach.

Despite reports in the papers, I was not present as the likes of Nicky Butt, Teddy Sheringham and Jonathan Greening were soundly beaten by the real boys from Brazil. In their own element, the kids flicked over the sand like beach hoppers and showed off their superb quick feet, or so the returning losers claimed.

The embarrassed few came back to camp ready to suffer humiliation at the hands of their team-mates, but to their surprise the quips never materialised. I think the feeling among the rest of us was simply: 'There but for the grace of God go I!'

Although I kept mainly to the hotel I wasn't a total hermit and I did manage to take a stroll along the famous Copacabana beach, although it was a let-down. After hearing all my life about what a magical place it was, I could hardly wait to find out for myself. Unfortunately, my impression was that it was just a very big beach.

I was more interested in taking the cable car up to the top of Sugar Loaf Mountain with Raimond van der Gouw and Ole Gunnar Solskjaer, mainly due to its appearance in one of the James Bond films. It's the one where Jaws tries to cut through the cable with his teeth and I felt I had to give the ride a try. Never again though, it was too high for me.

To be honest, I'm a bit scared of heights. When I'm in a plane looking down I'm quite happy, but when I found myself in a tiny little car dangling what seemed like miles up in the air and swaying from side to side, I seemed to be seized by some sort of phobia. I gripped on tight and tried my hardest to make sure no-one else in the car noticed my reaction. Whether they did or not, I'm not sure.

'Are you alright there, Jaap?' Ole called out at one point.

'Yep, I'm fine,' I lied back. 'I just want to get a better look at the view.'

'Why aren't you looking down then?' he replied.

My threatening smile must have said enough, as that was the last I heard of the matter. It was an experience, though, and after that I decided to concentrate even more on winning football matches. Certainly I wasn't adventurous enough to try out the long trek up to the Corcavado to see the famous statue that sits high overlooking the city of Rio.

It was built in 1931 to mark a century of Brazilian independence and, standing more than 30 metres tall, it was an amazing sight – especially from my hotel window. However, the view also indicated clearly the energy-sapping climb needed to reach the top and I baulked at the thought of clambering up there in the heat.

As well as having the press on our backs about the supposed holiday, rather amusingly we found ourselves under the microscope for our lack of PR work. Other teams made a special effort to go round the slums, or favelas as they were known locally, creating plenty of good photo opportunities. Our absence was noted with disdain by the media and their 'holier than thou' attitude annoyed me intensely.

'Why should we spend all our time doing PR work?' I thought. 'We're here to win a tournament, not to be politicians.'

Our primary task was to play in the Club World Championship, not to visit schools and entertain people. All we wanted to do was train, rest and think about winning the trophy. To this day I think we were right just to play football and concentrate solely on winning games. We did take a break to meet some youngsters to promote United's work with the children's charity UNICEF, and we enjoyed watching them play their tin drums before joining in a kick-around. But concentrating on the next game was always more important to me.

Training and playing football in Brazil was hard work. We worked out as normally we would in England, despite the heat and the jet-lag which bit deep into our energy reserves from the moment we touched down on January 3.

It's difficult to explain how temperatures of nearly 40 degrees centigrade can affect you when you're playing at the highest level of competition, but the heat tends to squeeze the very last drop of life out of your body.

After 20 minutes it's so warm you can't breath properly; filling your lungs with air gets more and more difficult. In turn that plays havoc with concentration levels; not that it's easy to concentrate anyway with sweat running constantly down your face and stinging as it gets into your eyes

Walking straight into those conditions after leaving the cold of England came as a real shock to the system and so we needed time to adjust. With a mere three days from touching down to running out for the opening match, we didn't have long enough. We trained in the mornings before the burning sun hit its peak temperatures, so I stuck on an extra top to help my body get used to the fluid loss and the heat.

But hot as it was then, that was nothing compared to the haze which enveloped the pitch as we ran out for our first game against Necaxa in the afternoon sun. The Maracana Stadium is oval-shaped and it allows no breeze to enter to lift the stifling heat. As I soon discovered, trying to run for long periods in that sweltering atmosphere was nearly impossible.

Some of the lads were desperate to play in the great Maracana, and mentioned how famous it was in England, but to me the place was neither historic nor attractive. I have to confess I had never heard of it before we flew out, as the Dutch don't seem to have the same feelings for the stadium which is labelled the home of Brazilian football.

Furthermore, there were few fans in the antiquated stands, which didn't endear the place to me. Perhaps I'm missing the point, but I was untouched by the Maracana myth. It did nothing for me and was simply another football ground.

While we suffered in the heat, the Mexicans, well used to such conditions, were buzzing around like flies, and when David Beckham was sent off for a challenge which caught his opponent high on the leg, looking worse than it actually was, we were really up against it. Yet even with all those obstacles, we managed to force a 1–1 draw and we would have started the competition with a victory if Dwight Yorke had converted a penalty.

We walked off the pitch in total bemusement. United are used to playing in front of some of the biggest crowds in the world and we are always powered on by the amazingly fervent support which follows us wherever we pull on our boots. This game was played in a surreal atmosphere, with few Brazilian fans interested in the match, and those that did make the effort to turn up early – it seemed that the main event was local side Vasco da Gama's evening match – soon got behind their neighbours from the southern hemisphere.

That disappointing draw meant it was crucial for us to beat the Brazilians and Ferguson rammed home the point before kick-off two days later.

'We've not come half round way the world and put up with all that shit from the media to go home with our tails between our legs,' he boomed in his pre-match team talk. 'We are the best team in the world and now it's time for you to go out and prove it.

'Let's show everyone here and at home what this club is really about, and that's winning matches no matter who we play or where we play. That prize is there for the taking. Do you want to be champions of the world?'

With his words rattling around our brains we started well and Vasco were struggling to break us down, even with the combined threat of the great Brazilian strikers Romario and Edmundo.

But two misguided back-passes from Gary Neville were snapped up and punished by the home side, to the joy of their manic support, as Vasco da Gama built a 3–0 lead by the interval. The more their self-confidence burgeoned, the faster we tired, and once they started show-boating, the game was over.

Their technique is sensational, they just love rolling out the tricks, and that is something to admire in itself, although there are plenty of players in our dressing room who can perform similar party-pieces. Ryan Giggs, for one, has exceptionally quick feet and could teach the Brazilians a thing or two. But on that occasion, we didn't have the confidence to try them on the park when a slip could have left us looking stupid.

Once we went 3–0 down the game was up. We spent so long pressing for the ball that our legs were heavy, and although Nicky Butt pulled a goal back nine minutes from time, the competition was over.

We played South Melbourne in the final game without a chance of progressing, so with the hard pitches causing my troublesome Achilles to flare up, I sat on the sidelines and sweated that one out.

It was an anti-climactic end to a disappointing tournament which failed to live up to my expectations. Maybe it can grow into something worthwhile. To do that, though, the location has to be changed to a part of the world that loves the game and is prepared to embrace every aspect of it. Our clashes with the Mexicans and the Australians were simply sideshows for the Brazilian fans, who were interested only in their team's ability to conqueror all challengers.

Playing to a handful of fans in a 100,000-seater stadium hardly gave the players the impression that this was the biggest and most prestigious club tournament in the world. The whole set-up was second-rate compared to the Champions League and the World Cup, even though I must admit the locals loved watching their side cruise to the crown.

In future, it would be better to play the tournament regularly in Europe, where the competitors would receive more appreciation from the fans of the host nation. The promotion of the event on television also needs to be looked at and improved. When I mentioned the Club World Championship on trips back home, my friends looked at me blankly. Most people in Holland didn't even know I was out in Brazil.

At the moment I think people tend to look upon the Toyota Cup winners as the real champions of the world as it's become part of the world football calendar. It's going to take plenty of years for the FIFA Club World Championship to catch on.

However, as Alex Ferguson pointed out while we were there, just being in Brazil meant United had left their mark on the competition.

'It's good to be part of something big,' he said. 'We can always say we were there at the beginning.'

CHAPTER EIGHT

The Gaffers

A fuming Alex Ferguson was already waiting in the dressing room as timidly I crept back in at half-time. It was obvious a bollocking was on the cards, but what I didn't expect was seeing the gaffer lose his cool to such an extent that he nearly wiped out my season – and the prospects of collecting three medals in May.

It was November 1998. We were drawing 1–1 at Sheffield Wednesday when the rant began and, to be honest, we hadn't been playing too well. Spotting the thunder in his face as my studs clattered against the tiled floor, I took a seat behind the treatment table; ample protection, I reckoned, to be safe from a face-to-face showdown.

'What the fuck is that?' he started. 'What the fuck are you lot playing at?' No-one was willing to answer, so he carried on.

'That is the biggest load of shite I've ever seen. Not one of you can look me in the eye, because not one of you deserves to have a say. I can't believe you've come here and decided to toss it off like that crap you're playing out there.'

As his rage grew, Ferguson's face began to burn with fury and his cheeks developed a harsh red glow. 'He's going to explode,' I thought – and he did.

The gaffer lashed out at the treatment table with a kick strong enough to send a ball flying out of Hillsborough. It took me a second to realise what was about to happen as the heavy table came flying my way. Suddenly the notion struck me that it was heading for my lap or, even more worryingly, my toes.

Drink bottles, rubs and tapes smacked me in the chest as I

pulled my feet back and stuck my hands over my bollocks to try to save myself from damage. There were gasps around the dressing room as the metal-legged construction crashed to the ground just inches from my retracted toes. I thought: 'What's going on here then?'

If the table had smashed into my toes or on to the top of my feet, it would have crushed several bones and ruled me out for a lengthy spell, probably costing me my place in the team for the rest of the season.

But even the fact that he'd nearly crippled his most expensive defender didn't stop Ferguson. Maybe he learned his lesson, though, and picked out other targets for his anger. As he singled out players one by one for a personal verbal bashing, Ferguson picked up the plastic water bottles now scattered across the floor and hurled them into the shower. That's how furious he was. I've witnessed him angry before, but it was one of the best outbursts I've seen and is folklore in our dressing room.

Can you imagine the headlines if he'd broken my foot and put me out for the season? 'Furious Fergie cripples his own player.' Certainly that would have enhanced his ball-busting reputation.

By the way, we lost the game 3–1! We tried to lift ourselves but had started the match too slowly, and once that happens it's hard to up the pace. It's always better to start aggressively with a high tempo and quick passing. It allows you to rip into teams and deny them the chance to settle into their stride. Some teams, if not beaten before they've started, are down and out after 15 minutes if we've launched into them from the off.

There have been plenty of other flare-ups since that day at Hillsborough and I'm sure there's a few more in store before Ferguson quits at the end of 2001/2002.

It's his way of letting players know they're failing to match the standards he's set for the club. If a red-shirted player is misplacing passes or losing out in tackles, he'll pick on him and give it both barrels. It's a man's game and at this level you can't afford to pussy-foot around, especially at half-time.

There's just 15 minutes to sort out any problem situations and the direct approach is the best way to make a point. It's not about personalities or egos. If Ferguson feels that he can improve the team on any particular day by a few well-chosen words, delivered in a rousing style, then he'll dispense them.

I've never seen a United player have a go back at him. He gets what he wants. You can say you don't agree in a calmer moment, but when he's got something on his mind he won't have any backchat.

When he is laying down the law, I'm not scared of him and nor are the rest of the team, though the respect I hold for the gaffer is so high that I wouldn't challenge his authority.

Ferguson always wants to win and you can feel the desire bursting out in every team-talk he delivers. There's no real deep, meaningful science in our pre-match chats. He just deals with everything we need to know. What system we have to play; what the other team's strong points are; how they like to play and how we go about stopping them.

If we haven't done well in a previous game he'll lets us know all about it and his address will be snappy or, if we're in form, he will merely cajole us to keep us on edge.

Most importantly, the gaffer talks only about winning. There's never an order to go out and keep things tight, looking for the draw. That's his psychology all over – victory is imperative. It's Manchester United's way and the tradition has seeped into his blood.

'Why should we fear anyone?' he asks. 'We are Manchester United!'

You can see that attitude spilling over on to the pitch in the way he spent a season with a stopwatch in his hand, timing matches to put pressure on referees. He felt his beloved United were being cheated out of time by officials when teams came and closed up shop at Old Trafford, and he made his point an in intimidating way.

Ferguson can be just as forceful with his own players and anyone in the Reds camp claiming not to have been subjected to one of his killer stares or venomous rants is a liar.

But also the gaffer has a caring side that has endeared him to all at United. His door is always open, and time and again he hears a knock from one of his boys wanting some help or advice on personal matters. At these times we all know there will be none of the famed hair-dryer treatment, so called because he gets up close to your face and yells so loudly that your hair blows backwards.

It's then that you realise the compassionate side of the man. His man-management skills have gone beyond the text-book guides. Ferguson cares deeply for his players and his willingness to help has turned him into a father-figure to many of them.

I know from personal experience how Fergie can be compassionate when the time calls for it. I was suffering with my Achilles injury at one point when it was my turn to pop into his office and ask for a favour.

'My wife, Ellis, has recently given birth, and I want to go home to Holland so my relatives can see Megan,' I proposed hopefully.

'What a good idea,' he replied without even thinking about it. 'You've been sat around for several months with your foot in plaster so the break will do you good.'

It was a huge relief for me knowing I could have a break. He understood how I was feeling and, rather than keeping me chained to a weights machine, he happily wished me a safe trip.

His relations with the rest of the team seem to run along similar lines, even with guys with whom he was said to have fallen out. David Beckham has had the odd run-in with Ferguson, most notably over missing a training session before the crucial match with Leeds in my second season at the club, but soon the row was forgotten and the pair were as friendly as ever.

Mark Bosnich is another player with whom Ferguson is supposed to have feuded. He was signed on a Bosman-style free transfer to replace Peter Schmeichel, carrying a reputation as one of the best keepers in Britain and with a string of international caps for Australia to his credit.

But a series of injuries left him struggling for his place and the press had a field day with rumours that the manager was unhappy with Mark's weight, and had not wanted to sign him in the first place. He was a 'board signing' in their eyes, meaning the directors had moved for Bosnich because he was available without a fee.

I never heard Mark and the manager have cross words in the 18 months he was at the club, and there were many times when the pair were laughing and joking with each other – hardly the sign of a hate-filled relationship.

But Ferguson's no pushover, and when he's on the training ground you sense he's watching like a hawk, even though he rarely takes a break from his mobile phone! When first I joined up with United in Norway in 1998 on a pre-season tour, I was amazed to look up from training to see him chattering away, with the phone glued constantly to his ear. I thought it was strange and I looked around at the other players to see if they were as shocked as me. They must have been used to it, as none of them batted an eyelid.

Back in Holland the manager was always in command, barking out instructions, but at United Brian Kidd was the one in charge of training with Ferguson making sure everyone was on their toes. Occasionally he pulls a player to one side and has a little chat or offers some advice, but generally Brian, before he left to take over as manager of Blackburn in December 1998, and then his successor, Steve McClaren, were left to get on with the job.

Ferguson does like to get involved with some of the ball work, though, and you can hear the groan when he joins in with one of our least favourite exercises, known as the box.

We call it the box because a group of eight players stand around the outside of a coned-off rectangle with two men in the middle hunting down the ball as it's passed around. If anyone in the eight-man phalanx makes a mistake it's their turn to chase as the ball fizzes around in a 60-second lung-busting spell of mad ten-yard sprints.

When we set up for our regular stint he tends to wander over and we jockey for position to make sure we don't stand next to him. If you're unlucky enough to lose the jostling battle and are positioned next to the gaffer, watch out, because he always stitches you up. Standing just two feet away, he'll pelt a ball at you with such ferocity that it's impossible to control, before giggling away like a school kid. It's a trick he must have pulled a thousand times but still he laughs like the first time he's seen it happen.

It's the only time you can talk to Ferguson as if he's one of the players. Most of the time he keeps his distance and you know who's the boss. But if he's tricked you in the box, then he doesn't mind you jokingly having a dig. To him it's just a seal of approval for how successful his little game has turned out.

Ferguson does love his psychology as Kevin Keegan found out in 1996 when United and Newcastle were battling it out for the title. The Reds had struggled to beat a Leeds side reduced to ten men after their keeper, Mark Beeney, was sent off. Ferguson voiced his hope that Leeds would fight just as hard for a result in their final few games, one of which was against Newcastle.

Keegan, then the Magpies manager, saw this as an insult to Howard Wilkinson, Leeds' boss at the time, and in an amazing outburst on Sky TV Kevin lost his cool. Talking about the race for the title, he spat out the never-to-be- forgotten phrase: 'I'd love it if we beat them, just love it'. Newcastle didn't, though, letting a 12-point lead slip and handing the crown of wind-up king to Ferguson.

It's a style of management which he's used hundreds of time in the past to get us in the right frame of mind for the big games. He's always on at us about how the whole world is against United.

'They hate you,' he'll yell, about no-one in particular and everyone in general in a pre-match team talk. 'Look at what the papers are saying today. They claim you're arrogant, they reckon you're too big for your boots.

'They are saying you're not anywhere near good enough to beat the best in Europe. And look what their centre-forward has said about you, Jaap,' he'll continue. 'He reckons you're slow, easy to turn. Are you going to stand for that?'

We all know what he's trying to do, but it works a treat every time. All the players read the papers, know what he's talking about and it seems to get the right reaction. We go out furious, determined to prove our doubters wrong, motivated to the extreme.

However, he doesn't urge the players to use gamesmanship in a bid to pressure referees into giving us more than our fair share of decisions. That charge was levelled at him when we conceded a penalty against Middlesbrough in January 2000 and Roy Keane, myself and several other players chased referee Andy D'Urso half-way across a muddy Old Trafford pitch to remonstrate with him.

But our anger was not a contrived plot hatched pre-match in Ferguson's brain. It was a spur-of-the-moment thing which came from the players and the mentality we all have towards winning. It's embedded in the team. If the referee gives a bad decision, we go up and tell him, but the gaffer is not one for encouraging us to intimidate the official.

I know people might think, when reviewing his earlier days at United, that Ferguson signed players who liked a little moan at the men in black. Paul Ince and Mark Hughes were not shy in coming forward, and in the current team Roy Keane likes to have his say.

But Ferguson prefers us to leave the referee alone. In fact, after the Middlesbrough match he sat us down and had a chat about the situation, telling us firmly that he didn't want to see such a fracas happening again.

In team talks he even insists that we don't get involved with the referee or players from other teams and just concentrate on our own game instead. But while he wants us to focus on the football, he does seem adept at using the media to get his own message across, even if that is done merely to gain a psychological advantage over other teams.

Reading between the lines, I can see him turning the screw and piling on the pressure. I think that's a good thing, although it's not just Ferguson who uses the media. Plenty of players do it as well.

When we won the Champions League, opposing players tried to use the press to unsettle my concentration. My old sparring partner, Filippo Inzaghi of Juventus, and some of the Inter Milan players tried to create doubts in my mind by claiming I was too slow. They need to work harder than that if they're going to upset me. I know from contests with some of the best in the world that there are not many players quicker than me.

I don't think Ferguson is that keen on the press anyway, and I know some journalists think that, at times, he is downright rude. Their opinion is not going to bother him and his reaction to the media doesn't bother me either.

In some cases I feel he has every right to be discourteous, considering the things that are written about him personally and the club as a whole. In the face of some of the criticism he's received in the past, why should he be the perfect gentleman all the time?

I don't feel I have to defend him, but part of his manner might be down to his desperation to win each and every game of football. During the week he is charming around the training ground, but on match day you can sense he is on edge.

His comments are sharp and designed to get ideas across in a serious and incisive manner. You can almost see his brain ticking over and the only thing he is thinking about is how to win.

He was backed up in that by our coach at United until the summer of 2001, Steve McClaren. When I arrived, Brian Kidd was taking all the training sessions, but when he went to Blackburn it was essential that Ferguson recruited a top right-hand man. He chose well, as Steve played a big part in ensuring we stayed at our best and his use of new technology gave training an extra dimension.

Steve used a rather nifty laptop which allowed him to download videotapes of each match and he employed special software to dissect the action. So rather than telling me that the central defenders were too far apart or mentioning how the midfield failed to pick up a runner, he could show me. That made it so much easier to visualise the situation and understand the point Steve was trying to make.

Against certain teams we can get away with mistakes. Better-quality players have a bit more upstairs and will find any gaps. So the awareness Steve brought to our game helped on the big European nights against the world's top stars.

Like all assistant managers and coaches, he was the link between the gaffer and the players. He could afford to joke more, join in with the banter and listen to gripes and moans, knowing that probably the players would open up to him more than with the manager.

McClaren proved a good listener and he won the trust of the players by earning their respect through his work on the training ground. Football clubs are all about players proving they have the ability and attitude to be on a par with their peers. If a player, manager or coach isn't good enough, they're found out quickly and the respect is lost. Often you hear about a manager losing the dressing room; that's when the players no longer hold him in enough esteem to follow his orders to the word.

McClaren changed training routines constantly, and the intelligent way his coaching was delivered achieved results. He worked hard in 2000/2001 to improve our defence and it paid off as our goals-against tally testified.

It was an area the management were keen to improve as we were conceding too many goals, considering the quality of players we had at the back. We spoke about it as a team and agreed that we weren't operating well enough as a unit. There were other teams in England and Europe whose individual defenders would struggle to get in the United team, but they played better as groups.

When we won the title in 1999/2000, the four teams below United – Arsenal, Leeds, Liverpool and Chelsea – all let in fewer goals and that was a warning to us. So from the start of the following campaign Steve got the back four together and impressed on us the need to work as a unit.

If the ball is in the left-back's area, the defenders have to shuffle across with the right-sided player almost coming in as a third central defender, and if the play is switched to the other flank we move across to counter the danger in a line. It's almost like having a piece of string tied through us, as the barrier has to remain intact. I heard that the former Arsenal manager, George Graham, does a similar exercise with players touching each other's shoulders as they shuffle across the pitch.

Also we talked about playing for offsides and came to the decision that it's not a game-plan we intended to use rigorously. We have enough pace in defence to cover players running from deep or strikers trying to catch us on the turn. In addition we decided to sit deeper when a player had possession in midfield and had no pressure on him. If he had time to look up and pick out a runner, like Freddie Kanoute did in feeding Paolo Di Canio for the winner in the FA Cup defeat by West Ham, we would have to stay back.

On that occasion I had to go and close down Kanoute, although I was never going to get there in time to put a challenge in. If the rest of the defence had sat just inside the box there would have been no room into which Di Canio could run. But we all charged out and the Frenchman had acres of space to slip through a pass for his team-mate to beat Fabien Barthez.

Of course, it was not just the defence on which McClaren worked. He was trying constantly to improve every aspect of our play, but I've concentrated more on the back-line here as it's the area which involves me the most.

It might have been expected that Steve's name would be in the frame to take over when Ferguson retires in the summer of 2002, but he accepted the job of coaching Middlesbrough a year earlier. Anyway, he would have been up against some tough competition for the Old Trafford role as obviously it is one of the top berths in football.

Probably it's a more enticing prospect than even the likes of Real Madrid and Juventus, as United don't have the politics of those clubs. In general terms, the Reds can point to a track record of sticking with their managers, rather than changing at the end of every season when a new president is voted in.

Ferguson has been at the club since 1986 and was given time to develop a treble-winning team. Loyalty like that in the modern game appears to be rare and has to something any manager considers when eyeing a job.

Whatever, it will be difficult for United to find someone to fill the gaffer's boots. Picking someone with the same presence in the dressing room and status in the game will be very difficult. With that in mind I think the club must go for someone who has played recently at the highest level and understands modern football.

The game has moved on in the past ten years and the pace and technical skills are of such high quality that players don't get time on the ball or to think about picking up runners. Everything has to be instinctive and managers have to appreciate that rather than living in the past.

In Euro 2000 the Dutch team had just that type of manager in Frank Rijkaard. His knowledge of the game was excellent and the squad respected his international record as a player. He had quit playing only recently so he knew how difficult it was out on the pitch and could relate to the problems we had.

Of course, it's no good appointing someone simply because they were once a great player. The right candidate also needs to have the ability to get his message across to the players and not everyone can do that. Ferguson is excellent at communicating and one of the messages he drills into us constantly is that we should have fun.

In the dash to win trophies, too many people forget the fun factor, but it's one of the reasons I will always look back at my time under Ferguson with a sense of immense gratitude. We had a ball!

CHAPTER NINE

In my pocket

Ronaldo, Rivaldo, Batistuta. Name any top striker and I can recall a battle with him at some point in my career. And after those experiences I can say, hand on heart, that when I'm on form I don't fear anyone. If I'm going into a game feeling fit, with confidence flowing through my veins, I believe taking on anybody is possible.

I'm not saying I'm Superman, it's merely that I'm positive about my ability. Of course, there are always matches in which I'm not at 100-per-cent capacity. Indeed, with the amount of games I play and the necessity of having to carry knocks, it's impossible for anyone to be at his peak all the time.

It's at that point that I have to rely on my technique and experience to come to the fore and get me out of trouble. There are ways to control any forward once you know the type of game he intends to play, and at the top level it's difficult for someone to throw up any surprises.

Almost every game is televised now and it is easy to pick up players' strengths and weaknesses without constantly studying videotapes. I'm not about to get caught in the trap of dismissing some of the top players in the world completely, though. What makes them so good is their ability to surprise a defender; men such as Romario or Kluivert can dupe any opponent with a clever touch or a burst of electric pace. A quick flick-on and they're away.

Speed is a dangerous commodity which defenders hate coming up against, but strikers need more than just an electric set of heels to cut it in the higher echelons of the game. There has to be an end-product.

Andy Cole, Nicolas Anelka and Patrick Kluivert can all leave most defenders dragging behind, but the difference between them and a nippy Third Division marksman is that they've learned how to make the most of their prize asset by delivering goals.

Playing against the likes of Roma striker Gabriel Batistuta is a massive test of nerve, as such men have a tendency to sit on the shoulder of a marker, waiting to pounce. Not often do they drop deep to look for the ball and get involved in link-up play. You have to be aware of where Batistuta is all the time. You can be sure he knows where you are and is backing himself to beat you to a ball delivered in behind the defence.

The Argentinian has the advantage of knowing where he is going to run, either left of you, past your right shoulder or straight behind your back into space. That knowledge gives him a split-second advantage over his marker and once someone with his kind of ability is in front, then it's time to start praying. You aren't going to catch him and if there's a sniff of a chance he's going to put it away.

Batistuta's goal against United for Fiorentina in the 1999/2000 Champions League group game was the perfect example. As we all charged out after each attack had been cleared, always the Argentine made sure he was level with me, the last defender, and when Roy Keane tried a back pass to get us out of trouble, Batistuta was off in a flash to collect possession and score.

I was close to him, but his anticipation was fantastic and there was no hope of me cutting him off as his pace turned Keane's backpass into the perfect through-ball. Any defender will say that playing against this type of forward is extremely difficult. When a striker sits in front of you, it's easy to see him and watch him make a run, but when he's next to you it's harder to keep tabs on him.

So you tend to drop off a bit more because you want him in your eye-line and in those circumstances he can get closer to your goal. A clever striker will stand between two defenders to confuse a pairing by posing questions about who is going to mark him. While you are thinking about whose responsibility he is, he has nipped past you and is bearing down on goal.

You have to find a player's weaknesses when he has this kind of pace. Take Michael Owen, for example. In this country everyone seems to believe the Boy Wonder can do no wrong, and I find the hype that surrounds the Liverpool striker a bit over the top.

When he broke on to the scene with that amazing goal against Argentina in the World Cup he was hailed as world-class. There's no doubting that he's a good striker, whose primary strength is running at the heart of a defence with the ball at his feet and utilising his fantastic pace.

But opponents such as England's Euro 2000 rivals have learned to combat that by dropping off him, ensuring there isn't the space behind them for Michael to attack. Without that option he loses much of his potency. Michael's not such a big threat when people play balls into the channels for him to latch on to.

I'm not saying he's a bad player, but his first touch isn't the greatest. As a defender you know a particular striker's weaker foot and with Owen you try to jockey him towards his left side. Then you feel there is time to get in a tackle or block before he has total control of the ball and is ready to set himself for a shot.

To be fair to him, as he seems a nice guy, whenever I've seen him interviewed I can tell he doesn't think he's the best striker in the world and admits he needs to work on his game. But I don't think the English press, with their desperation for a new hero every week, help him in that respect. He scores a few goals and all of sudden the newspapers scream that Milan want to buy him for £25 million. That's absolute rubbish and I'm sure he knows it.

On the flip side of the coin is Luis Figo. He's a player who picks up the ball deep in his opponents' half and reaches full pace before he even gets near a defender. Most people will remember his Euro 2000 strike against England, although I felt he had a bit of luck with a deflection off Tony Adams for that one.

A vision of the future – playing for PSV against Arsenal in a pre-season friendly in July 1997. Little did I know at that point that the Gunners would become one of my main adversaries just one year later.

Signing for United in May 1998 in the days when I used to have a little more hair.

Fitness fanatic – working up a sweat in training with Jordi Cruyff and Roy Keane. I'm not the biggest fan of distance running.

We have lift off – introducing myself to Michael Owen in my first season in the Premiership.

My former PSV manager Dick Advocaat looking thoughtful in his managerial role at Rangers. He was interested in taking me to Scotland but could not afford to match PSV's asking price.

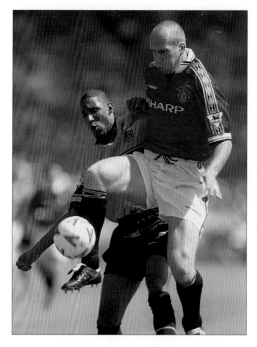

Making sure Nicolas Anelka does not get the better of me during the 1998 Charity Shield. Unfortunately he did slip away and score later in the match as Arsenal won 3–0.

Winning by a head – beating massive German striker Carsten Jancker to the ball in the Champions League final. He is just the kind of player I enjoy going into battle against.

Champions! – enjoying the most dramatic night of my career after we scored two goals in the dying minutes to beat Bayern Munich in the Champions League final.

Party time – proving I can carry a tune, while being nimble on my toes with a celebration jig during the Champions League winning party.

Cup kings – Peter and I had our run-ins on the pitch but they were forgotten as soon as the final whistle sounded.

Turning Japanese – hitting the back of the net in training as I prepare
for the Toyota Cup final in Japan's National Stadium.

No carnival in Rio – keeping my
eye on Romario during the World
Club Championships in Brazil.
Despite coming to the end of his
career, the Vasco da Gama striker
is still a handful.

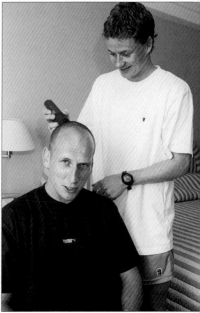

Short back and sides – room-mate Ole
Gunnar Solskjaer gives me a trim.
Ole was a joy to room with after putting
up with Jordi's late-night phone calls.

My one and only –
drilling the ball past
Leicester's Kasey Keller
for my first goal in
United's colours in
January 1999.

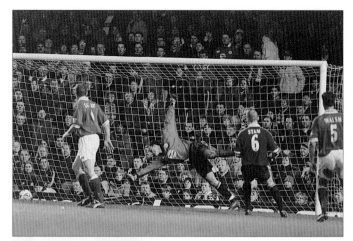

Boiling over – I'm joined by
David Beckham, Nicky Butt
and Roy Keane as we confront
referee Andy D'Urso after
he awarded Middlesbrough
a penalty in the clash at
Old Trafford.

Own-goal – I felt gutted
for Roy Keane and
the team after he had
diverted the ball into
our net as we lose out to
Real Madrid in the 2000
Champions League
quarter-finals.

Dutch delight – congratulating Patrick Kluivert on his hat-tric against Yugoslavia during Euro 2000. The 6–1 win was the highlight of the tournamen for Holland.

Mr and Mrs Stam – with my wife Ellis after being awarded the Golden Shoe for being voted the best player of the year in Holland in 1998.

Heading for row Z – my missed spot kick in the penalty shoot-out against Italy contributed to our disappointing exit from Euro 2000 at the semi-final stage.

The Kaiser – meeting Franz Beckenbauer one of the game's great defenders.

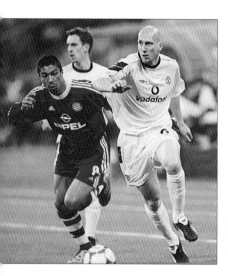

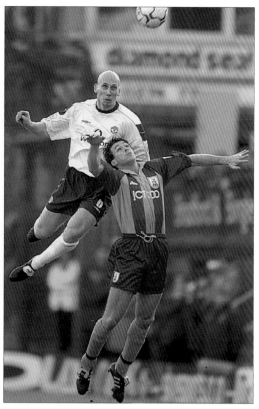

éjà-vu – chasing down Bayern Munich's iovane Elber as we lose out at the uarter-final stage of the Champions eague for a second year running. was a defeat that overshadowed Premiership winning season.

Fit again – out jumping Bradford's Ashley Ward in my comeback game after an Achilles tendon operation had left me stuck on the sidelines for four frustrating months.

Popping corks – tasting the champagne after securing the Premiership for the third season in a row. The presentation did not take place until May but the title was effectively won by the New Year.

Van the man – summer signing Ruud van Nistelrooy is sure to boost our bid for Champions League success in the coming seasons. Winning that trophy again is top of my hit-list.

In full flow – worrying Sir Alex Ferguson by breaking from the back with the ball. I enjoy taking on defenders but the boss has urged me to add some caution to my play.

Little Lisa – carrying my daughter Lisa during a lap of honour at our 2000/2001 Premiership victory celebration. She was frightened by the post-match fireworks and didn't enjoy the occasion as much as I did

If you let a player like Figo run at you, as the English defence did in that game, there's no-one better at punishing you. When I've played against him I make a point of closing him down as soon as possible, once he comes into my zone, and at that stage I leave someone else to pick up my striker. That's essential, as you can't give Figo any time to get in motion.

If the ball is played into him, you have to be tight or even try to get in front of him to nick possession. Once he turns and runs you're playing into his hands and often the penalty is seeing him wheel away in celebration after finding the net. If anyone is unfortunate enough to be left one-on-one with Figo coming at him like a charging bull, I guess the best plan is to run with him. Go diving in and he will skip past in a flash and be on his way to goal.

My United team-mate Ryan Giggs is a similar sort of player and as a member of the imaginary Defenders Union, I feel for opposing players who are forced to leave their positions and move across to challenge him. Even if there are two or three defenders in his zone, still Giggs can skip past once he hits full pace.

At United we don't like to play man-for-man marking, so when we faced Figo in his Barcelona days, it was a case of whoever was nearest picked him up. As centre-halves we tend to split the pitch down the middle. The left side is mine, with my partner Wes Brown taking the right. Wes, Gary Neville and most of my fellow stoppers at United all favour the right side, and although I'm not left-footed, I'm comfortable on that side so I don't mind covering that area of the pitch.

Then it's down to talking. We won't follow a striker right across the backline just because we are marking him, we'll pass him on when he swaps zones, and with people like Mikael Silvestre and Gary Neville often playing at full-back, we can even let a big guy drift to the flank knowing he won't be winning aerial contests too easily.

Carsten Jancker tried this a lot by sitting on the shoulder of Silvestre when Bayern Munich beat us 1–0 at Old Trafford in the Champions League quarter-final in the spring of 2001. He is a monstrous size, but Mikael's no midget and the German didn't get the joy in the air he was expecting.

Passing players on like that is a great example of the kind of communication needed on a football pitch, and that's never more important than it is for two central defenders. They have to work in tandem no matter what the combination.

One player might be better on the ball, while the other is stronger in the tackle and climbs well to win aerial challenges. Leeds have a good combination in Rio Ferdinand and Lucas Radebe. Rio likes to come out from the back with the ball and beat a man or spray around his passes, in contrast to Lucas who, although he can play a bit, is keener to get involved in battles with strikers.

The key is knowing how each other prefers to perform and that kind of knowledge comes with playing together over a long period of time. It's something Wes and I are working on at the back for United. We are quite similar in being physically strong, quick over the ground and good in one-on-one situations.

Just as importantly, I am starting to read Wes' game and vice-versa. When he's on the ball I can work out whether he's going to dive into a tackle or just hold his player up, and then I can cover the right area of the pitch instinctively.

I'm hoping we can grow into a formidable partnership, dreaded by opposing strikers in the way that Steve Bruce and Gary Pallister squeezed the enthusiasm of forwards during the first half of the 1990s.

Their daunting alliance was the backbone on which Ferguson built the first of his winning teams. People talk about them to this day, and the fact that Pallister struggled when first he came to Old Trafford has been forgotten. Ferguson stuck with him after his £2.3 million move from Middlesbrough and in time, with the domineering Bruce alongside him, Pallister transformed himself into one of England's premier centre-halves.

Like Pallister and Bruce, I love battling with a forward, but not as much as seeing his number being called from the touchline. Watching him drag himself off to be substituted tells me I'm having a good game and he hasn't done enough to keep his manager happy. The situation is a little different when there are just two minutes to go, though, as he's probably man-of-the-match.

When a new striker comes on I don't let it break my concentration, I try to keep doing the things I have been doing well, although if a quicker forward is up against me or a striker who likes to drop deep, I may have to change my positioning.

At United we have had two of the best exponents of pulling defenders out of position in Teddy Sheringham and Dwight Yorke, and luckily, at least until Teddy rejoined Tottenham Hotspur in May 2001, I have not had to worry about coming up against them in anger.

What makes these link-men special is their willingness to head back into the midfield jungle to lose a marker and find some space. If they can't lose their immediate markers, they will move out into the channels between full-backs and central defenders.

Facing a striker who drops deep can be tricky, and it's definitely harder to mark a forward who tends to do that. Very early on you have to decide how far into the midfield you are prepared to go with him. Even that's not as easy as it sounds. Dropping into the middle of the park with an opponent leaves a big gap for other midfielders to run into.

Personally, I decide before a game how far forward I'll push before I pass the strikers over to Roy Keane, Paul Scholes or Nicky Butt to pick up. If you're going to leave your post and keep a close tab on your player, though, the team has to make sure it doesn't allow other sides to take advantage – especially if you start playing the offside trap when the deep-lying striker has the ball.

The golden rule is not to push out if the man on the ball has time. He can pick a colleague running into that gaping hole you've just left and thread a pass into the space. As I mentioned earlier, Kanoute did just that to send in Di Canio when we were knocked out of the FA Cup in 2001.

The type of players I really enjoy going up against are in the mould of Emile Heskey, Duncan Ferguson and Alan Shearer.

Their whole game is geared to my assets and that's one of the reasons I was convinced I could be a success in England. I just lap it up when playing against this style on a regular basis.

They want to muscle it out, and love an aerial confrontation. Considering my size, that's not a problem for me and being a physical player I really enjoy it when a striker wants to get into a battle. I would rather have someone stood in front of me, contesting long balls, than a whippet hanging on my shoulder and looking to use his pace to get in on goal.

The other good side to these physical players is their refusal to play-act when the going gets tough. Okay, Shearer might moan a bit and Heskey did have a spell where he went down too easily, but they're not on the same planet as the Italian international Filippo Inzaghi.

Maybe he's a friendly guy off the pitch, but the way he plays football annoys and frustrates me greatly. It's not his penchant for running offside so often that winds me up, because the reason he does go offside is one of his strengths. He's always right on the borderline and maybe after being offside ten times, on the eleventh he'll go through and score.

What I despise about his game is the way he's always diving and moaning to the referee to engineer an advantage. The slightest touch and he goes down. Even if you are just walking by him and give him a nudge he's down like he's been hit by a sniper. What angers me the most is that referees fall for it. It's an Italian trait, but he takes it to extremes. Most of them do it, but in my experience he's top of the list.

The best way to respond is to ensure that the guy doesn't get the upper hand against you, and as a defender that means you do not let him score. Unfortunately, over the three occasions on which I've played against Inzaghi for United and my national team, he's found the back of the net twice – both in the Champions League semi-final in 1999.

I have to hold my hands up and say the first one was a good header, although I wasn't marking him at the time, but his second was courtesy of a wicked deflection after the ball struck my leg. He seems to have been born lucky.

But good fortune has nothing to do with the type of players who are deadly in the box. Strikers such as Ole Gunnar Solskjaer and Ruud van Nistelrooy just have that brilliant knack of being able to dispatch any chance that drops their way. Ole, especially, has what we in Holland describe as a nose for the goal and wherever he is in front of the net, that's where the ball will drop.

If the Norwegian was at any club other than United, there's no doubt in my mind that he would be a legend. He's got to be one of the best finishers in the country – just ask the keepers at United who face him in training! He doesn't think a lot and isn't one for trying out fancy tricks. When he's got the ball there is only one thing on his mind, and that's hitting the back of the net.

Sometimes he puts it away neatly, but also Ole can blast it, and both methods seem to be equally effective. He's my room-mate when we travel and I know he's not always happy when the manager tells him that a place on the bench is the best he can hope for that day. Outwardly he takes it well, but it is hard for him, especially as every time he comes into a game he does well and scores most of the time.

Ole's got more competition now. My former PSV team-mate Ruud van Nistelrooy has joined the Reds with a huge £19 million price tag and a warranted reputation for scoring goals. Both factors could yet cause him problems.

Firstly he has to live with that huge sum of money hanging round his neck. No player is worth that kind of cash and the fee shows how crazy the transfer system has become. The figure won't be a problem to Ruud if the goals start flying in straight away, but if he struggles to find the target the money will suddenly turn into an issue.

I faced that situation; so did Rio Ferdinand at Leeds, who cost £18 million; and tomorrow it will be somebody else. Ruud has to be mentally strong, ignore the critics and listen to the people who count, like Sir Alex Ferguson. His opinion is the only one that matters. He picks the team, not the newspapers or television pundits.

I firmly believe that Ruud will score goals. His track record is good, and although the standard in England is much higher than in Holland, the variety in his finishing should help him to keep keepers guessing about his next move and buy him the time he needs to settle in.

If he does come good he'll be following in the footsteps of another former PSV man who took the world by storm after leaving Holland. Ronaldo, now at Inter Milan after a spell at Barcelona, is still the biggest star in football despite being hit by injury ever since the 1998 World Cup.

When I worked with him at PSV, he was still young and learning how to play the game, but his pace, with or without the ball, was electric and what made him special was that he could do everything at full speed, even his tricks. He was hard to handle even though his play was naive.

There was no doubting that the talent was there and we could all see why Barcelona wanted him. He grew as a player from the moment he arrived in Spain, with his mind stronger and more concentrated on how he had to channel his game in the right direction to make sure he capitalised on his talents.

Not surprisingly, as he got older also he became physically stronger, helping him to ride the flying boots and hold off shirt-pulling opponents. I remember watching him a few times in Barcelona and marvelling at how inspirational his play had become.

When he's firing on all cylinders, Ronaldo is capable of winning a game on his own, although I never bought into the hype heralding him as the best player the world had ever seen. Before his painful knee injury at Inter, Ronaldo was up there with the best, but not alone on the podium.

There has been a lot of talk about him being as good as Diego Maradona, but personally I don't think he rates that highly yet. He possesses the same skills and probably is a bit quicker, but Maradona played at the top for more than ten years, so Ronaldo still has to prove he can stay at his peak in the long term. He's got the aptitude and if he gets back to his old form, when finally he regains fitness following his knee problems, he could be a true great.

Even the best in the world can't find the net unless he is given the right service, though, and that's where tactics come in. Kicking the ball long and high, hoping for the best, might have worked in the days of long shorts and laced-up balls, but in the modern era, how the game is played as a team is just as important as who can parade the best players in the world. A good set of tactics can deny opponents possession and nullify the main attacking threat of any side.

At United we play 4–4–2, with one of the strikers dropping deep to play off a main hit-man, who is usually Andy Cole. It's a system which most teams in England, and even in Europe nowadays, have adopted. There are a few sides who like to employ three defenders, with wing-backs going up and down the flanks to add more support to the midfield when needed, but at United we found a flat back four has suited us best.

It allows us to play good attacking football while still having strength when we lose possession. The other advantage is in allowing David Beckham and Ryan Giggs to attack their full-backs without the added worry of having to dash back for defensive duties on the rare occasions they lose the ball.

During my time in Holland I played sometimes in a 4–3–3 set-up. It's even more attack-minded because it involves three strikers with one player in the centre and one on either flank. It's a system which quite a few teams used at Euro 2000, with Portugal, helped by the presence of Luis Figo, one of the best exponents of the formation as they battled their way through to the semi-finals.

Playing this way means you need a trio of midfielders capable of working their bollocks off. They have to close down opponents quickly to make-up for being a man short in the heart of the battle.

One way to counteract the deficit in the midfield numbers is for one of the central defenders to step forward when the team goes on the attack. It's a job I've done on numerous occasions back home, but the most important thing is to ensure that I perform my primary task first – that of stopping the other team scoring. When we play 4–4–2, there is less space to go into midfield as already there are two players sitting in front.

Occasionally I get a chance to break out and leave my defensive shackles behind me, and I have to admit that's something I love doing.

I started out as a midfielder, and like most players I couldn't wait to get on the ball and start attacking. It's something we were brought up with in Holland; it's what the fans love to see and how I enjoy playing.

Still there were chances to charge forward even after I was converted into a central defender in my days before joining PSV. But I guess at United there is more pressure and I can't take as many risks as we are playing against better teams. Top-quality strikers would see me moving forward and dive into the space I left, pleading for the ball if our move broke down while I was stuck upfield.

I've had a few chances to go on forward runs with United and the response it has brought from the Old Trafford fans has sent shivers down my spine. There aren't too many defenders these days who receive the ball and try taking on two or three players before looking for a pass into the box, and when our supporters see me on the move they are quick to get on their feet.

My pace helps me as I can knock a ball past players and get around them while they are turning. When that happens and the fans start roaring me on, it's not a case of my head going. I don't try and dribble around 11 men before slotting home a sensational strike from twenty yards as if I was George Best. I'll look for the best pass and if I can play someone in on goal I'm more than happy – happier still if it brings a chorus of Jip-Jaap Stam from the stands.

If I had my way I would bomb forward in every single game. Who wouldn't get a buzz from hearing nearly 70,000 people getting to their feet and calling out their name? But the manager has had a word and told me to do so only on rare occasions. Although that's frustrating I can see his point because if it goes wrong and I'm out of position it could cost the team dearly.

That nearly happened when we played Leeds at Old Trafford in 1999. Although we won the game 2–0, the manager was upset with me because I'd gone on a dribble and when I passed the ball, the second phase of the move broke down. I was left standing next to Ryan Giggs as Harry Kewell broke away and nearly scored.

'It's all right playing the bloody hero,' he snapped in the dressing room afterwards. 'But look what happens when it fucks up. You were left in no-man's land and we had a massive hole at the back. If they'd scored we could have been shafted. Think about it next time!'

There wasn't much I could say to that. He was right, and from then on I've picked my moments a tad more carefully, and said a few prayers if we have then lost the ball.

The other difference between playing in Holland and starring for United is that I'm no longer taking free-kicks. Anything from just inside the opposition half to around 20 yards from goal was mine during my spell at PSV. I didn't do anything fancy, just blasted it at goal as hard as I could. You'd be surprised how many times the direct approach paid off.

At United, though, we have someone who's a bit special from dead-ball situations and I've had to take a back seat. I'm not complaining, as it would be hard to walk up to David Beckham as he's setting his sights on the back of the net and convince him he should leave this one for me.

But occasionally I do line up a few in training and have a dig at goal, glancing over my shoulder at the manager just to make sure he's aware that if Beckham suddenly loses his magic touch, I'm capable of stepping in and doing a job. I've got a feeling that's not going to happen, and although Ferguson knows what I can do, I wouldn't blame him for sticking with David.

But back to the tactics. I have to admit, although I take note when a blackboard is placed at the front of a team-talk and the manager hooks out the chalk, that I'm not a great one for sitting around a coffee table and talking about how the great Italian sides reinvented the defensive game with catenaccio.

And the only time I really think about other teams is when I watch 'Match of the Day'. If there's a side we are coming up against in the near future, then I will have a look at how they defend, and where their forwards like to run. Most of the time, though, I just enjoy the game.

The most effective system I've seen used against United was when we drew 1–1 with the Greek side, Panathinaikos, in the Champions League during 2000/2001. They had three strikers but only one who played tight against our defenders, with the other two in deeper positions, just in front of their midfield.

It was hard to know whether to go deep with them or pass them on to our midfielders. The problem started when Wes Brown and I were being dragged further and further upfield, but were unable to tell Roy Keane and Paul Scholes to pick up our men because they had their own players to mark.

We were left in a state of confusion and needed Fabien Barthez to be on great form that night. Twice he saved when strikers ran through on goal, with Wes and myself badly out of position following our runners, before finally being beaten.

On that occasion in Greece, it didn't help that we defended so high up the pitch. It gave their midfield plenty of space to put the ball over the top for their strikers to run on to. That match came in a run of bad form for us and we were pilloried in the press for much of the week. For once it was hard to defend ourselves against the attacks both on and off the pitch, as although the Greeks had their tactics spot-on, players of the calibre we possess at Old Trafford could be expected to react a little better to the challenge.

Paul Scholes scored in the final minutes to secure the draw and as we boarded the plane for home, despite the rhetoric about our character and ability to find important late goals, we all knew we'd been downright lucky.

Tactics can win matches, but just as vital is coming out on top in personal battles. If all 11 players on the pitch are better than our rivals on the day we will win, it's as simple as that. But in the modern game, it's not just about being able to play football.

You have to scrap and battle for the right to be involved and for a defender that means not letting a striker get on top. I know the old-fashioned way to ensure that didn't happen was by booting your target up in the air when he was about to get his first touch of the ball.

'Letting him know you're there' is one way to describe it, and I can see why some players adopt this method. If the striker doesn't fancy a running battle and is scared you're going to make an imprint on his ankles every time he receives a pass, he won't go looking for the ball very often. If he has little mental strength, he will run scared throughout the game, but that policy won't work against everyone. Alan Shearer, for example, will get up and laugh about it and then use that tackle to work on the referee. Before you know it, even your normal tackles are getting called up for fouls.

In recent seasons the laws have changed to ensure that nasty tackles from behind – the type which caused Dutchman Marco van Basten to quit because of damaged ankles – are no longer part of the game. I think the change has been good for football. It lets strikers play a bit and that's what fans want to see, rather than a slow defender breaking someone's leg.

The referee has to read the challenge, though, to determine the intention of the tackler. It is possible to tell if the defender is going for the ball or for both ball and man, and too many times players are being booked or sent off for innocent challenges which looked bad because of play-acting.

I'm not one for raking my studs down the back of a striker's calf. I can be quite physical and tough and if I need to make a tackle, I won't back out. But I'm not planning ahead and working out the best moment to go through a player with the intention of breaking his leg. If I can't get in front of him and nick the ball, I won't resort to crude methods. I'll try and solve the problem technically, with football skills, such as standing up strongly against him, forcing him to go backwards and lay the ball off.

A lot of the time that is just as important as diving in and winning the ball. Even if you've won the tackle, the loose possession could fall to an opposing player and you are on your backside with a big space behind you. At least if he's passed the ball you're still in the game and capable of cutting out the danger.

Steaming into an unsuspecting forward from behind is an obvious offence for a referee to spot, but too many of them are missing the amount of sly shirt-pulling which is rife in the game at the moment – and for a defender that's mightily frustrating.

It makes it increasingly hard to play my natural game as forwards get cuter about tugging on tops out of the referee's eye-line. The classic instance is when I'm chasing back toward my own goal with a forward. At this point, usually the referee is behind me and can't see the striker's outstretched arm across my chest holding me back. He can, of course, see me grabbing a handful of the striker's shorts in retaliation. The result: a free-kick and a smug forward. It's gone too far in the favour of the attacker.

I spend plenty of time screaming at referees to watch the strikers' arms and sometimes even when the offenders are facing the official with an arm wrapped around me, the man with the whistle will miss it. Maybe it's because I'm a big guy, maybe they think someone of my size should be able to cope with it, but that shouldn't come into the equation. A foul is a foul.

The situation can be even worse when corners and free-kicks are taken. At times it's a lottery and against most teams I don't even get a run at the ball, never mind a chance to head it. Markers aren't even watching the ball. They are watching you and when you make a move they just hold your shirt or block the run. They've no intention of going for the ball. It's got to the stage where it's the law of the jungle because the referee is never going to blow.

When we played Bayern Munich in the Champions League in 2001 I managed to get past Jancker to attack a corner and he just grabbed my arm and hauled me back. It was blatant. My arm was at full stretch behind me, but no penalty was given. Referees are too scared to point to the penalty spot in that situation and until they do it's only going to get worse.

These might be small matters to the fan but can make a huge difference to footballers on the park. I'm not stupid enough to think shirt-pulling will ever be eradicated from the game, and neither will diving and play-acting, but the governing body should look at ways to stamp down on the tactics before they get out of hand. As a defender who's always penalised, I can't wait for the day when FIFA takes some positive action.

CHAPTER TEN

Life through a lens

I find the way the English press have delved into my personal life to be extremely offensive.

I had grown to distrust the nationals, as the daily newspapers are called in Britain, after they had jumped almost tempestuously on to the bandwagon when my capabilities were being questioned during my first months in England.

But one act I can never forgive is the way the *Daily Star* decided my eating habits were worthy of front-page news. I was horrified when I arrived at training one day to find the lads offering me chocolate bars and making jokes about my sweet tooth.

'What are you talking about?' I asked, totally bemused.

'Have you not seen the *Star?*' came the reply.

A copy of the paper was thrust into my hands and I couldn't believe what I was reading. Their claim that I had filled two bags with sweets during a recent trip to the cinema was true, but the fact that I had stuffed the lot down my throat wasn't. Actually, the sweets were emptied into various glass bowls around the house and were intended to last for several weeks.

'Ellis, you won't believe this!' I shouted as I walked in the front door after training, holding up the paper for her to read. 'Surely the fact that we ate a few sweets is not that important!'

'I wondered what all this was about,' she said showing, me another bag of sweets. 'Some guys came to the door and handed me these.'

I put two and two together and cursed the journalists who had walked up my driveway. They'd been lucky I was out as I wouldn't have been as graceful and understandably confused about the incident as Ellis. If I'd been there they'd have found one irate Dutchman chasing them down the street, hurling expletives and jelly babies at them.

The unwanted knock at my door was bad enough, but the next day I was rudely made aware of the depths the English press will go to get a story. Not only had the two guys disturbed Ellis, they had an associate sitting in a bush with a camera snapping the whole episode.

If it wasn't so pathetic it would have been laughable, but their front-page story that day was completely made up. Every spit and cough of the so-called article was a complete falsehood. It claimed that Ellis had gleefully welcomed the Star reporters and thanked them deeply for bringing more urgently needed sweet supplies. I was staggered and this time so was my wife. Certainly she didn't consider a story which boiled down to her having a bag of sweets pushed into her hand to be front-page news.

It was an extreme lesson, if ever I needed it, about the desperate lengths papers will go to for a story, and my involvement in it shocked me. I'm not a superstar whose ugly mug is going to stop people in their tracks and make them want to buy the paper. I'm just a guy who liked playing football when I was a kid and has been lucky enough to make a career out of it.

I try to live my life as normally as I can with my family, and I definitely don't like all the press that seem to hover around the periphery of the game. I just want to play football and win prizes.

I guess I'm lucky at United. It's easy to stay away from journalists if you don't feel the need to talk about yourself. There are press conferences before each game, but usually they are for the manager. We do the odd piece for the local newspaper, the *Manchester Evening News*, and local radio stations, plus regular pieces for the club's own television channel MUTV, but that tends to be our only real club obligation and I know none of these media will sensationalise anything I say. They'll report it straight.

Also I have a newspaper column in the *Daily Telegraph* in which I express my views on general footballing topics, and I find that an enjoyable way of discussing the game, safe in the knowledge that my words will not be misconstrued.

The only other time I come into contact with the media is after the European games, national team appearances and when my kit sponsors, Puma, organise special press days. The Champions League nights are the worst as the press line up along a crash barrier with cameras, microphones and tape recorders, a gathering little removed from a massive scrum, all wanting instant opinion.

I don't hide away, though, and despite not being the type of person who wants to spend ages chatting to the press after every game, I will do my fair share. I take my responsibility seriously and I try to talk even when I've had a bad game or we've lost the match. You can't do it only when you win.

The problem is that everyone asks the same questions and you have to give the same answers again and again. For someone with little patience, like me, the repetition is maddening. Then there are the times when I've looked at the paper the next day and wondered who they interviewed, because the quotes are totally different to what I said.

Sometimes I forget I'm running the press gauntlet and stop to say hello to someone I know and instantly hundreds of microphones appear out of nowhere and are shoved under my nose, bringing to a premature end any hopes of a friendly chat.

With all the interview requests, I suppose I'm a prime candidate to undergo a spot of media training, but I feel I've got by okay without it. Not everyone is in the same boat, though, and that's hardly surprising. Footballers are sportsmen, not a separate species. We all have different backgrounds with some players more articulate than others.

Press coverage of football is different back home in Holland. When there's a game they write a match report, then the day after there might be round-ups of injury and transfer news, and then the views of players and coaches follow during the week. But there's nothing about players' personal lives.

In England it's so different, with people like David Beckham on the front page as much as the back. You could accuse some players of courting the publicity, and it's hard to accept all the grumbles about the press never leaving people alone if they were once desperate to use the media for their own good.

At this point I expect everyone is thinking about Beckham and his wife, Victoria, but although David does have his picture in the paper a lot, rarely does he give interviews and never has he been one for searching out the journalists.

The pictures of David and Victoria tend to be taken on nights out, when he has been invited to dinners and fashion shows. He wants to go and why not? Why should he sit in just because there's a chance a photographer will be there? It certainly hasn't affected his form.

But when he does have a little moan in the dressing room, I don't run up to him with tissues at the ready. He can't have it both ways, attending the glitzy nights without his picture being splashed all over the paper.

Another of my team-mates who gets blinded by his fair share of flashbulbs is Dwight Yorke, although this seems to have dropped off since he met his girlfriend, Jordan. In the days when he was pictured out partying, I don't think it caused a real problem with anyone at the club. He was out on a Saturday night after a game – what's wrong with that?

Personally, I'm not a party animal. I like to go out every now and then but the invitations I get to the *Hello* magazine-style parties are quickly torn-up and binned.

Sometimes my wife says: 'Come on, let's go out.' She must dread hearing me reply: 'Why? I'm always away. I want to sit at home.' I can understand her feelings as she wants to lead a normal life, but when I do relent, it's to go for a meal or the cinema, and not a nightclub.

The paparazzi are something we've all had to learn to live with at United, and no doubt there are similar conversations in the Liverpool, Arsenal and Chelsea dressing rooms as well. Footballers appear to be turning into the modern-day pop stars and it's a price we simply have to pay. I can't see a way of stopping it from happening, unless we sit at home every night.

It's not like that in Holland because the game is not so high-profile and the big-name players do not enjoy the superstar status attached to the top stars of the English game. Certainly, the atmosphere between the press and players in my home country is a lot less hostile.

I don't mind journalists writing their views about football; the game is all about opinions, after all. I don't even mind them saying I'm a poor player – that's their point of view. But some English journalists seem to have a hidden agenda. I went through it when I first arrived and so did Andy Cole when he hadn't scored for England. It seemed like the reporters were ganging up on him and had decided among themselves that his international career should be brought to an end.

One picture in the *Daily Mirror* before the match in Albania in March 2001 showed a net with a caption telling Andy: 'This is where you are meant to stick the ball.' It was disgraceful. Andy scored that night and I bet there was a massive smile on his face when he spotted those same reporters running around after him asking for an interview.

Andy has every reason for ignoring journalists, whereas I don't have a personal shutter I pull down when meeting a reporter for the first time. I'm quite happy being with reporters if they write honest stories and deal with football. But when it gets to the stage where I am misquoted mischievously and I see a piece of rubbish written about me then I say: 'Okay, if you want to write that, fine, but don't expect me to keep talking to you.' That's why there are only a select band of reporters who have my number.

Now I tend to look at papers only when they're lying around at the training ground and the biggest laugh of the week is checking out the marks each journalist has given a player for their performance in the most recent match. All players do it and there must be hundreds of disbelieving shakes of the head up and down the country on a Monday.

What makes me smile most, though, is the huge discrepancy in the marks handed out. In one paper I might have an eight and in another I've picked up a five. It merely adds to the feeling footballers get that most journalists don't know what they are watching.

The whole media circus appears to be a game now, with the chances to talk to the top players decreasing. So one of the situations they feed off is the way sponsorship deals are set up between sports firms and footballers.

I am contracted to Puma and part of the deal means there are press days set aside when I sit down with journalists to discuss football matters. In return for getting the chance to speak to me, the media are encouraged to mention the Puma link in their stories.

I have a good relationship with Puma and signed for them because I think they have the best product, but I draw the line at what I am prepared to do for publicity, especially when my dignity is at stake. I was not happy with them over one particular media day that was organised soon after I joined the Reds in 1998.

I could handle the hour upon hour of being asked the same questions about my background, playing for United and our chances of winning the Champions League. But I baulked at their plans for a publicity photo-shoot as soon I walked out on the lush green Old Trafford turf. In front of me was a throne and one of their staff was holding a crown, waiting for me expectantly.

'What is it you want Jaap to do, exactly?' My UK agent Mike Williams asked their representative cautiously.

'Well, because the boot is the Puma King, we thought we'd get you sat on a throne with a crown on, holding the boot,' he replied. 'With the North Stand in the background, it'll look superb.'

I stood there aghast before asking: 'Don't you think I might look a little silly?' All of a sudden this confident Puma rep lost a little of his cool and began desperately on the impossible job of convincing me how impressive the picture would look.

Unfortunately for him I'm not easily impressed, nor was Mike who pointed out there was only one King of Old Trafford in the eyes of the fans – Denis Law. There was no way I was going to change my mind about it. I don't mind having a bit of fun, but I won't be made to look stupid for any amount of money. He must have figured this out quickly as soon the throne was removed and we reverted to that old photographers' favourite of having the boots slung over the shoulder.

Worse was to come when Nicolas Anelka joined me for a Puma promotional campaign in Brussels two years later. At the time body-paint, where you strip pretty much naked and have your skin decorated with an image, was in vogue. Soon after arriving I was told they wanted to paint a boot on my foot which grew up my leg and eventually covered my body in a Puma logo. Freshly garnished in that way, I was expected to walk up and down a catwalk for the admiring photographers.

Anelka was being asked to do likewise. I took one look at Nicolas, he took one look at me and we shook our heads. There was no way I was interested in doing that. For one thing, I'm no model, and for another, the whole body-paint idea was definitely not my style.

I don't know why they didn't ask me before setting up the event, or even put the question to one of my representatives. It wouldn't have taken long to fax back a polite rejection and that would have saved everyone a lot of time, effort and money.

The body-paint wasn't the only bizarre thing I turned down that day. A local television station had set up a lorry with a glass dome on the back, housing a mocked-up mini-football pitch. Slap-bang in the middle of it was a pair of massive boots and a seat for me in front of a television camera, all ready for an interview.

If that wasn't ludicrous enough, they wanted to chat to me while we drove through the streets of Brussels on the way to the airport, with the rest of the world watching the ridiculous situation. You can guess, by now, my reaction to that!

I don't have any problems working with Puma and I'm happy to fulfil all interview obligations, but I just wish they'd get in touch before setting up these crazy promotion schemes. I signed up with the company because I find they make the best boots, not because they organise the most creative PR stunts.

CHAPTER ELEVEN

Falling foul of the men in black

I was boiling with rage as I looked up to see Andy D'Urso pointing at the penalty spot seconds after I'd clearly swiped the ball away from Middlesbrough's Juninho in our box.

The game was hanging in the balance at 0–0 when the little Brazilian darted into the area and became my responsibility. If he beat me, the angle would have been perfect to slip a shot past Mark Bosnich and give Boro a lead that would have been difficult to haul back. He tried to throw me by dropping his shoulder, but I read his trick. As he attempted to go past my left side I stuck out my right boot and nudged the ball away before Juninho crumbled over my outstretched leg and collapsed to the ground.

I jumped to my feet to collect the loose ball which was running away from danger, parallel with the goal-line, when I heard a loud blast on a whistle.

My head went for a second. 'He can't be giving a penalty,' I thought. 'I won the ball. All he has to do is look at the direction the ball has taken after I made contact to realise that.' It was never a penalty in a million years.

By the time the reality of the situation had sunk in, Gary Neville was off already, chasing the referee and demanding that he change his mind. I was close behind and, as D'Urso kept backing away, I strode forward, furiously wanting to air my disgust.

'Ref, that's never a fucking penalty, I got the ball,' I screamed. He waved me away as an angry Roy Keane joined the fray.

'How can you give that? It's a fucking joke. Talk to your linesman, he must have seen what happened. You can't give that as a penalty.'

'It's a penalty,' he replied nervously. 'That's it.'

I'm sure you've all seen the television footage of that infamous picture of us crowding around the referee, with Keane's veins on his face and neck standing out so much they could burst. It doesn't look pretty, but it was never as bad as everyone made out at the time.

I was livid. My head was full of injustice and frustration and I wanted to make my point known. We were talking about losing three valuable points. With hindsight, our actions were daft, as the referee was not going change his mind. Deep down we knew that, but we felt we had to do something. We were desperate to tell him he'd made a big mistake.

I refute the claims that it was an ugly incident, though. We didn't punch him, push him or anything like that. He kept running backwards and that made it look worse. If he had stood still and talked to us I doubt whether so much would have been made of it. Probably the fact that he kept retreating and waving us away got the fury pumping through our veins even more.

Bosnich saved Juninho's penalty and I guess justice was served by that, as we went on to win the match thanks to David Beckham's 87th-minute goal. It was a crucial win coming just after Christmas during the 1999/2000 campaign and it helped to extend the narrow gap at the top of the table over Arsenal at the perfect time. But that was all lost to the world as the situation, fuelled by the press, blew up into a national debate.

'Is this a good example to set children?' radio shows asked, while ex-pros insisted on disciplinary action in their paid-for newspapers columns.

In the end Ferguson acted. He called us all into a dressing room before training and laid down the law. It was never to happen again!

'I know you all want to win desperately,' he said. 'That's why you are here. I want only winners at this club. But you have to be more careful about the way you approach situations like this. It didn't look good and has put us in the spotlight again for the wrong reason.

'There are ways of letting referees know what you think without chasing him around the pitch. Talk to him during the game, but for fuck's sake not like that. If you keep doing it, it will have a negative effect. I guarantee it.'

Ferguson was right. For a few games after that we started to notice that linesmen and referees were giving decisions against us. Just subtle ones, nothing 'Match of the Day' picked up on, but we noticed it. The odd offside going against us here, the occasional foul not given there. It happened, I can assure you.

I don't know if there is a referees' union, as some people have suggested, where they all get together, discuss who has pissed them off and then agree to take some understated action. Maybe they were just unhappy about what they'd seen on television, but there was a sinister spell.

It's so hard to keep your mouth shut in those situations. Managers and players are human beings and the emotions are running high after 90 minutes of adrenaline-fuelled action. When you've put your heart and soul into something and been robbed by a decision that was blatantly wrong, it's difficult to bite your tongue.

Occasionally, still, we get bad decisions at Old Trafford simply because we are Manchester United. In the past a lot has been made of the Reds having everything their own way at home, with a referee scared to blow for something that might lead to 67,000 fans jumping on his back.

But I believe now it's got to the stage where we are at a disadvantage, at times, because referees are determined to show they are not intimidated by the place. Maybe some day a football fan will undertake a study to prove it, but I've seen with my own eyes. Just look at the amount of times we are awarded penalties at home – we had only nine in my first three seasons. Now, for a team which plays as much attacking football as we do, possessing tricky players with quick feet such as Ryan Giggs,

Andy Cole and Dwight Yorke, does that sound right? I don't think so!

There, I've got that gripe out of the way, so the officials can take their tin hats off now as they may be pleasantly surprised to read that, overall, I'm quite pleased with the standard of refereeing in England.

You're always going to get split decisions that you don't agree on, but that happens in every country. Actually I like the way English games are controlled and allowed to be a lot more physical than in other countries. The Spanish and Italian referees, encountered in the Champions League and in internationals, tend to blow up at the slightest contact. I find I can barely touch a player without the man in black charging over and delivering a blast on his whistle. It can be hard to adjust on those occasions, as I'm so used to playing in the Premiership style.

On European nights I have to tread carefully, stay on my feet and hold my player up rather than dive in to win the ball. If I can't be sure of getting in front of him when the pass is made, I have to make sure he doesn't go past me, and if he lays the ball back to someone else then my job is done.

There's no black book in my sportsbag when it comes to referees but certainly the gaffer does his homework and he will always have a word or two with us before the game to let us know how to handle ourselves.

'Don't even talk to this guy or you'll get a yellow card,' he will warn. On the other hand he might say: 'This guy lets a lot go, so get your tackles in and don't back out.'

In Europe most referees speak English, which can be a help to team like United. We can understand straight away what he is unhappy about and, with no language barrier, it's easier to get our own feelings across.

The image of an English referee to some people may be of this petty man waving away players in an arrogant manner, but I find it's possible to speak to most officials in the game nowadays, and I have to disagree with former England striker Ian Wright's claim, made a number of years ago, that all whistle-blowers are 'little Hitlers'.

With most of them, you can have a joke or a laugh if something genuinely funny happens, and although I'm not the type to spend the whole game chatting with them, I like a more informal atmosphere during a match. I prefer them to say 'Jaap, I want a word', rather than screaming: 'Number six, come over here.'

Also I like to give referees and linesmen a thumbs-up or a little clap if they get a tough decision right. It's not a case of gamesmanship. I appreciate that they are doing a very tricky job and I want them to know that they're doing well when they get it right.

As I've said, in England there aren't too many bad 'uns and even the best like Graham Poll, Andy D'Urso and their colleagues can have the odd couple of dodgy games. But one guy I'm glad they did drop from the Premiership list was Uriah Rennie. Quite simply, he was not good enough.

I've been led to believe he was fast-tracked through the system after building a good reputation in the lower leagues. Certainly he had a physical presence and supposedly he was handy at marital arts, but looking the part and being the part are two different things. If he was pushed to the top quicker than other referees by football chiefs, I think they made a big mistake. I believe that if a referee is good enough, then he will work his way through to the Premier League of his own accord.

There's been a groundswell of support recently for professional referees, with FIFA president Sepp Blatter seemingly keen to introduce full-time officials. I don't see it making a huge amount of difference. They might be a touch fitter, but it's rare these days to see a referee out of position, and what are they meant to do with their time when they're not fitness training?

There was talk of referees joining clubs for training sessions. I can't see the advantage of this. What will they pick up from watching a bunch of players stretch and play five-a-side games at three-quarter pace? We don't have special diving sessions, or a spell of learning new tricks on how to foul players in training. We just play football. They would be better off at home watching re-runs of 'Match of the Day'. At least on television all the flashpoints are replayed in slow-motion and they can spot any skulduggery.

In my opinion, the best thing to do about referees is to leave them exactly as they are.

CHAPTER TWELVE

The good, the bad and the downright ugly

I was never too happy when I picked up a paper in Holland to read that yet another foreign player was heading for Dutch shores. It used to rankle with me that more and more money was being thrown at overseas talent rather than used to develop home-grown Dutch kids. Now the boot is firmly on the other foot; I'm the foreigner and, to be honest, although this may sound hypocritical, my opinions haven't changed too much.

First let me qualify the beliefs I held while playing in Holland. Playing alongside Ronaldo, as I did at PSV, only helped me to become a better footballer and I'm convinced that top-quality players should be welcomed to any league.

But, quite simply, too many of the overseas intake are not good enough. At PSV we had a Brazilian striker called Claudio, who was a small and tricky player but too light to hold his own in Europe. Also we had a Russian, Dimitri Khokhlov who, despite struggling to get into the team, earned more than most of the Dutch players. The foreigners knew how much they were wanted and demanded good money to leave their homeland – and got it.

Once the news of their wages got out, and the rest of the squad realised they could hardly be considered value for money, all the petty jealousies which exist in any dressing room started to rear their ugly heads, and the atmosphere around the team suffered.

It would have been better using that money on the youth team, buying in top coaches and ensuring the best available advice was passed on. Also there is the option of stuffing the cash into the wage packet of a poorly paid local player, which might save him from having his head turned when a rival club hints at a pot of gold just over the horizon.

Foreign players continue to like the Premiership because of the huge following it has and the big names already playing in England. Don't forget that in mainland Europe a lot of clubs play to half-empty stadia. The whole product looks attractive to them and, of course, the money is pretty good as well.

I'm sure that in the past some of the foreign players looked at a spell in England as a chance to enjoy a decent pay-day before hanging up their boots, and I think that still happens.

I don't want to tar everyone with the same brush, but there are a lot of players out there focusing solely on money and it's not just the foreigners. You can look at every Premiership club and find players who are taking home a very good wage, yet who never play.

I can't understand why footballers don't leave a club when they fail to get in the side. Even a loan spell at another team, where they would have a much better chance of playing a game on a Saturday, surely ought to be more attractive. But still these individuals seem to be happy making a good living and enjoying the status being in the Premiership brings, all the while possibly feeling scared to test themselves in a lower division in case they fail to impress.

Personally, I couldn't do that. People might read this and think that it's easy for me to say it, as I get picked for Manchester United every week. But I'm the type of guy who loves his football and if I can't play I'm not going to sit on the bench for a year or two. I'm hungry to play every match day. Still I get a buzz knowing that I'm going to be running out and performing in front of thousands of people.

If, suddenly, I found I was being left on the bench and it didn't look like I was going to play long-term, I would need to find a solution very quickly, whether that was at Manchester United or somewhere else. If that meant earning less money to play, then so be it.

Unfortunately greed seems to dominate the game these days, and it really disappoints me when good young players from abroad move to the top clubs in England, Spain and Italy simply because of the money.

If they went to what is perceived as a second-rate league like Holland's or Belgium's for a couple of years, they would learn how to play technically good football, develop as players and build up the confidence that comes only from playing first-team football week-in, week-out. It may not be the best level in the world but, after a couple of years, if they really are true stars and not just talented teenagers, they can pick a big club and arrive confident of making a big impression.

When I was at PSV, that was how the system seemed to work, with Ronaldo the most telling case in point. He joined the club from Brazilian side Cruzeiro in 1994 and still had a lot to learn. He was ready and willing, but I feel that he might have got lost at Juventus or Barcelona at that age.

To a club like PSV, despite the fact that he was only 18 years, already he was a jewel to be treasured and the dedicated coaching he received helped him draw scouts from the top teams in the world. When finally he moved to Spain, Barcelona were desperate to have him in their team and pay very good money for his services.

Also the list could include Nigeria's Kanu, who started at Ajax; AC Milan's Fernando Redondo, an Argentinian willing to play for little-known Tenerife before getting his big break at Real Madrid; and George Weah, the Liberian whose career took off after joining Monaco.

Nowadays young players don't want to play for PSV and Ajax, they just want to go to a big league and a big club, probably without realising or really caring that it's hard to go and live in a different country, adapt to an unusual style of play and impress a new coach. That's when greed takes over and the money on offer from Holland or Portugal fails to impress when compared to the lire or pesetas being thrust into their hands.

It's not all the players' fault, though. Don't forget they can't just turn up on a training pitch and join in without being asked by the manager, and for all the carping about too many overseas stars, no-one has seriously questioned Premiership managers' involvement in the problem.

I know United's boss prefers to look for an English player who fits his needs when he decides to strengthen his squad. Only if he can't spot a home-grown candidate with the right qualities will he go abroad.

That isn't always the case. I get the impression some managers prefer to buy foreign footballers simply for the sake of it, and there seems to have been a lot of money wasted on them. It's the same in all divisions in England at the moment; there are too many foreign players clogging up the system.

It would be far better for clubs to take youngsters on loan from the fringes of Premiership sides and give them a chance. Manchester United have benefited from this approach with David Beckham, in particular, enjoying a spell at Preston. It helped to toughen him up and brought his game along in leaps and bounds.

He needed to sample the physical aspects of football which he wasn't going to do in the reserve team, where players may not be playing at 100-per-cent fitness or have the determination they would show in a first-team game. If you have First and Second Division clubs using foreign players there is no place for youngsters to develop and it's got to be bad for the English game as a whole.

So far, all I've pointed out are the negatives but, equally, the introduction of someone with different experiences and values in life and football can have a positive influence on any team. To this day I hear the name of Eric Cantona bandied around Old Trafford as a role model everyone should follow. His dedication to the game is legendary at United and Cantona's good habits, such as extra training, rubbed off quickly on his team-mates following his arrival from Leeds for £1.2 million in 1992.

Just as important was his winning attitude and strength of character which helped United to overcome the mental hurdle which seemed to block their bid to win a League title before his arrival. It's hard to think of any British players at the time who could have made so much difference to a team as good as United.

The attributes he brought to English football are now being picked up by young home-grown players from other foreign imports at clubs across the country. How difficult it is to visualise the Premiership being such an exciting competition without the skills of Gianfranco Zola, Thierry Henry and Dennis Bergkamp.

Of course, with the thrills come the spills and some of the foreign habits are not so appealing, most notably in my book that of diving. Players from Scandinavia and Holland aren't divers, but the signings from Spain and Italy tend to go down far too easily for my liking. Even players in Germany are used to taking a dive, and in all these countries it looks like they've been brought up with it from their schooldays.

I don't think it's caught on with English youngsters yet, as their fair-play mentality stops them from taking a tumble. Coaches at academy levels are honest and would stamp out that kind of cheating from their team, although I admit to becoming frustrated by the frequency of this malaise in the Champions League. It has got to the stage where Ferguson has even told us: 'Don't try and stay on your feet if you are in the box and get a slight kick.'

He wants us to copy other sides we face in European competitions and go down to win a penalty. Far too often English players seem determined to keep running after getting a whack on the leg, even though the chance to get a shot in has gone.

It's tricky for me to take a dive, though. If I go into the penalty area and fall down under the slightest kick I'm going to look stupid collapsing to the turf like I've been shot. I can't see referees giving me a spot-kick unless someone chops me in half.

Another difference between central Europeans and Scandinavians is the incessant moaning from certain individuals. From the English game being like a war, as claimed by Markus Babbel and Robert Pires, to Patrick Vieira's whingeing about being picked on by referees, it never seems to stop.

English football is a tough game and there are some hard tackles, but I've never seen someone going in deliberately to harm an opponent. Of course, it's more physical than in other countries and that's one of the charms of the game here, but the players are honest and fair. Can you always say that about the Spanish and Italian game?

As for Vieira's claim that he is picked on by referees, I'd have to dispute that. The Arsenal midfielder is a magnificent player, who covers so much ground, imposes himself on the game and wins tackles he just shouldn't be able to make. But his whole style involves playing on the edge, and if you play like that you can expect to get on the wrong side of a referee every now and then.

The other thing that makes me smile is when I hear players complaining about too many matches. Didn't they look at how many teams there were in the Premiership before signing their contracts? If they can't handle it, the only solution is to leave.

We are fortunate at United to have such a good squad with a large pool of talent. The manager uses it well and if players look tired he gives them a rest. When David Beckham was struggling in March 2001, the gaffer was able to leave him out for two games knowing that Luke Chadwick could step in and do an excellent job in his absence. A month before, Paul Scholes and Roy Keane were given a breather. Every top Premiership side has a huge squad now, and could follow United's example if they wanted to.

The only thing which could help stop the cries of 'Too much football' would be a winter break. When I was in Holland I used to love having a few weeks off in the middle of the season. We were brought up with it, so every time Christmas came I used to rub my hands and think: 'Great, a holiday.' Some of us went away to Spain, while others stayed home, spent time with the family and relaxed without the pressure of playing football.

But I knew that by coming to England the break was going to be a thing of the past, so I had to adjust to that. It was something I had to deal with and although it meant the season seemed to go on a lot longer and I didn't feel so fresh in the second half of the campaign, it wasn't too hard to cope.

No doubt people will point to the 1999/2000 season and claim that we had a break by jetting off to Brazil for the FIFA Club World Championship. But as I've already pointed out, that was not a holiday. We trained every day in the searing heat and played matches in temperatures that were so hot it was hard to breath. A true break is exactly that – a break. No football, no running, just feet up and taking it easy.

Now I've grown to understand the English culture I feel it's almost impossible to have a winter break here, although I'm sure it would benefit the game and increase the chances of winning in Europe. A gap in the season would allow players to recover for the second phase of the campaign, they would be fitter and sharper, while the number of injuries would be reduced as it's easier to get injured when you are tired.

But in England the games over Christmas are some of the most eagerly anticipated of the season. People seem to enjoy a freezing Boxing Day watching their heroes in action. It's a tradition and even a naive Dutchman knows it's hard to separate the English from their traits.

CHAPTER THIRTEEN

Under pressure

I've known players who have come up through the ranks, read too many tales about their own stunning exploits for their own good, and turned into big-time Charlies. I'm not like that.

Maybe it's because I came into the game late; possibly my family keeps me from getting too big for my boots; or perhaps it's down to who I am. Whatever, I haven't changed, and my close pals would tell me soon enough if I did. But although I haven't become a different person, people around me have changed in the way they treat me.

Probably the worst for that are the people I have known the longest, the guys from my early days in football at Kampen. They look strangely at me now as though I should be two feet taller, wearing designer clothes or looking down my nose at them. They can't seem to realise I'm the same old Jaap who walked out of the town all those years to forge a career in football.

'You must have changed,' they challenge me. 'You're a big football star now. You play for Manchester and are on the television. You have to be different from the way you were!'

Also, the way people speak to me when I go home has changed, quite literally. There is a Dutch dialect spoken in my area and it's very distinctive. I use it still, but when I go home everyone who stops me in the street speaks regulation Dutch to me.

I suppose in one way they are right. I've changed a little. I'm older, wiser and a much better judge of people's characters. I have to be. I'm suspicious of people who want to get to know me well without any apparent reason; hangers on I believe they are called in England. They don't get a chance to get their claws in for long enough to take a firm grip.

But I notice it most when I go home, as that is where most of my oldest friends and family are, and my first club, which is still close to my heart and my parents' hearts. My father always goes there to watch the matches, just as he did before I played, while my mother works behind the bar pulling pints for the supporters club.

Despite my allegiance to Dos Kampen, I left the club with a lot to prove when I went to FC Zwolle in 1992, and not just to the football world at large. There were a lot of fans and committee men who suggested openly that I would fall flat on my face and return begging for a game. I could handle that, as it's in my nature to prove people wrong.

What has irritated me, though, is that those same people now want me to provide them with tickets, signed shirts and David Beckham's phone number. The worst part is that they go through my parents to try and set things up. They are forever handing them letters because they need tickets from me or they want to use me to raise money. They didn't give me a hope in hell of succeeding when I left, yet now they need a new kitchen ceiling and floor for the clubhouse, they claim to be my best friend.

I'm told that as I'm the club's most famous old boy, I must sponsor them so they can buy a new astroturf pitch. They wanted £50,000 for it and told me that in return my name would be on the boards around it. It was an idea I didn't fancy.

People I don't even know phoning up my parents with requests is stomach churning. 'My husband is having a birthday next week and I want to surprise him with two tickets for United,' was one recent demand which they received from a supposed old pal. My parents are always polite and ask me, but they know what I'm going to say. They are not a ticket office or my messaging service!

There was even one guy who wanted me to find out flight details for him and book a hotel. I wouldn't have done that even if I had known him. What does he think I am, a travel agency? I would never ask someone a favour like that.

There have been similar requests in England, but not as many as I stick to a close circle of friends who would not try to take advantage of me.

But unfortunately, I was forced to move home two years after joining United because of frequent knocks on the door. The first home Ellis and I chose had no big gate or any of the security trappings you might expect an international footballer to need. It was just an average suburban house which opened on to a small garden and the street. Regrettably people seemed to believe we were welcoming them by living in that house, and although I could handle the requests for autographs, it all proved too much when I was disturbed after having my ankle surgery.

This guy, who I didn't know, stood in my doorway. Although he arrived with the best intentions, as he went into a deep explanation about what I should do to cure the injury, I began to get annoyed. Didn't he realise that a club like Manchester United might have brought in the world's top men to look after a player who had cost them just short of £11 million? Quickly I hurried him away with a string of unconvincing excuses and called out to Ellis: 'We're going to have to move.'

When I'm out shopping with my family the people of Manchester have always been courteous and I like that. Big groups don't charge up to me in the Trafford Centre and I'm happy to stop and say hello to the odd fan who might spot me.

But the fear of clans of youths looking to cause trouble is one of the reasons I don't plan for a full night out if, as happens occasionally, the United squad decides to go for a drink. Last Christmas we went to Tiger, Tiger in the recently opened Printworks complex in the centre of Manchester. The bar is superb, with different rooms depicting different themes, from a Canadian hunting lodge to a Moroccan bar complete with seating cushions.

But within minutes of arriving our whole party was swamped by people wanting to talk about United and football. It was our

Christmas party and all we wanted to do was relax, so standing with complete strangers discussing who's going to take over from Ferguson was not on my agenda. I made my excuses and left way before closing time.

I want people I meet when I'm out to realise that I like my privacy. It's one of the reasons I came to England as I had been told that people would know I was there but would leave me alone. I've heard from some of my Dutch team-mates, such as Dennis Bergkamp, that when they played in Italy a trip to the shops would take hours because they were mobbed everywhere they went.

People may think I'm a miserable sod for not wanting to spend my time off speaking to fans, and I know that the supporters pay my wages. I understand all that, but all I ask is that they realise that playing for one of the most successful clubs in the world takes a toll on a player's personal life.

With European games and internationals I seem to spend half my life in an airport lounge or stuck on a coach, so when I'm home I want to be with my family, doing all the things any family guy wants to do. So I hope fans can appreciate the frustration of having a rare lunch with my wife interrupted by an queue of autograph hunters, or how infuriating it can be if I make a trip to the shops and spend more time talking to people than picking out new clothes for my daughters. I know David Beckham had a problem fighting off the autograph hunters when he went to his favourite restaurant. He's now reverted to take aways, but luckily I have not had similar problems.

Don't get me wrong, I will never snub another well-mannered human being who wants to talk to me, but I guess it's like most things in life – good in moderation.

While the shopping expeditions can border on the frustrating, I always enjoy popping up to one of the hospitality suites after a game to meet supporters who have asked me along for a presentation. Contrary to popular belief, these are not all 'prawn sandwich-eaters'. Also there are true fans, and discussing the afternoon's events as seen through someone else's eyes can be very interesting.

Despite my gripes I realise that the pressure, the sometimes unwanted adulation and the press intrusion is all part of playing for Manchester United, and comes with the territory. It did get to me at first when I moved to Old Trafford, but that was only natural as it was something I hadn't really come across during my time with PSV.

Once I got used to the idea of people wanting to meet and talk to me, and understood why – after all, all I do is kick a football around a park – it became part and parcel of my life. In fact, the up side of it is superb. It's impossible to convey the feeling of pride that races through my body when a packed Old Trafford rises in unison to sing my name. Few people will ever feel that sweet sensation, but I am one of them and proud of it.

CHAPTER FOURTEEN

Keeping the faith – United's keepers

Keepers? I've known a few in my three years at United, including two of the best in the world, but sandwiched between the imposing Peter Schmeichel and the maverick Fabien Barthez was a season of uncertainty and disruption.

Mark Bosnich and Massimo Taibi arrived and eventually left, with my old Dutch friend Raimond van der Gouw the only real common denominator as Ferguson chopped and changed to accommodate dips in form, the occasional injury, and a change in stud length for the Italian.

But despite the alternating faces behind me, the only real difference I noticed during my second Old Trafford campaign was that my life had got a whole lot quieter. Schmeichel took his eardrum-shattering rants to Sporting Lisbon after captaining us to the Champions League trophy in Barcelona, and although we had lost the world's best keeper, at least I knew I could concentrate on my game without a weekly rollicking.

Peter was a terrific goalie but, at times, he could be a real pain in the arse as well. Before I signed for United I knew all about his explosive temper and had seen on television how dishing out criticism was just as important to him as making vital saves. The hot-tempered shouting matches with his own players kept Peter on his toes and also ensured that the defenders in front of him never slackened off. Despite his ever-increasing years, the temper didn't tail off when I arrived at Old Trafford.

He was always shouting at me, and most of the time I was wondering what the hell he was talking about. If one of my headers dropped ten yards short he was on my back about it, and if I let someone enjoy too much time on the ball, there he was again staring daggers into the back of my head. I lost count of the number of times I turned round during play to yell back: 'Shut up!'

Finally it got too much for me and, in front of a packed Stretford End, I lost my cool. I can't even remember what he was moaning about at the time, but I bit, and he knew about it.

'What the fuck are you talking about?' I snapped as we went toe-to-toe while the match carried on around us.

'You've got to get rid of the fucking thing properly. That header was piss poor,' he yelled back.

'What do mean?' I answered. 'I cleared the problem, didn't I? Get back in goal and shut up will you, you idiot!'

'Don't tell me to shut up,' Peter raged. 'Just fuck off.'

I turned around to find out where the ball was and that signalled the end of our row. Once the game was over the incident was forgotten and we never mentioned it again. But while the shocked full house at Old Trafford might have gone silent in amazement and wondered why we had fallen out, I didn't mind a bit.

In fact, I think that probably it had a positive effect on both of us. From that point on, we were desperate to prove each other wrong and tried even harder to step up our performances.

Conflict on a football pitch between team-mates is always seen as a negative situation and portrayed as a clear sign that there is no spirit in the camp, but in my experience it's exactly the opposite. The players are all determined not to lose and if anyone makes a mistake they get worked up about it. But, in general, slanging matches blow up only because team-mates know each other well enough to realise no long-term damage will be done if views are aired there and then on the pitch.

You'll struggle to find anyone in the United camp wanting to criticise Peter, that's for certain. He has the respect of everyone who played with him and saw the amazing saves he pulled off. Peter had a massive presence in goal. It could put off a striker even before he thought about shooting. He put doubts which probably had never existed before into forwards' minds. He charged out and almost jumped at players with his arms and legs spread like a star. It was an imposing sight. All of a sudden, with Peter hurtling out of goal to stop them with his huge frame blocking out the sun, they must have wondered: 'How can anyone get this ball past him?'

Also Peter was blessed with brilliant reactions and produced some of best point-blank saves I've ever seen, especially for a man of his size. Despite being a giant he had remarkable flexibility and could twist and turn in the air to get a glove to the ball.

One save that sticks in the mind was his stop from Ivan Zamorano in the 2–0 Champions League win over Inter Milan at Old Trafford in 1999. The Chilean striker had slipped free at the far post and got his head to a deep cross. Everyone in the ground, including me, thought it was going in, but Peter threw out his left hand and kept the ball out with his wrist. It was inspirational stuff.

Peter's kicking wasn't as good as Barthez's, but he could send the ball long and high, and frequently he threw it out with deadly accuracy to David Beckham and Ryan Giggs, setting up quick breaks in the process. His vision meant that from being under pressure, we had our opponents desperately chasing back to try and deny us a goal-scoring opportunity.

The classic example was Giggs' goal at Coventry in February 1999. Peter collected a cross from our left and hurled the ball to Dwight Yorke on the half-way line. Two passes later and the ball was in the City net for the winner.

Peter shocked the football world and his team-mates by announcing that he intended to quit United in the summer of 1999, the bombshell coming a full seven months before the season ended. No-one in the changing room had a clue what was on the cards and I found out only by reading a newspaper.

It was a massive disappointment for me to hear he was going, but I could understand his reasons. He had played nearly 400 games for United over an eight-year period and wanted a new challenge, one he found by helping Lisbon to the Portuguese title the season after he left us.

I was gutted to see him go, but I knew that he needed a fresh start to keep him on his toes and Peter was a brave man to face up to those facts. It must have been hard to walk away from the biggest club in the world, but he had a decent send-off present – the treble.

Alex Ferguson was also frustrated by his decision, but the manager refused to stand in Peter's way by holding him to his contract.

'It was a surprise,' I recall Ferguson saying at the time. 'But I understand why he wants to go. With the service he's given us over the years, he deserves us to be understanding.'

After Peter left, nearly every top keeper in Europe was linked with the vacant spot and my Dutch international team-mate, Edwin van der Sar, was hotly tipped to take over, but then he joined Juventus. In the end we signed Mark Bosnich on a Bosman-style free transfer from Aston Villa.

The Australian was close to Dwight Yorke, his former team-mate at Villa Park, and the chance to play for a club which had won so much the previous season obviously appealed to him. Mark had been at United before as a kid and was forced to return home after work-permit problems. In retrospect it seems that when it comes to United and Mark Bosnich, things are fated not to work out.

He was injured after just four games and, worried about having no cover for European competition, Ferguson brought in Taibi from Venezia. Ironically the paperwork was not completed in time for the Italian to play in the Champions League and once he suffered a sudden demise, Bosnich had a straight fight with Van der Gouw for the number-one jersey.

Inspirational against both Palmeiras in the Toyota Inter-Continental Cup and Real Madrid in the 0–0 Champions League draw at the Bernabeu, Mark showed he was capable of holding down his place. But he never seemed to convince the man who matters most, Alex Ferguson.

Bosnich was dogged by rumours that he never got on with the manager, and that he was bought by the board rather than the boss. Certainly he became depressed about spending lengthy spells on the sidelines. Mark was always friendly and, typical of most Aussies, he was a loud and confident character, but towards the end of his time at United probably those traits let him down a bit.

After the arrival of Barthez, it became blindingly obvious to all and sundry that Mark was never going to be given the chance to stake a claim to be United's long-term number-one, but his pride refused to let him walk away.

He was told to play in the third team and then snubbed offers to go on loan before his contract was cancelled and he signed for Chelsea in January 2001. In his situation, I would have gone much sooner. If I'm not wanted, I'll disappear.

Bosnich will be hoping to prove Ferguson wrong by making a massive impact at Stamford Bridge in 2001/2002. I wish him all the best, except when he plays against us.

Mark's spell was interrupted briefly by the appearance of the Italian keeper, Taibi. When I heard we'd signed him from Venezia for more than £4 million in September 1999, I must admit to being surprised – I'd never even heard of him. Like Mark, he was a friendly guy, despite not speaking a word of English. We tried to make him feel at home by conversing through hand signals but it was hard work to get a point across in any split second's break from action in a Premiership game. His lack of conversation almost certainly played its part in his early exit after just four games.

He never settled and, as a foreign player, I know how important it is to feel comfortable with your personal life when it comes to handling the pressure of playing top-class football in another country.

Massimo didn't get off to the best of starts, either. Early in his debut, the televised morning kick-off against Liverpool at Anfield, he charged a long way off his line before flapping at a cross, which was headed home by Sami Hyypia. However, let's not forget that he went on to make some brilliant saves and after we won the game 3–2 he was named as man-of-the-match.

Over the next few weeks he amazed me with his ability as an outfield player. He had all the tricks and could fool anyone with a slight feint or dummy when on the ball. Of course, that's not why we bought him.

Eventually his inability to communicate with the United defenders started to take a toll. He couldn't command his area or talk us through a game like we had been used to in the Schmeichel era. With Peter, we knew exactly where all the runners were heading, but now there was almost silence.

His lack of English started a rash of false claims about him. There was even a myth flying around that in the Liverpool game he had someone behind his goal translating for him. The story goes that whenever he shouted in Italian, the guy behind his net translated the phrase and bellowed it out to the rest of us. A great idea – but just a myth!

Still, we had confidence in his ability and we could see in training that Massimo was a decent keeper, but his stock started to slip after a shocking mistake in the match against Southampton in late September.

Matt Le Tissier's under-hit shot from 25-yards was trundling so gently towards him that I'd turned and was walking back upfield, waiting for his punt to sail over my head, when I heard a groan. I looked round and saw the ball trickling over the line.

I saw later on television replays that the ball had skidded from his grip and rolled into the net through his legs. It was unbelievable. To make matters worse Southampton went on to draw level and take a point out of a game they had been losing 3–1.

If that had happened to me I would have come clean afterwards – put my hands up, admitted my error and got on with the rest of the season. Instead Massimo made a rod for his own back by claiming his studs were too long and caught in the turf. It all sounded as ridiculous as it looked and, as soon as I heard that statement, I knew it would come back to haunt him.

Another glaring error in the next match, a 5–0 defeat at Chelsea – in which he came almost to the edge of his area to punch clear and missed to let Gus Poyet nod an early goal – brought the excuse to the fore again.

The gaffer decided to give him a break and let things calm down a bit. He was told to sit out for a few games and work on things in training, with Ferguson obviously hoping the consequent easing of pressure might change his game.

But Taibi never got back into the team and went back to Italy to play for Reggina. He scored with a header last season to win a vital match as they fought against relegation, and he said in interviews that he wanted to come back to England to play for a smaller club than United, just to prove he is not a flop.

The disruption in goal that season gave Van der Gouw a chance to prove once again that he is an extremely valuable member of United's squad. My fellow Dutchman moved to Old Trafford in July 1996, but because of the presence of Schmeichel for most of his time in England, he has played only around 50 games.

But he came in when Bosnich was injured and Taibi lost form to prove what we all knew from the occasional day when he stood in for the Dane. Without a shred of doubt, Rai is a Premiership-class keeper.

He must feel part of the furniture, and while fans can talk about David Beckham's or Ryan Giggs' allegiance to United, it's hard to see past Van der Gouw when it comes to real loyalty. He has suffered the pain of having to drop out of the first team on too many occasions, but always he has battled away and waited for another chance.

Now the obstacle he's got to overcome is Barthez, currently the best keeper in the world. Fabien is unique in being comparatively small yet dominant in the air. Meanwhile the fact that he hasn't got a hulking big frame means the Frenchman is agile and has a great burst of speed off the line.

In addition, he's a genuine entertainer, and having won a World Cup and European Championship before joining us from Monaco for £7.8 million in the summer of 2000, there was no way he would struggle to handle the intense pressure all players come under when signing for United – even though he was heralded instantly as the long-term successor to the legendary Peter Schmeichel.

I missed the first half of Fabien's debut season because of my Achilles injury, but it wasn't hard to build up an understanding with him after returning in the match against Bradford City on January 13.

It's vitally important to have a good relationship with your keeper and with Fabien being so quick off his line we can defend high up the pitch, safe in the knowledge that he is almost like a sweeper behind us.

Before a game the manager will tell us how much space we can leave behind us. Against sides with pacy strikers we leave less room for them to exploit, but normally we push out and leave Fabien with space to pull off some of his party tricks. It can be heart-in-the-mouth time when he tries to beat a striker before clearing and, although he rarely gets caught out, I don't stop and stare in admiration. I will try and pull wide of him to give him an option if he needs to offload the ball.

Barthez brought a smile to my face as I watched from the bench against Derby County in May 2001 when he took on and beat Malcolm Christie and Lee Morris just outside his own box. Later he sprayed a 50-yard pass over two defenders to the boot of Beckham, a ball the England captain would have been pleased to deliver himself.

The one criticism normally levelled at Barthez is his lack of height, but he possesses a great spring and such good timing that he can climb as high as any keeper in the Premiership. When crosses come into his six-yard box, we tend to leave them and generally he'll eat them up all day.

But if the ball is arrowing towards the penalty spot than Fabien has to make his mind up and we wait for a call. In general terms, if the cross is pumped in from distance and almost floats into the area he will gather the ball quite comfortably. We would expect him to charge off his line and collect. But if there's pace on the ball and it starts to dip, I expect to get my head on it, as Fabien would have less chance of making it in time.

I can't finish this chapter without a quick mention for Andy Goram, who joined us for a short spell from Motherwell in March 2001 to cover when Barthez and Van der Gouw were injured.

We hit it off straight away as he was at Glasgow Rangers for a long time and still has close contact with people at the club. I wanted to find out how some of my Dutch team-mates were faring up there, and he filled me in.

He's a friendly guy who possesses the kind of exuberant character needed in the dressing room, and he proved on the training pitch – and a short stint against Coventry in the April – that despite being 37 years old he retains the ability to play on for a while yet.

CHAPTER FIFTEEN

Dutch disappointment

As I collected the ball and strode purposefully towards the penalty spot I was more than aware that Holland's chances of winning Euro 2000 rested firmly on my shoulders.

If I missed my penalty kick we were pretty well on our way out, as Frank de Boer had seen his effort, our first attempt, saved by Francesco Toldo. Now Italy were 2–0 ahead with a 100-per-cent success rate.

Failing to find the net was not an option as I stared at Toldo and watched him bounce up and down on his goal line. If I couldn't beat him, an Italian side which I considered to be second-rate compared to the Dutch would be well on their way to celebrating a place in the final against France.

The Amsterdam Arena had been a cauldron of high-intensity excitement throughout the burning-hot afternoon, but now it hushed as I started my run-up. I knew exactly where to put the ball, straight down the middle with enough power to carry it home, even if Toldo stuck up a lucky leg and picked up a slight deflection.

But as I struck the ball I didn't get over it far enough and skied my penalty high into the massed ranks of orange-shirted fans behind the goal. 'Shit!' I thought. 'We're out.'

There were more kicks to come and although Patrick Kluivert converted his kick, Toldo got down to deny Paul Bosvelt and once again I had been beaten on penalties at the semi-final stage, as in the 1998 World Cup, and it hurt. It was a crushing blow, but I refuse to take the blame for our exit on an afternoon of high drama and wasted chances.

'Don't worry about it too much,' my best friend Arthur Numan told me as he put a consoling arm around my slumped shoulders. 'I won't,' I said to myself. I took my responsibility and it's easy afterwards for people to say maybe someone else should have taken the spot-kick, but they wouldn't have said that if I'd buried it.

I should never have been left to trudge back to the dressing room with my head bowed, though. The game should have been over before reaching that point. In the 90 minutes we could and should have finished it off. We missed two penalties in normal time and numerous other chances after the Italians were reduced to ten men following Gianluca Zambrotta's sending-off in the 34th minute.

It will be my name that goes down in history as the culprit, but it's far too easy to blame the penalty-takers in the shoot-out. They are just the unlucky ones who have to put up with the sympathetic words or nasty verbal attacks from mindless fans for years to come.

It still rankles with me that we lost to the Italians, as they were not a good team. They played so defensively throughout the tournament and ended Euro 2000 with plaudits for being strong at the back. But they didn't impress me. Certainly they didn't defend well against the Dutch. They gave us two penalties and chances galore. Is that the sign of a team acclaimed as the masters of defensive football?

Everyone thought they would win the tournament once they'd beaten us and, indeed, they should have taken the title after leading 1–0 with seconds to go against France in the final, having wasted a good chance to make it 2–0 when Alessandro Del Piero missed.

Despite the Juventus man's slip, the Italians thought they had won it. The substitutes linked arms on the touchline and started bouncing up and down in a triumphant celebration, only to be halted by a dramatic French equaliser from Sylvain Wiltord. Their faces dropped and I swear there were tears. How embarrassed they must have felt. Sitting at home watching, I felt a sweet sensation and it got even better when David Trezeguet scored the golden-goal winner.

Italy weren't the best team in Europe. They didn't deserve to win the tournament, and didn't even deserve to be in the final. I'm convinced that if we'd beaten them in the semis, Holland would have been crowned as champions of Europe. That isn't meant to belittle the French as they have a great team, but at that time we were playing so well and I think we had a wonderful chance to win in front of our home fans.

I flew to New York the day after the final. It wasn't a case of getting away from it all, as I wasn't sitting at home like a manic depressive because of missing that penalty. It was simply a chance to go somewhere Ellis and I had always fancied visiting, so we left Lisa with relatives and jumped on Concorde.

Back home the press were still talking about my blazing miss from the spot. I, meanwhile, had put it out of my mind. I'm not the type who sits on the couch every night for the rest of his life feeling sorry about a footballing incident or pitying himself. It was gone. It hurt, but it was gone.

To the merry-makers it was still a source of fun. Some comedians claim the ball hasn't hit the ground yet; other jokers say they were hit by the ball while innocently wondering around outside the Arena. I just let them laugh about it.

Maybe it's their way of handling the fact we didn't win. We had gone into Euro 2000 playing on our home pitches with our coach, Frank Rijkaard, steadfastly claiming he expected us to win, and although we weren't producing our best football in the warm-up games, there was an air of confidence around the team.

We had our doubters, especially after drawing 5–5 with our co-hosts, Belgium, before the tournament. We knew at that point we had to improve, but importantly we knew there was improvement in us. Once Euro 2000 started the pressure would be intense and that would add another 20 per cent to our play. In the friendlies the Dutch side just weren't sharp enough.

To be honest, we weren't much better in our opening 1–0 win over the Czech Republic, secured thanks to a controversial 89th-minute Frank de Boer penalty after his brother, Ronald, took a tumble in the box. Referee Pierluigi Collina was adamant that a shirt-tug was to blame, but after seeing it on television I have to admit it was a dodgy decision.

By that point I was off the pitch after a thumping crack of heads with the man-mountain Jan Koller which had ripped the skin around my left eye. I had gone up with him for a long ball and caught the back of his head with the soft flesh just above the eyelid.

I was led off the pitch straight away with blood pouring down my face and the team doctor didn't need to look twice to tell that stitches were required to seal up the wound. However, they needed to be inserted in a rush and without an anaesthetic. To make matters, worse the cut was so close to the eyeball that a slip of the needle could have blinded me.

The lack of anaesthetic I could handle as the blow had made the whole left side of my face go numb, so the Rambo-style instant-stitching was okay by me. The one thing that did worry me was what a loose needle could do, especially when I saw how shaky the doctor's hands were.

I could understand his nerves as everyone on the bench was urging him to hurry the task and get me back on the pitch, while he was insistent on doing a decent job and making sure that I went back on without a needle protruding from my eyeball.

'I'm not going to mess this up,' he told me. 'It might take a bit longer than they want but I have to get this right.'

'I'd rather you did,' I replied. 'My wife isn't too keen on pirates in patches.'

He took his time to slot in five stitches and before too long I was back in the thick of the action, while probably the doctor was enjoying a nip of brandy to steady himself. In hindsight he need not have rushed as the sight in that eye was still blurred and in the 75th minute I was hauled off to be replaced by Bert Konterman.

With my eye still sore, I missed the next game as we hit form to see off the Danes 3–0, but I was back in the side for the final group match against a second-string French side. It was a game we needed to win to ensure first place in the group and we edged home 3–2 in an exciting encounter.

Now the pressure was really beginning to build. Playing at home we were always expected to lift the trophy, but although some of my team-mates might have been feeling it, the strain didn't weigh too heavily on my shoulders. As a Manchester United player, I was used to having 60,000 fans anticipating a home victory – you could call it ideal preparation for a tournament like this.

We booked a passage into the semi-final with a 6–1 win over Yugoslavia on a night when, metaphorically speaking, our opponents failed to turn up. They have some cracking players and boast guys with brilliant technical skills, but on the night we began to wonder if they really wanted to know. They gave us so much time and space it was easy for our passing game to cut them open time and again.

There have been few games in my career when things have gone so well for one side. Every chance that dropped our way was taken with Patrick Kluivert scoring a hat-trick and Marc Overmars getting two, while an own goal made up the tally.

Kluivert was fantastic on an occasion when the De Kuip stadium in Rotterdam produced one of the best atmospheres of the tournament. He got on the end of three brilliant passing moves and his finishing was clinical.

We had been getting better as each game was won and, roared on by a wall of orange-shirted fans, the side felt more than capable of matching the success of the class of 1988, who won the trophy in Germany.

Certainly we didn't see the Italians as a massive barrier in the way of our ambitions, not at the start the match anyway. We were on fire from the first whistle with Overmars and Boudewijn Zenden getting down the flanks and behind the Italian defence, and when they went down to ten men we took control.

Frank de Boer had a spot-kick saved and then Kluivert scuffed his effort from the penalty spot. We weren't concerned about the Italians scoring. In fact, they didn't have a shot on target until the 83rd minute. But as the chances came and went I began to wonder if it was going to be our night. It wasn't!

Once it got to penalties, probably the Italians had a

psychological edge. We had wanted to win in normal time and hadn't. They had played for penalties from the first minute and had achieved their aim. In addition, we had missed two spot-kicks in the game.

Still, I believe that anyone who had watched us in training would have remained full of confidence as Frank Rijkaard had made us practise beating the keeper from 12 yards in every session. No-one missed.

It made a lovely statistic for the commentators, but I didn't set much store by that fact. A lot of people say you can train for penalties but I think it's very hard to do that. Of course you can tuck the ball home, but it's impossible on a training pitch to simulate the pressure you are under from performing in front of 50,000 fans and a massive television audience, knowing that if you miss you are out of the tournament. You can't practise that.

The pressure told in the end, but probably just as memorable as my penalty miss was the image of Rijkaard sitting in the stands crying as we were eliminated. Little did I know as I trudged off the pitch that those tears would lead to an exasperated decision to quit.

'I set myself one goal when I started as national coach and that was winning the 2000 European Championships. I failed and I think it is now time for a new coach,' Rijkaard explained afterwards.

The first I knew about Frank's decision was when I walked out of the dressing room and straight into a pack of reporters desperate to know my feelings on Rijkaard's exit. My face must have given away my emotion – I was deeply shocked.

'I can't believe he's gone,' I babbled. 'I expected him to take us on and fight for a place in the World Cup.'

Frank had been a controversial choice for the post in the first place, having taken over the position without a previous coaching job. He'd not even been listed as a contender. But he'd worked with the national team as an assistant in the 1998 World Cup and the training sessions he organised were well received by the players for their intelligence.

So once he got the job he was given the immediate backing of the squad, some of whom he had recently played alongside at Ajax. The fact that he'd stopped playing only a few years previously was definitely a help to him. He knew when and how the players wanted to train and was happy to let us call him by his first name rather then endure the regimentation of 'manager' or 'gaffer'.

Frank even allowed us to go home after games and have days off with the family, and his actions boosted the team spirit. It's hard being shelled up in a hotel for a long period with nothing to concentrate on but the next game, and popping home to see Ellis and Lisa helped to break the mental strain I was under. The idea was forward-thinking and not approved of in every circle, but I believe it worked.

Also, he sat in the stand for a lot of the games and looked at the tactics, preferring not to be constantly in touch with players and trying to get messages across from the bench in the manner of my former PSV coach Dick Advocaat.

I remember during my time at Eindhoven that our captain, Arthur Numan, always picked the opposite side of the pitch to the dugout if he won the toss. That would save him an ear-bashing when Advocaat was at his most vociferous in the opening 45 minutes.

Arthur didn't have to follow suit with Rijkaard, whose immaculate dress sense and calmness in his dealings with the media hid an intensity and desire to succeed which seeped out only at the end of his reign.

Frank's ambitions are to start managing again and I hope he returns to the game soon. He has much to offer and I'm surprised he's not been tempted back to the fold already.

Rijkaard suffered in the end from the inevitable pressure which comes from being involved in Dutch football at the top level, and which has confronted every team since the 1970s. I must admit I don't know too much about the Dutch sides which finished as runners-up in the World Cup in 1974 and 1978. I'm not a big historian and, despite seeing the action on television programmes, I can't name line-ups from past tournaments.

But I do know about the style of football they played and the legacy it left for the sides which have followed in their wake.

Johan Cryuff's team played 'total football' with players able to interchange positions while looking as though they had played in their new roles throughout their careers.

Inevitably with such skilful players, the team was geared towards attacking football. There's no point in having a defender who can beat two men with a trick and score from 30 yards if he never leaves his right-back position.

The Dutch supporters have grown up with this philosophy and now all subsequent national sides not only have to win, but win in style, with goals flying in from all angles. We have to play attacking football, because that is the way we've always performed in the past. The fans have been spoilt and now they demand entertainment relentlessly. They aren't even happy if we win having spent 90 minutes catching a team on the break.

That can make it difficult in an era when defensive football is the norm for successful sides in international football. Just look at the Italians. Current Dutch manager Louis van Gaal has upset some followers already by occasionally abandoning the all-out attacking policy of the past, but he must get the right results if he intends to play that way.

We've played with three strikers, but also we've played with one and we can't afford to employ a style reminiscent of the great sides of the 1970s just because it keeps other people happy. In fairness to the manager, his hand has been forced slightly in that he's gone into games without key attacking players. But he knows that he cannot under-estimate the depth of feeling among our supporters about adventurous football.

One of Van Gaal's assets is his strength of character. He won't buckle under the weight of public pressure and go gung-ho against his better judgement just because that is what the pundits are screaming for. I've had the impression in the past that such a cool approach has not always prevailed. I'm not talking about the bosses I've played under – including Guus Hiddink and Rijkaard – they've been clever enough to work out the best system for the match. Previously, though, I've wondered about some of the formations.

The current line-up have to live with the need for stylish

success, just as we live with the prerequisite that we must win a major tournament to prove we are as good as the Dutch masters of the past. It's nothing new. Ever since 1978 each new team has needed to prove they are more than just a good side; they have to live up to reputations built by legends.

The 1988 team had the same problems, despite containing the brilliance of Ruud Gullit and Marco van Basten. Until they lifted the European Championship title in Germany that summer, they were considered unworthy to be compared with Cruyff's side. Now they are deemed a superb team on a par with anything the Dutch have produced previously.

The likes of myself, Patrick Kluivert and Edgar Davids have to follow in their footsteps to avoid being regarded as Dutch failures. We have to win a trophy to ensure we are ranked up there with the best. Having reached the semi-final of the last two major tournaments, we are not far off, but not good enough yet to please the demanding Dutch fans.

They have every right to be demanding because we have every chance of winning any tournament we enter. Despite being a small country, we always enter the competition with one of the best teams.

That was the case in Euro '96, when I was called into the squad for a senior tournament for the first time, and later in the 1998 World Cup. Guus Hiddink was manager for the former, and when he phoned me just two days before the Dutch were setting off for England, as I hadn't been named in that squad I wondered what he wanted with me.

I picked up the handset and was ready to hear one of my friends attempt to put on a dodgy impression when Guus spoke to me. His next words came right out of the blue. 'I want you to come to England with us,' he said.

I still wasn't sure it was him after putting the phone down and stood there dazed, staring at Ellis, whose confused look matched mine.

'I'm in the Euro '96 squad,' I told her, almost apologetically as if frightened to reveal too much in case someone was playing a trick on me.

The news was a major surprise in the Stam household, and probably many others across Holland as only recently had I moved to PSV after years of playing for smaller provincial clubs. My sole international experience was 15 minutes as a substitute against Germany as a replacement for Michael Reiziger. There had been a few warm-up games for the tournament since then that I'd not been involved in, so I was counting down the two weeks until my summer holiday in Tenerife.

You can guess how astonished I was when the reality began to sink in. That didn't really happen until later that night when we were watching TV with my father-in-law and I heard Hiddink admit that Frank de Boer's injury was going to rule him out.

'Who are you going to take instead?' he was asked.

'Jaap Stam.' You could hear the cheer for miles.

When I joined up with the squad I felt I was rubbing shoulders with the stars. The likes of Kluivert, Danny Blind, Aron Winter and Dennis Bergkamp were big footballing celebrities and I'd spent very little time in my career with players of that stature.

I felt awkward around those guys, not knowing how to speak to them. I was the little guy from the small club who was almost still a pretender at PSV. These guys were gracing the top clubs in Europe like Lazio, Barcelona, Arsenal and an Ajax team that had just played in two European Cup finals.

One of the first things I noticed was that although Holland were one of the favourites for the tournament, and the guys all expected to do well, there was no real sense of conviction in the answers when the question was asked: 'Can we win it?'

Scotland was our first game and, watching from the bench, I couldn't believe we didn't get a penalty when Ronald de Boer's shot was handled on the line by John Collins. The referee missed it and when Clarence Seedorf headed wide towards the end, we knew the Scots were going to hold on for a draw.

It was a satisfactory, if not a great result, but after our next game with Switzerland our tournament exploded into a nightmare when Edgar Davids was sent home following a blazing row with Hiddink.

Edgar can be abrasive at times and the pit-bull image he has built can spill over into his relationships with people off the pitch. When you get to know him he's a decent, honest lad, but strangers find him an odd character and there's no point in them trying to start up a conversation with him. He would be likely to walk away!

He even got snappy with me when I poked fun at him over the goggles he has to wear due to an eye problem. 'You haven't got time to go skiing,' I told him when I first saw him put them on. 'We're about to play a football match.'

'Fuck off,' was the short and sweet reply.

Davids, along with Frank de Boer, has since been dragged into a messy drugs controversy after testing positive for the banned substance nandrolone, a performance enhancer.

I refuse to believe either player knowingly took nandrolone. At the time, it was thought the substance was contained in some vitamin pills handed out by the Dutch team doctor. I am not convinced by this theory as I was given the same pills and even checked with the Manchester United doctor. I was given the thumbs-up to take them. I can only think it was something in a meal they ate or a drink they had, as having known Davids and De Boer for more than five years, I would willingly stand up in a courtroom and plead their innocence.

Getting back to the Euro '96 bust-up, it was not – as the media claimed at the time – due to a racial split in the camp, which many people tagged the 'Rasta revolt'. It was simply Davids arguing with the manager over which tactics we should be using.

Nobody, apart from those two, will know exactly what happened because the other members of the squad were in their own rooms at the time of the row. When we came down to eat at 5pm, a team meeting was called.

'We just want to inform you that Davids has left for Holland,' Hiddink told a stunned audience. 'There has been a disagreement and he was asked to pack his bags.'

They didn't give us a specific reason, but we heard rumours that a few names had been called and Davids told the manager where to shove his team selection. Apparently he didn't like the system we were using, with Seedorf playing as a central defender and then moving into the midfield to create an extra body when we had the ball.

Players were slipping past Seedorf as he tried to cover the two roles and Davids wasn't happy that his friend had been put in that position on the pitch. Hiddink, seeing his authority being challenged, put his foot down and booked the midfielder a ticket home.

It was a brave move and was a surprise even though Davids had been dropped for the 2–0 win over Switzerland, but I guess that the manager had to show who was boss. So ignore what you might have read at the time, there wasn't a racial split or anything like that in the team.

Always there are specific groups of players and, although I'm not a cliquey person, I hung around with Numan, Philip Cocu and Wim Jonk simply because they were at PSV with me and I knew them best. Kluivert, Davids, Seedorf and Winston Bogarde were always together, but it wasn't as though we were at odds with each other. I've heard the word 'camps' used when describing the supposed factions among the Dutch players, yet it couldn't have been further from the truth. In fact, I thought the atmosphere was good and honest, with the players working very hard for each other. There wasn't then, and isn't now, one dominant player who stands above the rest. We are all the same; we want the best for the team and we want to win.

There has, of course, been a history of internal rumblings in the Dutch squad, but although I can only talk about my own experience, I do know that the current side doesn't have the kind of hierarchy as existed in the team which won the European Championships in 1988. Clearly, that situation was prone to cause jealousies.

In those days players like Gullit, Rijkaard and Van Basten were looked upon and treated as superstars. In an era when few Dutch players were invited to move abroad, these guys were excelling for the likes of AC Milan and conquering Europe.

If you run through the current Dutch line-up, you'll find more than half the team are plying their trade with such clubs as Juventus, Barcelona and Manchester United. The star status no longer survives and that has led to calmer waters in the squad.

There are still rumblings to this day about splits in the camp, though, and several pundits on top sports shows back in Holland continually raise the issue. When I hear it I think: 'What a load of nonsense!'

They have never been invited inside the inner sanctum of the team and haven't even met all the players, so how can they possibly know how we are feeling?

We weren't helped in our bid to show there was a united dressing room by slipping to defeat in our next game against England. I know folklore has it that Terry Venables' team were able to rip apart a Dutch side torn in two by internal arguments, but despite the departure of Davids, that was not true. We were ready and well prepared, and we walked on to that Wembley pitch feeling we could upset the home nation and book a place in the quarter-final.

How wrong could we be? Watching it from the bench, I couldn't believe how well England were playing and there were quizzical looks all around the pitch as the host nation simply took us apart. For the first time in my career, I was happy to be sat in the dugout rather than out on the pitch. I was desperate to stay there and I wasn't the only one.

Actually we started well, once again shooting down the conspiracy theory, but once Blind brought down Paul Ince and Alan Shearer put away the penalty it was all over for us.

England came at us again and again, controlling the match in midfield. They scored three in a ten-minute spell after half-time with Alan Shearer and Teddy Sheringham ending up with two goals each as the Wembley crowd around us sang Football's Coming Home, the theme tune of the tournament.

We had a radio by the bench to monitor the Scotland game and, as it petered out to a 0–0 draw, we knew that just one goal would give us a chance to fight another day in the quarter-finals. Personally I thought it was more likely we would let in another five than see someone on our side finding the net.

But after going on as a substitute, Kluivert popped up to score in the 77th minute and, amazingly, we could celebrate a place in the last eight – not that we did much celebrating.

The scoreline might have been a shocker, but the post-match reaction to the 4–1 drubbing by our manager was unbelievable. The players had walked into the dressing room with heads bowed, trying to hide their embarrassment. When Hiddink strolled in, we all sat down and waited for the inevitable bollocking.

But, amazingly, he smiled and said: 'Well done lads, you've qualified for the next stage. That was our aim and we've achieved it. Obviously the press will be after you because of this result, but don't let them get on to you. Ignore what they are going to say and prepare for the next game. Don't forget that we're still in the tournament and can win it.'

You could almost hear the gasps of astonishment as the expected tantrum turned into a triumphant moment before Hiddink strode off, leaving behind the most bemused squad of players Holland has ever known.

Our build-up to the next challenge, against France, was all about trying to get confidence flowing through the squad again, and it seemed to work as we played well, being denied what we thought was a certain penalty when Marcel Desailly handled in the box.

The referee didn't give it and after Cocu hit a post the match went into a penalty shoot-out. All five French players scored with their spot-kicks. Seedorf missed, and we were out.

To be honest, I was quite happy to be going home. Of course, it would have been nice to win it, but I hadn't played at all and with the initial excitement of being involved starting to die off, the time was beginning to drag.

Sitting there through game after game, knowing there was not the remotest chance of getting on the pitch, started to take a toll and it was a whole new feeling for me to deal with. In my career I've been lucky not to have spent long periods on the bench and although I'm glad I know how it feels, the depressing factor of not playing matches is hard to fight against.

The only fun I had was with my PSV team-mate, Numan, as we enjoyed a running joke at our manager's expense. It came about as we sat behind him, kitted up on the bench and drilling holes into the back of his head with our eyes. We were trying to send messages to his brain about putting us on.

We sat there without even stretching our legs for 90 minutes, because whereas in England players tend to go for a run along the touchline every 15 minutes or so to keep loose, in Holland we wait until the manager tells us to get warmed-up. Arthur and I kept waiting and waiting for the nod and every time Hiddink decided he needed to make a substitution he looked over his left shoulder at our excited faces but not once did he ask us even to warm up.

In the end we decided he was only looking over to try and figure out who the hell we were, taking up space in his dugout. We had grown so resigned to the fact that we weren't going to be used that we sat with our laces open and would have been happy to sip a coffee as we enjoyed the game.

Back home, of course, everyone was disappointed with our showing, but not having played I hoped to avoid the inevitable backlash from the Dutch press. That proved to be the case when I got off the plane in Holland and strolled through customs to the waiting throng of journalists and autograph hunters. I was one of the first to face them and was expecting some stick, but a path opened up for me like the Red Sea for Moses.

As I walked past I could hear people saying: 'He only plays for PSV, don't bother with him.' I manoeuvred my trolley through the crowd to see Ellis waiting and we headed home and on to a holiday in the sun.

It was totally different the next time I joined up with the Dutch squad for a big tournament – the 1998 World Cup. I'd just signed for Manchester United as the world's most expensive defender and there were more than a few eyes watching my performances.

We drew 0–0 with Belgium in the opening game, hardly a surprise considering the local rivalry with our neighbours. As always the game was physical, but never turned nasty and we were disappointed not to grab a winner after outplaying them for long periods.

Then South Korea failed to cause an upset as we dispatched them 5–0, but the Mexicans were different. We were 2–0 up after 20 minutes through Cocu and Ronald de Boer, and it felt good to rub their noses in it after watching them dive all over the place from the first whistle.

Luis Hernandez was so bad that on one occasion he went down as though shot when he was at least five yards away from Numan's challenge. The next chance I got I sidled up to him.

'Hey cheat,' I yelled. 'I hope you'll be as embarrassed as your family will be when you see that on telly.'

I was desperate to win and make a bigger point at the final whistle but the Mexicans pulled one back with 15 minutes to go through Ricardo Pelaez, and then the problems started for me in the final seconds. There was a cross fired in and as I ran backwards I stuck my foot out in a last-gasp bid to clear, only to see the ball run underneath it. It dropped to Hernandez and he slotted home the equaliser.

That was when all the trouble started with the English press. They had been waiting for a slip-up to use as a hook to hang me, simply because of the huge fee on my shoulders. That moment had handed them the perfect ammunition. They went to town on me!

But to this day I still can't see what more I could have done. I was running back and was off balance when I stuck my foot out. They didn't care about technical matters like that. As far as they were concerned I was a lumbering fool and Alex Ferguson had wasted nearly eleven million quid.

What really angered me was the fact that for 90 minutes I had enjoyed a good game. I was on top of Hernandez throughout and looked composed in bringing the ball out from the back and instigating play. But, of course, all of this was forgotten once the Mexican's equaliser hit the back of the net. I was going to get slaughtered on that one moment.

It didn't help that I gave away a penalty in the next match, a second-round clash with Yugoslavia, although this decision by Spanish referee Garcia Aranda was extremely debatable.

I did have a handful of Vladimir Jugovic's shirt as he twisted towards the byline but his touch was poor and the ball had run out of play before I heard a whistle. I thought it was going to be for a goal-kick and was shocked when he pointed to the spot.

Luckily Predrag Mijatovic missed the penalty, because by then Slobodan Komljenovic had cancelled out Dennis Bergkamp's opener and the match looked set for extra-time before Davids drilled home a brilliant winner from 20 yards in the last minute.

The diving and late goals continued in the quarter-finals against Argentina with little Ariel Ortega leaving me sick to the stomach with his cheating. But finally he got his come-uppance in the best possible way after a unsightly clash with our keeper Edwin van der Sar.

The striker had tried to win a penalty by tumbling in the box, but Mexican referee Brizio Carter wasn't conned and as the Argentine got to his feet his head came close to Van der Sar, who crashed to the ground as though he'd been head-butted. Ortega hadn't caught him and tried to protest his innocence but, as the red card was shown, it was a sweet case of what goes around, comes around.

Argentina, who equalised through Claudio Lopez after going one behind to Kluivert's early goal, hoped to hold on and force the game into penalties but their plan was ruined by a brilliant piece of finishing from Bergkamp.

With immaculate comntrol, he plucked a superb high pass from Frank de Boer out of the air, took one touch to steady himself and lose Ayala, then poked home the winner. It was the goal of the tournament.

The semi-final against Brazil was played in the squad's seventh week together. During the tournament we stayed at a beautiful hotel on the waterfront in Monaco, and with the location being Monte Carlo, rather than hiring out push-bikes to guests, there were jet-skis on offer. New toys like these were adored by we footballers and, every chance we got, a gang of Dutchmen would set off for some seaside frolics.

Unfortunately there weren't always enough jet-skis to go round, and our walking pace would increase as we neared the boathouse. It was a comical sight as the huge frames of Pierre van Hooijdonk and myself tried to edge subtly past nimble little Marc Overmars without breaking into a run.

But by the time the finishing line was in sight there was always a schoolboy sprint to throw on a lifebelt and grab a jet-ski. It was a good job Hiddink wasn't keen on water sports or he'd have been pulling his hair out at our antics.

'Come over here,' I'd call to Overmars, and when he was next to me I'd push him off his machine and into the sea. Then there'd be a frenzy of jet-skis circling around him, trying to build up enough waves to cover his head before, practically choking, he'd be allowed to swim to shore. God knows how much how the insurance would have cost if the money-men had spotted what we were doing. Mind you, it must have been pretty high anyway, as the squad was flown by helicopter to each game!

Our clash with Brazil was hosted along the coast at Marseille and was potentially the match of the competition. We had been in fine form, but so had the South Americans, who could field the likes of Rivaldo, Bebeto, Roberto Carlos and, of course, Ronaldo, who had been excellent throughout the World Cup and had taken Chile apart almost single-handedly in the second round.

My central-defensive partner Frank de Boer and I decided to ditch plans to man-mark my former PSV team-mate and agreed to pick him up depending on which side of the pitch he played. Also we had to be wary of Bebeto dropping deep to pick up possession and link play. With Ronaldo's speed and Bebeto's brain, it was an arrangement to test any pairing, but Frank is such a clever reader of the game and intelligent talker that I always believed we could contain our illustrious opponents.

Ronaldo got only one chance on that night of July 7, as he wriggled past Cocu by faking to go outside him, then nipping in front to touch home a cross from the right. It left us with 44 minutes to find an equaliser and we took our time before Kluivert headed home with 180 seconds left on the clock, sending the match into extra-time.

That was cagey at best, but ended in agony for me when I was struck down by cramp with minutes to go. A lump the size of a golf ball appeared on my thigh and every step sent a shooting pain through my body. I could barely walk at the end and when the names were pencilled in for the dramatic penalty shoot-out, I was number 11.

Van der Sar had every reason to feel confident about keeping out one or two of the Brazilians' spot-kicks. We had sent our video analyst to the South Americans' training camp to film their sessions and he came back with a compilation tape showing every penalty being tucked away low into a bottom corner.

If van der Sar could guess the right way to dive he was bound to get one – or so the theory ran. In fact, the Brazilians must have been tipped off that our man was there as they placed all their efforts into a top corner.

They only needed four penalties. Brazilian keeper Claudio Taffarel saved from Ronald de Boer and Cocu, and we were out. I was devastated. Who knows if I'd ever get the chance to reach a World Cup Final again? Losing out on spot-kicks made it even more painful. I'm sure Brazil will admit they weren't the better side; the match was far too even for them to claim that.

But while they were looking forward to a place in the biggest game in football, I was left to prepare for the ridiculous third-place play-off against Croatia.

'I'm shattered,' Dennis Bergkamp uttered as he walked over to me in the centre-circle while the Brazilians wheeled away to celebrate.

'Hey, Dennis,' I consoled him. 'What more could we have done?'

We turned up for the match with Croatia, who had been beaten by the eventual World Cup winners, France, and we went through the motions in the 2–1 defeat. No-one was interested and all we wanted was to head home. For me, in particular, there was good reason to return to my nest.

There were only two weeks to go before I joined up with Manchester United and Ellis was still no closer to going into labour. We decided she should be induced and that gave me a week to spend with my first child before leaving for the Reds' pre-season tour of Norway.

It was perfect timing as the thrill and anticipation of becoming a father for the first time helped to take the bitter edge off the World Cup defeat. When there was time for the memories to enter my head, I refused to become despondent. Life goes on and in football there's always another match to think about. Just as well, when my life's ambition to play in a World Cup Final had been ripped from my grasp so cruelly.

CHAPTER SIXTEEN

The dressing room

I have played in a European Cup Final and a World Cup semi-final, but still I get that unmistakable buzz on the morning of any match. The excitement rushes through me and there's a smile on my face as I leap out of bed. This is what being a footballer is all about. This is the day players live for – match day!

I live in a deadly serious world of high stakes and even higher wages, where winning is paramount. But that doesn't stop me enjoying my job. I'm privileged and I know it. I haven't got to crawl out of bed in the middle of the night and descend, half asleep, into a dark pit and hack away at a coal-face all day.

The hardest part of my working day is the worry of getting a bollocking from the gaffer for doing something wrong in a game, because that's all it is. A game.

The adrenaline starts pumping as I drive into Old Trafford. We have to meet up three hours before the match, which is a comfortable regime compared to the routine in Italy. In Serie A players have to stay in a hotel the night before a home game to ensure proper preparation without the distractions a wife and family can bring.

It's a system which no doubt suits some players, but would not be my choice. The night before a match – it used to be Friday but now often it is Saturday – offers a great chance for me to relax with Ellis and spend time with my daughters, Lisa and Megan.

Granted, they may wake up during the night and upset my sleep patterns. However, that's a price I'm willing to pay to be at home, and having kept the same routine all my career, I don't believe it's caused me too many problems.

After a morning with the Fisher Price toys, I drive into the ground and you can bet your life that Gary Neville and his brother Phil will be there aready. They're always first to arrive, whether it's for training or a match or even meeting up for the coach before away games.

Those guys are first and moaning about it. The pair of them never stop whingeing. 'Busy c* *ts' we call them, for their endless grumbling about everything in general and nothing in particular. Gary isn't happy unless he can have a good gripe and it's not too long after meeting up that the first shout of 'shut up' is sent flying down the dinner table.

Later in the afternoon Gary's desire to chatter actually turns into a benefit for the team. He has such a strong, forceful character that people find it hard not to listen, especially as it's backed up with a good footballing brain.

Before we take to the pitch he's always discussing how the particular game should be played. I've been around players who spout rubbish for the sake of making their voices heard. They'll say things like: 'That keeper's crap, have a go at him.' You think: 'What are you talking about?' It's almost like schoolboy rantings but, in contrast, Gary knows what he's on about.

He's impressed me so much that I'd even stick my neck out and say he'd make a good manager when he decides to quit playing. He's got the vocal element you need to get your ideas across to and has a way of expressing himself which conveys the point he is trying to make in a simple manner.

He's extremely experienced as well, having playing at World Cup level with England and in a European final with United. Those are pressure matches and it's obvious that Gary has watched how managers handle situations and adapt tactics. He's soaked up all the information and I'll be interested to see, if he takes up coaching, how he approaches his first managerial job.

Phil doesn't natter away as much as Gary, but it's obvious how much United means to the pair of them. The potential changes in the transfer system got everyone in football talking about how much players could earn and our dressing room was no different. A move to Barcelona or Juventus for the United boys could make them instant millionaires, and there were a few eyes opened at Old Trafford when we heard about the sums of money which could be on offer. But not Gary's or Phil's.

'I'm not going anywhere, no matter how much cash is on the table,' Gary would say. 'This club has given me everything I've ever wanted and they'll have to drag me out of here. I don't even care about the money. I just want to stay here and win things for United. Anyway where are you going to go that gives you a better chance of winning things?'

He has a point, and a huge allegiance to the Reds after coming through their youth system. Gary was in the side which won the FA Youth Cup in 1992 alongside Ryan Giggs, David Beckham and Nicky Butt, and he's known glory and medals ever since. I can't see him leaving the club, no matter what the inducement. I expect he'll ask to be buried under the pitch!

Once Gary has finished eating and got his head stuck in a newspaper to find something else to moan about, it's the turn of the terrible twins to start their pranks. Ryan Giggs and Nicky Butt are the Peter Pans of our dressing room, always wanting to play the kind of jokes most people forget about after leaving school, and too often for my liking I find myself caught up in their little games.

They know I bite on any comments about my game, my appearance or whatever they decide to pick on that day. I know what they're doing, but I can't stop sticking up for myself.

Ryan's wind-up antics are evident also in training games. He'll stitch me up in a drill by dropping a pass short or firing it hard at my chest, and when I'm pulled up for the error he'll say 'Oh dear!' in a comic voice.

At first it used to bug me, but now I see the funny side of it. Quite often I'm fuming, but at the same time I can't help smiling at the hilarious way they've set me up once again.

I have to hold my hands up here and admit that I'm partial to rubbing a team-mate's nose in it if he drops a clanger. You need a thick skin as a professional footballer since there will always be jokes made at your expense. You can't let it get to you. It happens to everyone and you have to ride it out.

Putting his jokes to one side, Giggs is a fantastic player to have in any team. He's one of the best wingers in the world and he can take any defence apart with his pace and ability to carry the ball at high speed. Just look at the goal against Arsenal in the FA Cup semi-final replay at Villa Park in our treble-winning year, and the wonder solo goal against Bradford City in 2000/2001 when he beat half their team before tucking the ball away.

At the speed he runs, his control of the ball is phenomenal. Ronaldo can do it, but not many others can, and that's what marks Ryan out as such a threat to defences. Also he can lift his game on the big European nights and prove an inspiration. He took on Juventus almost single-handedly in the Champions League in October 1997, and scored as the Reds won 3–2. Then he hit the crucial equaliser against the team from Turin in the home leg of the semi-final in April 1999, after which we went on to lift the treble.

They couldn't cope with the way he can either hurtle down the left wing or cut inside and open up so many more options. His play has numerous dimensions and working out a game-plan to stop Ryan Giggs must be a real puzzle.

Nicky's ability as a footballer is sadly underrated, simply because he doesn't get a game every week. He'd walk into any other team in the land, but at United he has the problem of trying to find his way into a central midfield department already home to two world-class players in Roy Keane and Paul Scholes.

His quality is not lost on other Premiership managers, though. Sunderland's Peter Reid has been reported to have shown a great deal of interest in him, while claims that Blackburn Rovers were willing to pay £7 million for him in the spring of 2001 offer indications of his true value.

Nicky can boss a midfield, and did just that for England against Italy in November 2000 before limping off with an injury. I'm sure that his influential display must have caught the eye of Sven Goran Eriksson. Butt has a little nasty streak which makes him more determined to win a 50-50 challenge than most players, but he can play a bit, too, so don't be fooled by any one-dimensional images of the player purveyed by the media. In fact, he can spread play with a 50-yard pass when the situation calls for it.

Nicky's clever, though, and accepts that David Beckham or Ryan Giggs can do more damage so, sensibly enough, he tends towards laying a ten-yard pass to one of them. That's intelligent football and he's intelligent off the pitch, too. Don't try to have a slanging match with him. He's direct, sometimes rude, and always funny. Launch a verbal bombshell at him and he'll bat it straight back with interest.

Once the lunchtime joking is over and we've killed a bit of time reading the newspapers, the players drift over to the dressing room to get massages and strappings sorted, and that's when the chat about the game really begins. We'll have had a tactical team-talk during the week so now it's a case of reminding each other of our tasks as the pre-match pressure starts to build. Usually the television is on, with a spot of horse-racing for the lads to cheer. And, of course, with 16 men in a small room the temptation to let a few farts go is something one or two of the guys can't resist.

Also there's a queue for the toilet, and I'm always in it as I need to get rid of all the excess water I've drunk during the day. I fill my body with as much water as possible so I don't dehydrate during a game, but before kick-off it plays havoc with my system.

In between trips to the loo I'll have a quick chat with Fabien Barthez about how much space we are going to leave behind us, and give him an idea about where I am happy to see him advance to sweep up.

Despite his reputation for being a crazy entertainer on the pitch, Fabien is actually quiet and calm in the dressing room. When I talk to him he doesn't understand all the things I say, because before he came to England from Monaco in the summer of 2000, he didn't need to speak English. That means big conversations with him are out of the question.

Probably the first time we were all keen to see Fabien take centre stage in the dressing room was after our defeat by West Ham in the FA Cup in January 2001. Paolo Di Canio had gone clean through on goal and Barthez just stood there with his arm in the air appealing for offside. 'What are you doing?' I thought at the time, as the Italian managed to evade Fabien's last-gasp challenge by slotting the ball into the far corner.

Afterwards he explained in broken English: 'I was trying to fool him, make him think it was offside. It did not work and I am a sorry but I am sure that if I ran out he would have scored past me.'

Rather than having a go at him, I realised that his actions were a classic example of his uniqueness, and that sharp brain of his is what makes him so good. He thinks so quickly and is always trying to figure out how to gain the upper hand in the mind-games he plays with strikers. Not all keepers are bright enough to do that.

Sometimes there is commotion in the dressing room when Roy Keane hands out the players' tickets. It's the captain's role and one I hate filling when wearing the armband in Keane's absence. We are allowed three tickets each, but no-one is happy with just three. They want four or five and even players who don't need them will join in the shouting match in an attempt to pick up some extras for a mate. It's like being on the floor of the Stock Exchange with the amount of bartering, bickering and squabbling going on. Suddenly all the lads are your best friends, or they remember the favours you owe them. It's a nightmare!

After the tickets are sorted we run out on to the pitch, sample the atmosphere and test the ground to see what studs we need to wear. When there were problems with the Old Trafford surface a couple of seasons ago, it didn't seem to matter what boots we wore, they all churned up the turf. But now we can stick to normal studs and be happy.

I like to get on the pitch, pass a ball around and stretch, but Andy Cole never leaves the dressing room until just before the kick-off. He prefers to stretch on his own and that sums up the guy. Andy likes to keep himself to himself, so much so that after three years in his company I still don't really know him. He's never interrupting conversations or making jokes, but just because he isn't the life and soul of the party doesn't make Andy arrogant. It's merely that he likes to stay in control of himself.

Andy's partner-in-crime up front, Dwight Yorke, is almost the total opposite. He loves a night on the town and we spend plenty of time in the dressing room trying to figure out how he dates so many attractive women. We're honestly surprised at the girls he's pictured with in the papers, and there's always a quip or two about how he's pulled his latest stunner.

Dwight loves the nightlife but won't go out when we're under an official curfew before a game. He's not stupid and knows the rules. There is a time to party and a time to be serious and no-one at United is fool enough to break the rules and upset the manager. We all know what the result would be and we wouldn't expect long careers at United if we stepped out of line.

In his book *Managing My Life*, Ferguson has admitted that the sale of Paul McGrath and Norman Whiteside during the early years of his Old Trafford reign was connected with his efforts to end a drinking culture at the club. At that time he was yet to stamp his name on United's history by winning trophies and had not become embedded in the powerful position he holds now. So if he was that fearless in his decisions to axe people then, he is hardly likely to have second thoughts after the success he's enjoyed. That's why Dwight knows to play it clever and keep his nights out down to a minimum.

Yorke has great presence in the dressing room and merely seeing him can lift a quiet group of players. How can you not feel happy around a man who has a permanent smile on his face? Also he possesses an extremely generous nature. He's willing to help everyone he can and if you ask him to do something for you, Dwight never refuses.

After returning from a warm-up on the pitch, Dwight, Ryan and Nicky will try to keep a ball up for as long as possible. It's not meant to be a test but any player who doesn't get to ten before passing the ball on certainly knows about it.

Their little games help break the tension. No-one is so nervous that they have to nip off to the toilet to throw-up, but as kick-off time draws nearer there is a definite change in the atmosphere, with voices acquiring a serious tone and faces no longer cracking up with laughter. You can feel everyone switching on and making sure in their own way that they are psyched up for action.

One player who's seen it all before is Teddy Sheringham, and not only has his huge experience been good for him, he seems to be getting better with age. Despite being 35 in April 2001, he was voted player of the year by both the Football Writers Association and the Professional Footballers Association. Quite a feat.

Sheringham started the season in majestic form and scored so many goals in the Premiership and in Europe that it was impossible for Sven Goran Eriksson to leave him out of the England set-up.

It was a powerful reminder of just how good a player Teddy is. His footballing brain is sensational and he sees things faster than the majority of his Premiership peers. Crucially, not only can he recognise the opportunities, but he can act on them as well.

In the summer of 2001 he made the difficult decision to leave Old Trafford and return to Tottenham, and from his displays during the previous campaign there is little doubt that still he has a couple of top-level seasons in him. I wish him well.

There was not a lot the gaffer could tell an experienced pro such as Teddy before a game, but Ferguson will always mill around, having the occasional word with individual players to keep them on their toes before kick-off.

Then he will go into his final pep talk, reiterating what he's told us to concentrate on, before building up to a climactic rousing speech.

'I want a good tempo from the start. I want you to keep the pace up and match them in the opening stages. They'll be in there now listening to their manager telling them the only way to beat us is by fighting harder, running harder and working harder than us.

'I don't care what he says; we can fight, run, work and play harder than anyone. Match them at the start, their heads will drop and we'll go on from there. Keep it tight at the back and enjoy yourselves.'

As we file out of the dressing room, David Beckham will tuck in behind Gary Neville. I don't know why he does it, but it has become a habit from their days in United's junior teams. David wears a brand new pair of socks for every game. Our kit man, Albert Morgan, lays them out tidily for him and that's probably the only time Beckham gets a little more attention than everyone else.

He's not big-headed and couldn't afford to be in a dressing room like ours. If he became cocky and started bragging about his superstar persona, he'd soon be brought straight down to earth. Just because he's in the papers all the time doesn't mean he'd get away with being arrogant around us, and certainly he isn't one for giving a big-time Charlie act.

David has so much pressure on his shoulders that he must wonder, sometimes, whether he's a footballer or a world leader. The press are always on his case about the smallest things, from his haircut to his new jeans, and his every move is watched.

It must be hard not to do the simple things in life without a photographer, autograph hunter or even a troublemaking fan wanting a piece of you. If we have a team day out and head for somewhere public, such as a racecourse or a bar, then David can't stay too long. There's always an idiot waiting in the wings to take a pop at him and sell it to the press.

I thought the attacks he suffered in the media and by fans after getting sent off against Argentina in the 1998 were totally unwarranted, but it changed him for the better and he grew up both on and off the pitch. Ever since that game teams have sent players out solely to boot him up in the air and wait for the reaction. In general terms, there hasn't been one, not in the sense of petulant flicks anyway. David has reacted in the best possible way, by creating and scoring goal after goal. Now that really hurts!

In addition he has had to shrug off suggestions that he's thick. Now I'll admit that David will not be asked to take a turn in the black chair of Mastermind, but I doubt whether I'd be wanted in there either. David's not thick, he's just a normal guy having to put up with a lot of shit thrown at him by people who don't even know his true personality.

I'm thinking about those mindless thugs who hurl abuse at him from the stands and terraces. Spiteful songs expressing the hope that his son catches Aids and referring to his wife's sexual preferences are disgraceful, and I hope anyone who has been childish enough to sing those things feels embarrassed now. It's a constant problem with football crowds. If one person sings an unpleasant chant everyone follows. I would love to see them stand face to face with David and then bark out their filth.

Beckham's play dipped a bit in the middle of 2000/2001, but overall he has been sensational during my three seasons at the club to date. I don't need to mention his ability on the ball; we've all seen what he can do. But not many people realise just how fit he is as well.

At United we have a dreaded bleep test, designed to find out who is the fittest man in the club. Each player has to run to a certain distance before the machine makes a noise and then sprint back to the starting point ahead of a second bleep. At the start it's not too difficult, but the bleeps get quicker and quicker as each man tires. I can tell you, it's hard work.

During one recent test David was the last man standing. He was still going as the rest of us crumbled to the floor in a sweaty heap. To be able to do that takes a fit man and if you watch Beckham charge up and down the right flank during a game, it should be easy to appreciate how much running there is in his legs.

David has been appointed England captain and I feel that his new role will help to bring out the best in his game. Already he's coming out of his shell in front of the media and seems more confident in situations both on and off the pitch.

Still there are those who doubt that he has the right qualities to lead his country. 'He's too quiet,' the media claim. 'He's not a leader,' they moan. But I think he will be hailed as a great England captain one day. David is vastly experienced at the top level of the game and has the trophies to prove he's a winner. You have to respect what he's achieved.

He doesn't need to shout all the time. A skipper can inspire the rest of the team by refusing to accept defeat, and always being aggressive – two character traits David has in abundance.

He will learn to talk more in time. I know from my experience of taking charge of United in Roy Keane's absence that, when you're the captain, you chat more because you feel you have to.

We've all met his wife, Victoria, in the players' lounge or, since the birth of Brooklyn, at the players' creche, and I always stop for a quick chat with her. She's a friendly woman and seems capable of handling all the pressure they are under. Rather them than me, though. I'm happy to enjoy an afternoon under the glare of publicity and then return home to my wife and kids to spend time playing daddy. I would hate to know that there might always be a camera lens lined up on either Lisa or Megan, with a desperate snapper out to sell their pictures.

The birth of Brooklyn must have changed David. Kids do alter people and in his case he seems to be a little more mature and enjoying the responsibilities of life as well.

I have been careful to dedicate myself to becoming a better player, but not dedicating my whole life to football. I have a lovely family and they are so important to me. They help me to switch off and taking a break from the game – even if only for short periods – is vital for me. Not everyone is the same, but I'm convinced you can't be at your best if you become obsessed with the game.

That drains you of your energy and leaves you pondering on the mistakes that will ultimately come at some point. I like to slip away, forget about it and come back refreshed.

Football is the only thing on my mind when I run out to the rapturous reception at Old Trafford. Once on the pitch I tend to line-up alongside Wes Brown these days. When I started at United, Ronny Johnsen proved to be my best partner, but 'Iceman', as he's known for always having packs of the stuff strapped to his legs, has been injured most of the time since the 1999 European Cup final.

Ronny's misfortune, which appeared to be receding as he made a successful comeback towards the end of 2000/2001, handed Wes and I a chance to gel and the partnership has blossomed. We don't speak much outside of football as he's young and has his own friends. Naturally enough, he wants to go out and enjoy himself while I'm happier having a meal or spending time with Dutch friends who pop over to see us.

But Wes is great to play alongside. Crucially he's always willing to learn and that's why he will only get better and take a regular slot in the England side, notwithstanding the challenge from Rio Ferdinand, Jon Woodgate and Sol Campbell, who are three excellent players in their own right. Most central defenders don't come of age until much later in their careers but Wes has so much quality that the gaffer threw him in during the treble-winning year when he was aged only 19.

In Holland there are players of his age thinking about ruling the world, butthat's not Brown's style. He wants to be taught new things and try out different ideas. Maybe picking up a truly horrific knee injury in 1999 has helped him in the long term. He knows how close he came to losing it all in just one tackle, which damaged his cruciate ligament, and he wants to make the most of his second chance.

Certainly the injury helped his character and made him more determined to succeed. Wes is bigger, tougher and stronger now, and having played so many high-profile games for United and England, he's already arrived. But there's so much potential in him that I can't wait to see how good a player he becomes eventually.

Performing on the left side of central defence, I've got Wes on one side and Mikael Silvestre on the other. The Frenchman began to prove during 2000/2001 that he is a fine player. Mikael had a hard time and struggled to make an impact when he first arrived. He was in and out of the side and in some games even had some of our own fans on his back, but the tide has turned since Christmas 2000.

He was handed Denis Irwin's left-back position and has thrived on the responsibility, looking like a young player ready to make the shirt his own for years to come. The way he has developed is no surprise to me. Everyone in the United camp knew he was capable of making a big impression at Old Trafford. That's why Gerard Houllier was so keen to sign him for Liverpool before our gaffer jumped in and nicked him from under the nose of the Anfield chief.

Having seen Silvestre's performances in training, we accepted him straight away, but it took a while for him to settle. Recently I've noticed a change in his style of play. Maybe, at first, he was scared of making mistakes, but all he wanted to do was win the ball in the tackle and pass it on simply. Now he makes runs down the touchline, skipping past opponents and getting into the box. He always did that in training, but excelling at Carrington is not the same as performing at Old Trafford. The gaffer kept believing in Mikael, though, and when his confidence started to grow we saw what a good player he really is.

Usually I'll give him a pat on the back in the changing room after the game to let him know I appreciate the great job he's done. Then the manager will have his say and, certainly at Old Trafford, it's not often that he has much to moan about. He might be a little upset about one or two aspects of our play in the game, but usually we've just secured three points so we are safe from a bollocking.

If something has gone wrong the players tend to sort it out anyway. We're all pals but that won't stop us having major rows after a game. It's never got to blows but names are mentioned. We're all big boys and if a player has been doing something wrong he has to be strong enough to stand up and take the flak in our dressing room, and that includes me.

At this level there's too much at stake to keep your mouth shut and stew. Simmering away and moaning to friends behind someone's back just causes more problems. If the stick is aimed at me and I feel it's justified, I'll sit there and take it. I'm not saying that's easy to do. How many people can handle being told they've screwed up? But as long as it's fair I'll listen. If it isn't fair, then I'll have a go back and even if it gets quite heated, there are never any grudges. We just leave it all behind in the dressing room.

As captain, Roy Keane tends to take the chair in these post-match verbal dust-ups and he's firm but fair. He has the respect of all the lads and won the armband through his desire to succeed. No-one can question his right to it.

Keane is an incredible player, a real one-off whose name would be first on the team-sheet of any side. It's not just the fact that he wins every tackle, or the way he can drive a team on with his powerful running and snappy passing; with Roy there's something more, a desperation to win that drags the whole team on to victory.

He has dedicated his whole life to winning and it's become even more noticeable in the past few seasons. He's almost a recluse off the pitch and probably he'd lilke to be beamed up to another planet as soon as the final whistle goes. Keane doesn't like to be bothered. He won't mind signing the odd autograph but if there's a crowd he'd rather walk away.

Roy's not afraid to speak his mind either. There was ample proof of that in his passionate rants about how prawn sandwich-eaters in executive boxes are ruining the atmosphere at Old Trafford, and on the controversial subject United's need to rebuild the team after losing to Bayern Munich in the Champions League quarter-final. He can say what he likes to the media; it doesn't really affect or interest me. If Roy wants to let me know something, he'll say it in the dressing room. He doesn't hide.

It took me a while to work out his character and discover that he's more sarcastic than nasty when he fires off his sharp little comments. If he doesn't agree with you, Roy will let you know and although sometimes he can be funny, there's a prickly side to his manner which is liable to offend people who don't know him well.

When I came to the club, at first I thought he had a real problem with me. He was on my case, pushing me to do better, and before long the snide little remarks started. Roy's always saying something about your game or your appearance and, unfortunately, when you're a foreign player it can be a bit difficult to answer straight back. I had to think how to translate my reply into English and by then, frustratingly, the moment had gone.

With Keane rattling on at me it was getting to the stage where I felt something needed to be said. That was until Jordi pointed out that Roy was saying everything with a dash of sarcasm, and then I realised that in his own way he is just as big a wind-up merchant as Giggs or Butt.

Everyone has seen the ferocity of his tackles but in training it can better playing against him rather than being on his side. He hates losing, whether it's a five-a-side or a cup final.

Once Keane has conducted any post-match inquisitions the players tend to drift off on their own and we don't plan a big night out after every match. Some of the youngsters may gang up and head off for a few drinks but a lot, like myself, will want to be with their families and enjoy a meal.

Certainly one player you won't see organising any parties is Paul Scholes. The man is so quiet, at times, that it would be easy to forget he's around. It's the same on the pitch. Paul won't carp on at team-mates or spend his time trying to annoy opponents with well-chosen digs, but if they let their guard slip for an instant then he'll ghost in and find the net. Often that happens at the death, a factor United have been thankful for on several occasions.

Paul hates being in the press, despises interviews, shuns any of the superstar trappings and avoids the big money sponsorships in favour of his privacy. A man of few words, he does his talking with his feet and has everything anyone could want in a modern midfielder. His technique is perfect: just look at the goal he scored for England against Tunisia in the 1998 World Cup tournament and the scorching volley he ripped home against Bradford City, direct from David Beckham's corner at Valley Parade in March 2000.

He can muster decent pace, he carries enough strength in his shoulders to hold on to the ball, and unlike a lot of people with his skill, he loves to get in the thick of the action and win tackles.

Scholes is one of the best footballers at United, without doubt a world-class player. The way he can connect first time with the ball, or shift it deftly between his feet, appears so easy, but players capable of doing that as well as Paul are far and few between.

I'm quite similar to Paul in that I won't be jumping on team-mates' shoulders after a game, demanding that we try out the latest club to celebrate another win. I have no desire to spend the night pretending to hear what people are saying to me above thumping music and avoiding conversations with drunken football fans.

I prefer to get into my car and drive home to Cheshire and spend an evening with my wife and children. We might go out to the cinema or sit in with a meal and watch 'Match of the Day'. That's how I like to unwind after a match.

Not quite the superstar lifestyle expected of a professional footballer is it? But then, I'm no superstar!

CHAPTER SEVENTEEN

A new contract

It's hard to think past my Manchester United days, but I suppose there's going to be a time when I wake up to the disappointing thought that Jaap Stam is no longer a Red. I hope that's a long way off, though, as it was only recently that I signed a new contract which will keep me at Old Trafford until I'm 33. So unless United make it blatantly clear that I have no future at the club, I won't be leaving before then. It's hard to think of a better or bigger club to play for, especially as I have no real desire to enjoy a taste of life in Italy or Spain.

I like my current lifestyle, and I don't mean the house, car and all the other luxuries footballers take for granted. Much more important is the relaxed approach to the game in England where, for all the pressure on the pitch, life is still pretty normal. I'm given spare time and allowed to live as a person rather than a machine, with afternoons and days off to spend time with my family, play golf or, if I was the betting type, to drop into the bookmakers' shop.

There is even time for activities away from my family and football. For instance, I like to keep up with what's going in the worlds of gadgetry and cars. I've always had a fondness for electronic toys and I'm lucky enough now to have the money to indulge myself. Unfortunately we seem to be behind the times here in England so I keep up to date with the latest devices in the market place by tuning into a Dutch show on my satellite system.

Also I'm a frequent visitor to the Internet, forever logging on to Dutch sites – which seem to be ahead of the game when it comes to gadgets – and reading magazines from my homeland.

Like most footballers I change my mobile phone far too often, but one of my recent buys went down a storm at Old Trafford. I snapped up a Siemens mobile phone that boasts an MP3 player and a dictaphone as features. At the time it wasn't out in England and the shiny silver case was soon noticed in the dressing room.

'Let's have a look,' David Beckham begged before grabbing the phone. 'What does it do?' he asked and he was almost salivating as I listed its characteristics.

'Can you get me one?' he asked and those words were like gold dust to Siemens. Within minutes the rest of the lads had crowded round and wanted a good look. Dwight was next to place an order and the list went on. That night I must have spent a couple of thousand pounds on my credit card ordering a job lot.

I don't change my phone with every new model that arrives, but if there are some outstanding features I give it a try and see if I like it. That's not uncommon in footballing circles and at least it gives me something to keep my mind ticking over on long coach trips and the endless hours spent in hotel rooms waiting for games.

I've mentioned my Internet interest and also I've got some other technical wizardry, such as a TV which beams pictures on to the wall and – pretty standard fare for footballers nowadays – a DVD player which can show films from America as well as Europe.

When it comes to cars I'm nowhere near as bad as David Beckham and some of the other lads who have garages cluttered up with raw power from the best motor manufacturers in Europe.

I have a big Jeep to help the family get around and also a Mercedes for when we want to travel a little closer to ground level. And I fulfilled a lifetime ambition after signing for United by buying a Porsche. It was something I had dreamed of owning since my early teens, and I still get a stirring of pride when I jump in and rev that purring engine.

Slipping into the comfortable leather seats is not so much an ego trip, but a chance for me to enjoy a material benefit from my career. It's almost like having a marker for what I've achieved in my life. I set out as a youngster dreaming about flying along country roads in that car and now I can drive it until my heart's content.

Also I have a fondness for classic cars and intend to start building a collection at home in Holland when I find the time. I'm forever skipping through car magazines, so now I have an idea of price it's a market into which I intend making forays in the near future.

Overall, in fact, I feel I've reached a stage in my life where I can make long-term plans while spending time with my children and entertaining family and friends when they come over from Holland. Even such seemingly basic activities are not always possible in Italy, for example, as I've found out from Dutch team-mates such as Edgar Davids, Clarence Seedorf and Edwin van der Sar.

They have all played at Juventus where they go into hotels or camps before each game and the training starts at 10.30am. There are rooms at the camp where they sleep in the afternoons and then it's training again at 5pm, before finally getting home at 8pm. That's not the kind of lifestyle I want to put up with. I guess in my world there are other things just as important as the beautiful game.

That's precisely why, when United asked me to extend my contract by another year, I jumped at the chance. In the original deal I signed in 1998 there was a clause which allowed both sides to sit down and talk in the third season if things had gone well.

Chief executive Peter Kenyon wasn't bound to present me with a whole new set of terms. I still had four seasons to go on a contract with which I was happy, a deal I wouldn't have signed in the first place if it wasn't up to scratch. But, with that clause in there, I would have been frustrated if United hadn't wanted to discuss a new offer. Not because of the money, but because it would have meant they felt my form had been poor and that I hadn't contributed to the club's success.

Certainly I didn't go into the talks with a determination to become the highest-paid player at the club or to even be the second-best-paid player – I don't need that status – but I did think I should pick up a salary in line with my value in the market place. The game is moving at such a rapid pace, with more commercial avenues opening every day, that it's inevitable that old contracts, which once looked extremely lucrative, now appear to underrate the value of a player.

Roy Keane is a classic example of this. When he signed his most recent contract for the Reds, a figure of £52,000 a week was bandied about and described as obscene. The media and some supporters were up in arms about a man receiving such a large amount of money just to kick a ball. It wasn't long before that deal paled into significance as big clubs started talking about paying £100,000 a week to keep their best players. It's just the way football has moved forward with changes in the transfer system and the power of the top stars in the game to demand, and receive, incredible amounts of money.

The financial side of the game is developing with almost indecent haste and that will become evident at Old Trafford when Alex Ferguson retires in 2002. The new manager is sure to want his own players as he looks to continue the success we've enjoyed. That's not a slight on the guys already here, it's just a fact of football life. Another fact is that any new faces won't be second-rate. They will come from Europe's top clubs and demand huge salaries for their services. The next generation of United stars who hail from abroad probably won't have European Cup and League title medals on their mantelpieces, but they will pick up extortionate wages. Quite simply, I wanted to make sure I didn't get left behind in the wage game.

So, with my immediate future secured, I guess I can look at what I'm going to do in the year 2005 when my United career is due to come to an end. Obviously it would be nice to stay on with the Reds but I have to be realistic and accept that, at the age of 33, they may no longer want me.

With that in mind there are a few options I hope would be open to me, and the first of those is playing in Holland. I have no intention of joining a small Second Division club and playing out my days in a team for whom success is avoiding relegation every year. I've played in the top flight and tasted the champagne so I fear that plugging away, fighting the drop for my final few seasons, would destroy me mentally.

I couldn't live every day with the frustration of seeing players make errors which the likes of Ryan Giggs and Fabien Barthez would never allow to creep into their game. This is not an attack on players in Dutch football, far from it, but not everyone can be a David Beckham.

Having set such high standards for myself, it would be hard to accept less than the best. So if I went back, possibly it would be to a club such as Ajax or PSV, where they would be challenging for the domestic title and playing in Europe. I couldn't play without that buzz in a league that I know so well.

The other attractive option is packing up the suitcases and heading across to America to play out my career in the MLS. I would love the opportunity to play in the States, and although the standard is not up to European levels at the moment, in four or five years time who knows how different the quality of the game over there could be? Don't forget that only recently the USA were above England in the FIFA world soccer rankings!

I love the country and with football coming in a distant fifth to baseball, American football, basketball and ice hockey in the sports rankings, I could live without the intrusion into my personal life that playing in European countries would bring. Also there would be so many things for my family to see and do. I could enjoy all the tourist adventures while I was out there and save a fortune in airfares!

A lot of this depends on how my body shapes up once I start hitting the thirties. I reckon there's plenty of bone-shuddering challenges left in me yet, although I can't see myself following in Richard Gough's footsteps and running down the tunnel to take on Premiership strikers at the age of 38.

The bones might be okay, but there is a slight concern that my early diet probably wasn't what the doctor would recommend for a player keen to stretch out his career for as long as possible. Gordon Strachan used to fill up on seaweed and bananas, and he played on until he was 40, but even when I was turning out for FC Zwolle at the age of 22 I ate everything I wanted.

If I was driving past a McDonald's and wanted a burger and chips I'd park up, order a big, fat, juicy meal and tuck in. I was a chocolate lover, too, and liked having a bag of sweets handy for a tasty dessert. It felt good and I could perform on that diet, so I refused to be bothered by the fact it might not have been the most nutritious meal.

Now I'm older I'm rather wiser, as I think the whole of football is, about the need for a decent diet. It's something which has come to England from abroad and certainly has been taken on board by all the players at United. Also, the benefit of supplements, vitamins and other dietary advances was extremely marked at Arsenal after the arrival of Arsene Wenger. The Gunners had an extra edge as they surged past United to take the title in 1998 by winning ten games in a row at a stage of the season when most sides were feeling the pace.

They left everyone in their wake and when a smart player realises he's been left behind, he welcomes the changes he might have resisted earlier in his career. Now every club employs dieticians and fitness coaches and, personally, I watch what I eat and make sure I rest to keep my body in the best shape possible.

Certainly I don't regret eating burgers, though, and even now I have the occasional one. My eldest daughter, Lisa, loves chips with everything so I have some as well when the mood takes me. The odd plate of chips now and then won't harm me.

To be honest, I'm glad I didn't have to grow up like the youngsters now coming into the game. I was lucky to enter the professional ranks at the age of 19 and didn't spend my formative years 'married' to a football club which controlled my life.

At a stage when most trainees in the English game are petrified that they may not earn a contract, and fear losing out on a chance of fulfilling their dreams, I was under no pressure. At the age of 18 I played my Saturday afternoon amateur game and then propped up the bar with my team-mates talking about the night out ahead.

It was a great life. I felt human and did exactly what I wanted.

Also there was a distinct lack of training. Just two nights a week took care of it and the rest of the week was mine to meet mates, go to the pub or cinema, and generally do whatever I preferred.

Sometimes I miss it, and for all the glory and the money I now enjoy, it would be wonderful if I could go back to those days. There was no pressure; I just played for fun. If I kicked the ball out of the ground or delivered a poor pass, nobody got on my back. It was just a game of football and a chance to socialise with my pals.

My formative years in football suited me and were in complete contrast to the way the majority of the world's stars in other sports have had to drive themselves to the top.

People such as the golfer Tiger Woods and the tennis players Venus and Serena Williams have had their whole lives geared to success, driven by ambitious parents and a determination inherent in very few individuals. Woods was on the golf course at the age of three and spent his waking hours chasing just one dream, while the Williams sisters were holding tennis rackets as soon as they could walk.

They are all extremely dedicated athletes and their road to success is not just down to the amazing ability they possess, but a purpose bordering on the obsessive which drives them to demand excellence in their play.

But for every Woods and Williams there are hundreds who drop out on the way. The early experiences of Jennifer Capriati offer a prime example of how the pressure of living an unnatural life can take its toll. She was at the top of the women's game before most people of her age had left school, but the rigid regime of the training, and pressure from those around her to achieve triumph after triumph, made her rebel and her life went off the rails for a few years. A cry for help, possibly, but certainly not an experience any parent would want their kid to go through. It is wonderful, by the way, to see that a more mature Jennifer Capriati has got her career back on track.

Unfortunately many youngsters are going through a similar hell, perhaps on a lesser scale, at football clubs all across Europe. That's why I feel so sorry for the young players being ushered into the academy system today, and I do mean young. Football clubs are looking for talented kids aged six and seven, then putting them on an assembly line and mapping out their whole life for them.

They are told how to play, what to eat, where to go, and when to sleep. They don't have their youth any more. They are missing out on something that can't be given back at a later date, something that should be innocently enjoyed.

By the age of 18 it must drive them mad. They must crave to go out with their friends and enjoy a real night out on the town. They must be filled with frustration when they hear the stories about the high jinks and parties they are missing out on.

It's no wonder that some of the country's most talented players never make it. They are burnt out by the routine of football life by the time they're 21. They've had enough because they've been pushing so hard for so long.

And what about the ones who are considered not quite good enough? How would you feel after giving up so much to chase a dream that never came true? It would be so hard to take and, unfortunately, too many youngsters are left to face a painful reality because their hopes have been built up by a one-way system that is suiting the clubs but failing the individuals.

Even the much-vaunted Ajax system, which produced top-quality stars such as Clarence Seedorf, Edgar Davids and Patrick Kluivert, is not as good as it was. The players aren't falling off the production line any more. Football has to sit down now and think through how we run our youth policies and give the youngsters back a little bit of their childhood.

CHAPTER EIGHTEEN

My Achilles heel

Sat on the Wembley bench, engulfed by the roar of the fans, I had my bootlaces undone and my socks rolled down to my ankles. It was the Charity Shield in 2000 and we were playing Chelsea, but unusually for a footballer I wasn't champing at the bit to get on.

I can imagine the number of players who have occupied that seat in the past, jumping up and down to catch their manager's eye in the hope of getting a run-out on that famous pitch. But I'd made my peace already with the 'Lord of Old Trafford' and I was there only for the day out – or so I thought.

With my legs still sore from a tough Euro 2000 campaign and my troublesome Achilles tendon having played up throughout Holland's run to the semi-finals, it had been deemed best for me to sit out the prestigious showcase opener to the club season.

But as Mikael Silvestre crumpled in a heap on the pitch after ten minutes, the manager rather reluctantly turned around and looked at me. I knew the score; I was going on.

As we stumbled to a 2–0 defeat in a game which saw Roy Keane dismissed, my ankle began to flare up once again and by the final whistle I was wincing with pain. I knew I had to sort out the problem.

But, as had been the case over the past 12 months, it eased off after the game and with proper warming-up and regular treatment I managed to drag myself through training sessions without too much reaction. I decided to start the season and see if paying careful attention to my condition would allow me to battle on.

In our first League game against Newcastle it looked as though the risky strategy might work. I felt as good as I had for a while and I lasted 90 minutes as we started the season with a 2–0 win.

But over the next three games my fears returned as twisting and turning on the Achilles sent an unbearable pain shooting up my leg. To make matters worse, I felt it was harming my performance. Even reaching more than a canter was beginning to hurt and this time I decided enough was enough, something had to be done.

The biggest worry was the possibility that the Achilles might snap if I carried on pushing it. That could have signalled the end of my career just when I'd worked so hard to get a top club and was enjoying the benefits. As ever, the manager's door was open when I knocked and strolled in.

'Gaffer,' I opened firmly. 'My Achilles is too tender to keep going. I've put it through enough, the pain is terrible and I can't move freely in games. I don't want to let everyone down but I need to get it sorted out.'

'No problem,' he replied calmly. 'I always thought it would get to this stage sooner or later. We'll get you booked in for the operation.'

Within minutes we were talking about how soon I could see a specialist and discussing what the results of the check-up could mean to my season. It was a brave move as we had a Champions League group just about to start and the odds were that I would miss the early stages of the campaign.

With Wes Brown only just coming back to form after his own career-threatening injury, and with David May and Ronny Johnsen missing through their long-term fitness problems, United were short of cover.

But I was packed off to see the specialists, who had no hesitation in giving me their opinions – if I was to play again without pain it was the knife for me. First I went to see the club surgeon, Dr Noble, and then flew down to London for a second opinion from a the specialist, who would actually carry out the surgery. Both of them diagnosed tendonitis and warned that the Achilles could snap if I played on.

Only then was the bombshell dropped that I was going to miss three months of the season. The news sent a shock through my system as I had been prepared for eight weeks at most, and expected to be turning out well before the hectic Christmas schedule.

A month in football is a long time with games coming thick and fast, especially over the festive season, and I asked Dr Mufolly whether anything could be done to shorten my absence.

He explained that the Achilles isn't a particularly complex part of the body and it doesn't matter whether you are a top sportsman or an old woman; everybody needs three months to allow the fibres to knit together before weight can be placed safely on the heel.

It was a massive blow, but I'd been lucky in the past and steered clear of nasty knocks, twisted knees and muscle tears, and in a way my situation was easier to handle as I had been given a date for my return before going for surgery.

A lot of players are fine one minute and then, without warning, they are struck down with a broken leg or medial ligament damage the next. Jesper Blomqvist, for one, was charging about in training and then, suddenly, he was facing possibly years on the sidelines after a serious knee injury. At least I'd had a warning and, mentally, that was priceless for me. I knew what to expect about the rough road that lay ahead and it was my decision to go down it.

I laughed out loud when I picked up the newspapers to read that I was at loggerheads with Ferguson over the operation. I was supposed to be keen to go under the knife while the manager wanted me to hold off and help United to negotiate their way through the opening group stages of the Champions League.

Apparently relations between us were frosty. Nobody had told us, though. In fact, it might have been yet another clever piece of kidology from Ferguson as we were facing some of our major rivals at the time, and he might have wanted them to be second-guessing our game-plan.

But behind the scenes I was booked in for surgery as soon as possible, with the manager making sure all the details were taken care of. That took three weeks and I was relieved to come round in the hospital and be told the operation had gone smoothly.

The basic job was to peel away rubbish that had collected on the Achilles, in the same way that layers could be lifted from a spring onion. The doctor confirmed that his half of the job was complete; now it was a case of recovering as quickly as possible.

Any desire I had to jump out of bed and get on the rowing machine straight away was wiped out by the state of my ankle. The skin around the Achilles is so thin that very little blood runs through it and putting in a stitch is like making a couple of new wounds. So rather than giving my already bruised ankle something new to worry about, the surgeon put paper stitches across the gash he had opened to work on my Achilles.

That meant two and a half weeks sat on my backside in a cast, waiting for the wound to heal before I could get on with building up the strength in my left leg. Those 17 days were pure frustration for me, as I had to sit at home and watch television with my foot up on the living room table. I was even fed up at not being able to do the household chores.

I like to warm the pots and cook up a dish in the kitchen, but that was out of the question. I was unable to stay upright without my crutches and all I could do was read stories to my daughter, Lisa, and feel guilty about my pregnant wife carrying all the weight of keeping the house together, as well as our next offspring.

Also there was the little problem of my health, as my body went through a bizarre withdrawal from not being able to exercise. I was so used to running every day, or doing weight-training, or playing games, that calling a complete halt to the activity overnight didn't go down well with my muscles and organs.

I spent a week suffering with a cold and lying around the house feeling incredibly weak and miserable. Even when, after the stitches were taken out, I was able to go to our training ground at Carrington for a massage on the ankle, I had to be ferried in by Ellis and then cadge a lift home.

Even worse was the sweaty daily grind of treadmills, steppers and pedalling on bikes which I had to endure before being given the okay to resume proper training. My day started at 10am and I worked through to 2pm with a short break for lunch. It was five times harder than a footballer's customary activity and, like a schoolkid, I spent most of my time looking out of the window, watching the lads train.

Every morning I would see them run out, laughing and joking and telling tales during the warm-ups, as I struggled through my fifth mile on the unrelenting black surface of the running machine. It was a bad time for me but it seemed nothing when set against the depressing experiences of long-term injury victims Jesper Blomqvist, Ronny Johnsen and David May.

Compared to me, these guys seemed to be serving life sentences, with Jesper still to kick a ball at senior level since the European Cup Final in 1999. I would have hated to go through the daily boredom they suffered.

Also Teddy Sheringham was out for a spell with a hamstring strain and, if nothing else, it gave us the chance to sample the wonderful facilities available at Carrington.

The new training ground was opened while we were in Brazil in January 2000 and I find it hard to imagine there are many better. We've got a swimming pool, an excellent rehabilitation centre and state-of-the-art weights and running machines. If I hadn't been so fed up about having to slog my way through two months in that gym, I might have asked about membership fees.

A lot of my work was done with one of the youngsters at the club, Michael Clegg. He was working on building up his body strength and he became my companion on the weights machines.

It wasn't always a grind. There was the odd bit of humour to brighten the day, but we looked on it as a prison sentence and we couldn't wait for it to end. I missed being out in the open air and running about with a ball at my feet. All the things I took for granted about being a footballer were denied me.

Even watching our games was hard. I went to all the home

matches and watched the others on television when I could, but not being involved messed with my emotions. I was glad to see the team play so well, but a big part of me yearned to share in the glory they were enjoying out on the pitch.

The big question on everyone's lips was: 'When would Jaap Stam be pulling on a United shirt again?' Although I had a rough idea in my head, I decided to keep it to myself. If I'd gone public with a date, or a match I'd targeted for a return, and I had failed to make it on time, then rumours would have surfaced about problems with my comeback. That was the last thing I needed. I didn't want to spend time dismissing false gossip when I should have been concentrating on getting my Achilles right.

There were some really low times before finally I could join in with first-team training sessions again. The worst came a couple of weeks into my rehabiliation and it was a real setback after my fitness bid had started so well.

Suddenly I started to get an ache in the Achilles after running and I thought the soreness was back again. Thoughts flashed through my mind. Is the problem still the same? Will I need another op? Will it ever go away?

But after I limped in to see the club doctor, he reassured me it was normal to reach a plateau after coming back from an operation. He explained there would be a time when I hit a brick wall and the injury wouldn't progress for a couple of days. And he was right. A few days later the pain eased and once again I was pushing myself to the limits and eager to get back into action.

With a hole in the reserve team calendar, Ferguson set up a friendly against Wrexham for myself and two other recently injured players, Andy Cole and Teddy Sheringham, to get a run-out.

Normally it would have been a low-key game, but with Wrexham keen to earn a few pennies out of the night there was a decent atmosphere at the Racecourse Ground, with plenty of United supporters filling an end and singing their hearts out.

Some players would have approached the match with apprehension but the manager had made sure before we travelled that we treated the game simply as a training exercise.

I was there to get some match action under my belt and not to make last-ditch tackles and dive into clumsy challenges. Already I'd had some rigorous training matches and had done everything I needed to convince my own mind that the Achilles was strong enough. The pitch was heavy so I played 45 minutes, came off, had a shower and was on the motorway heading home before the final whistle, feeling very satisfied with my night's work.

Seven days later I turned out in a behind-closed-doors clash with Burnley and I loved the freedom of being able to run again as we beat the First Division side. I felt as fit as a racehorse after the amount of galloping around Carrington I'd put in over the past month, and the only thing I was lacking was my touch on the ball and the high-end fitness that comes only through matches.

After the Burnley game, the manager pulled me to one side and whispered the words I'd been waiting nearly four months to hear: 'Do you fancy a go against Bradford on Saturday, son?'

'Stick me in, Boss, I'm ready,' I answered with a massive smile on my face.

'Okay, we'll put you in, but we won't have you play the whole 90 minutes. I don't want you to risk it.'

The relief on my face must have been evident to everyone and when I arrived home to tell Ellis she was just as happy as me. We don't talk about my job much around the house, but she could tell how frustrated I was growing, especially during long days I spent on the sofa getting square eyes from watching television.

If there was a bright spot in the whole injury affair, it was that the timing was perfect for me to enjoy the new addition to the family. Playing for United ruins any domestic schedule, with Champions League trips and FA Cup matches. Then there are international get-togethers which ensure as much time is spent on the road as it is at home with the family. But as long as I was on crutches or working out in the gym, Ellis knew I would be about when Megan was born and that must have been a relief. Also it was a bonus for me and something to take my mind off the crushing dullness of fighting back to fitness.

It was January when I made my comeback, against Bradford City at Valley Parade in a game we were expected to win. They were bottom of the table and struggling, while we seemed to be going through a purple patch.

I was nervous and I noticed an unusual tension in my mind as I prepared for a massage and then pulled on my boots. I didn't want to make any careless errors or, even worse, break down again as soon as the Achilles was tested to the full by the short sprints that Premiership football is all about.

It took me a little while to get used to the pace and by half-time I was knackered and ready for a breather, but once the second period started I knew there was 90 minutes in me. I looked across to try and let the gaffer know I was fine, but it was too late. The board went up and the fourth official was calling in number six. My time was up.

But that didn't matter. I was back – and just in time to fight for another Champions League medal.

CHAPTER NINETEEN

Just the League title, again

As the ball arrowed in towards Dion Dublin's chest, I took two quick steps to get in front of him and nick possession. It's a ploy I use every week, only this time the Aston Villa striker spotted what I was trying to do and put the block on me.

I was half around him by the time the ball arrived, and as Dion's boot came flying up, it caught me smack on the back of the hand.

It was my first game back at Old Trafford since the Achilles injury which had ruled me out from early September to January. I had come through 60 minutes against Bradford City a week earlier at Valley Parade. Now I was desperate to enjoy a successful return in front of my home fans.

As the ball spun away to safety, a shooting pain ran through my palm. I looked down to examine my hand as the throbbing turned to agony and found no blood-spurting gash, no bones protruding through my skin. There was no time to make a big song and dance about the tenderness in my hand. I just grimaced for the rest of the game as we ran out 2–0 winners.

Dion couldn't have known how much damage he did me that day, but his boot had actually broken a bone in my hand. The pain is still there now. It's in one of those awkward places I always feel when grabbing hold of everyday objects and I suppose it will be a weak spot for the rest of my life.

But that pain was nothing compared to what I felt on 28 January after West Ham knocked us out of the FA Cup in a fourth-round tie we fully expected to win.

We were rightly confident. Only Liverpool had come to Old Trafford and beaten us, so why wouldn't we be feeling assured? Up front the Hammers had Freddie Kanoute, a player I believe is extremely underrated in the Premiership, and Paolo Di Canio, but man for man we were a far better team.

Certainly the bookies expected us take another step on the road to the final, and so did I. West Ham had other ideas and played with a steely fervour before nicking the game through Di Canio's bizarre winner, which became a talking point for weeks afterwards.

I cover the incident in more detail elsewhere in this book so I won't repeat myself. Nevertheless, even after that strange goal we were convinced we could get back into it – we always do. On this occasion, though, Harry Redknapp had done his homework and we couldn't find a way through.

At the final whistle Gary Neville had an angry row with an assistant referee which eventually led to him being fined and suspended by the FA. I understood his frustration. As I slumped in my seat in the dressing room and stuck my head in my hands, I didn't know whether to be pissed off with myself, the referee, or the rest of the world. I just knew I was really pissed off.

We hadn't been allowed to defend the FA Cup the previous season because of entering the Club World Championship. With that still bugging me I was determined to make amends by lifting the trophy this time around. Although I cherish my winner's medal from 1999, I've yet to start in an FA Cup Final and there is still a huge yearning in me to fulfil that ambition by taking to the pitch at kick-off time in the biggest domestic cup game in the world.

The silence in the dressing room was broken by Alex Ferguson asking Barthez to explain why he hadn't come charging off his line, and we all accepted the fact he had done it his way. Even if Fabien had made a mad dash to close down Di Canio, probably the Italian would have slipped the ball past him anyway. There was no blame attached, I was too fed up to blame anyone. I just wanted to get out of there.

We had only three days before getting back to Premiership action and that helped us quickly to snap out of the FA Cup blues. We had a tough trip to Sunderland, who at the time were making a real charge and were being talked about as title contenders.

Their manager, Peter Reid, built his playing career on a reputation for biting people's ankles and hassling the big names out of their rhythm before picking up the pieces and playing simple football. His Sunderland side have been created from the same mould. The tackles come flying in and you have to be alert to ensure you're not left in a crumpled heap on the floor with a set of studs embedded in your ankles. I'm not having a go at their style of play – those are the tactics which work best for them – and, anyway, I love playing in physically rough games.

You just have to be strong in mind and body to make sure their intimidation washes over you and at United those qualities are something we have in abundance. The game was great to play in, a real battle that spilled over when Andy Cole was sent off for going toe-to-toe with Sunderland's Alex Rae. The pair had got into a heated confrontation throughout the match and when Andy scored the winner it looked like he'd had the last laugh.

Earlier Michael Gray had been sent off for dissent and then Graham Poll ruined Cole's night by ordering off the striker and Rae after one heated tussle too many. The constant aggravation from Rae finally took its toll and, unfortunately for Andy – even though later he appealed to the referee to change his decision – it meant a ban which was to keep him out of action for a large chunk of March.

By now I was back in the swing of things after my injury and pleased to hear that my defensive partner, Wes Brown, had been tipped to captain England. Wes has such great future ahead of him and I'll be amazed if he doesn't become a long-term fixture in the national side. At the time of writing he's only 21 and that's very young for a central defender. I didn't come into my own until my mid-twenties, so to have so much experience behind him when he's a relative baby in footballing terms is going to help Wes blossom into one of the very best. The pair of us love keeping clean sheets. It's a test of our effectiveness as much as scoring goals proves the deadliness of strikers.

Our next examination came against Everton at Old Trafford on the first day of February, when Walter Smith's side sat blatantly behind the ball and invited us to open them up. We managed it only once through Cole's deflected shot which was heading wide before leaping up off the heel of Steve Watson and foxing the keeper. I read later that we didn't have a shot on target and it has to be the only match I remember winning without having a strike on goal. How bizarre is that! We just couldn't break through and I was bored shitless thanks to their tactics. They seemed happy to go home without a point, as long as that meant they hadn't endured a thrashing.

Unlike Everton, Chelsea aren't the kind of side who will settle happily for a goalless draw and my Dutch international colleague Jimmy Floyd Hasselbaink made sure that didn't happen in our clash at Stamford Bridge. Jimmy capitalised on Paul Scholes' weak headed back-pass by getting a touch to nod past our stand-in keeper Raimond van der Gouw. He could have had a clincher but for a brilliant tackle by Mikael Silvestre which stopped his run on goal. We survived that scare and then started to dominate the game. Cole levelled but we couldn't force the winner, which would have claimed revenge for the previous season's 5–0 hammering.

Hasselbaink had a great season at Chelsea after returning to the Premiership from Spanish side Atletico Madrid, and that doesn't surprise me. He's found the net consistently in a side which has not always been at its best, and finished the season as the Premiership's top scorer. That's down to Jimmy's great eye for goal and the fact that he's a clinical finisher, something I've found out during training sessions with the national team.

Jimmy's an easy guy to get on with and he loves a joke, never more so than when he's stuck a goal past my team. But despite his desperation to get one up on me, I wasn't taking extra steps to stop him scoring. I don't care who I play against, whether it's

Kluivert, Ronaldo or a Third Division forward I've never heard of, I work just as intensely to make sure they leave the field without being able to claim they've put one over on me.

Our upsetting early exit from the FA Cup allowed us a weekend off to concentrate on the Champions League double header with Valencia. The Spanish side were definitely the surprise package in the previous year's competition when they made it all the way to the final before being beaten by Real Madrid.

Now Valencia had lost some of their stars, with the speed of Claudio Lopez being employed to spice up Lazio's attack and the guile of Gerard prompting Barcelona's midfield, but overall Hector Cuper's side were probably just as strong.

They brought massive Norwegian striker John Carew into their attack and could even afford to leave the experienced French World Cup winner Didier Deschamps on the sidelines because of their strength in midfield.

During the previous season we drew at their place, and beat them 3–0 at Old Trafford at the same stage of the competition. This year we couldn't beat them. We drew 0–0 at a rain-soaked Mestalla Stadium and unfortunately didn't fare much better when the Spanish side came to England, this time being held 1–1 following a late own goal by Wes Brown.

Interestingly, we didn't perform at our best against Valencia despite having the weekend break. For years our manager has called for more help in rescheduling the fixture list when we play in Europe. Most teams we face have the weekend off before the game, whereas United have to deal with 90 minutes of blood and thunder against a Premiership side desperate to turn us over.

Yet having seven days between the two Valencia games didn't seem to make a big difference to us, contrary to what Ferguson seemed to believe. Maybe we need the impetus from a weekend game to catapult us into European action. Maybe we carry over the fight and passion from the Premiership into the Champions League and that's what made us so successful.

On this occasion we struggled to find a rhythm or tempo to our play and allowed the Spanish side an easy passage throughout a game which they might have expected to be far more tempestuous.

The lads wanted desperately to put things right in our next League outing, against Arsenal. Here was a chance to gain a badly needed shot of confidence and kill off the Gunners' chances of catching us in the title race once and for all. We all knew the importance of the match, and realised that we had not been playing well. What we didn't expect was a monumental bollocking from Ferguson even before kick-off.

'You were shocking against Valencia,' he laid into us. 'I still can't believe how bad you really were. I have never seen a United team lack passion in the way you did. If you keep going like that we'll never win anything. It has to change, and it has to change today. Lets go out there and see these guys off. Do them today, knock them out of the title race and let's get our form back on track.'

By half-time, he wasn't so irate! We demolished them in the first period with Dwight Yorke playing out of his skin, grabbing a hat-trick and tearing apart an Arsenal defence in a way no other striker has in recent memory. Dwight had their defender Igor Stepanovs on his backside time and again as we ran riot to lead 5–1.

We couldn't keep the pace up after that remarkable first 45 minutes but it didn't matter, we finished that Sunday with an improbable six goals against a team second in the table. That result, more than any other, shows just how much we dominated the Premiership.

We were especially delighted for Dwight, whose season had been turning slowly into a nightmare. Poor Yorkie was always either injured or away on international duty and that meant he never had a regular run in the side. It's so hard to find your best form when you play one week and sit on the bench the next. You can't find a rhythm to your play. As a striker, goals are crucial to build confidence and after this match Dwight was brimming with it.

Arsenal had a couple of big guns missing, Tony Adams and Martin Keown, but the guys replacing them just couldn't handle the high tempo of our play. We came out of the traps with such pace and power that our opponents could not perform with any composure, and that's been one of Manchester United's trademarks over the three years I have been at the club.

Every season the Gunners represent one of our toughest conflicts and to walk off the pitch having thrashed them 6–1 was a major surprise to me. Normally the games are tight affairs, decided by one mistake or one moment of brilliance. This match was the opposite. They made errors galore and Dwight punished them with as clinical a display of finishing as I've ever seen.

Our lack of consistency struck again, though, and we couldn't repeat our form at Leeds. In the end we were lucky to walk away with a point from a 1–1 draw. Fabien was booked while giving away a penalty by kicking out at Ian Harte when the defender upset him by using an elbow as he jumped for a cross. The Frenchman saved the spot-kick, but after Luke Chadwick scored for us, Mark Viduka equalised with a header. Then Wes touched home a cross but what looked like being a decisive own goal was disallowed controversially for offside. In the end we were glad to hear the final whistle as David O'Leary's side put us under pressure.

Probably Leeds weren't at their best, either, but they came strong later in the season with a great run in the League and a fantastic campaign in Europe which took them to the semi-finals of the Champions League. O'Leary has fashioned a young side full of players seemingly willing to die for each other and who display a hunger to win games which should see them become a major challenger to United over the next few years.

We had the same qualities in our treble-winnig season and if they can keep that passion alive we'll have to watch out for our rivals from across the Pennines, both domestically and on the European front.

Our poor run continued at Panathinaikos in early March, when we were lucky to get out of Greece with a 1–1 draw. They used deep-lying strikers who were almost impossible to get to grips with, and we needed Fabien to save us time and again. Even he couldn't keep the Greeks out all night and we were indebted to Paul Scholes for a late, late equaliser which saved some face, if it did not prevent another blast from the manager.

Our form had dipped so disappointingly that Ferguson went as far to say, before the clash with Sturm Graz, that we were an embarrassment in Europe. It was a cutting statement designed to hit home, and it hurt. There was even a chance we could go out of the competition if the Austrians beat us 3–0.

A shock result of those proportions was never going to happen and duly we put three past them, cruising into the knockout stage where once again we were drawn against our old foes Bayern Munich. It could have been worse: Real Madrid were still in the competition and their Spanish rivals, Deportivo La Coruna, had come from 3–0 down at home to beat Paris St Germain in the group stage and were looking dangerous. Arsenal and Leeds had won through to the last eight, too, and were in the other half of the draw, adding to the growing anticipation of an all-English final.

It's only when we get to the knockout rounds of the Champions League that the competition truly comes alive. Far too often in the early stages we play games simply to make up the numbers for television.

No player wants to be involved in meaningless matches and, I'm happy to say, at United we don't have many of them in a season. To go through the motions in games which have no impact on the final outcome of the group is tedious. You can tell the difference in atmosphere when it's the knockout stage; the players, fans, and just about everyone else have an extra spring in their step. The excitement of the cup is back and that is something UEFA should concentrate on when they restructure the tournament in 2003. Certainly, fewer teams and not as many group games would be a start.

We went into the rematch with Bayern ignoring all the ridiculous hype about the Germans seeking revenge. That was rubbish. Bayern may have some bad memories after our late goals in Barcelona tore the Champions League trophy from their grasp in 1999. But that wouldn't make them run faster, it wouldn't make them tackle harder or shoot straighter. This match was the quarter-final of the biggest club tournament in the world and nobody on either side needed additional motivation.

United dominated the opening half of the first leg at Old Trafford without creating too many chances, and as the game wore on the Germans gained the upper hand before striking with minutes left. A Stefan Effenberg free-kick was flicked on by Alexander Zickler for Paulo Sergio to touch home at the far post. It was a terrible goal to concede and we knew it. The manager knew it as well.

'What the fuck was going on at the end?' he blasted as we walked into the dressing room. 'Why the hell were you all ball-watching? That's schoolboy stuff. Who was meant to be picking up Paulo Sergio's run?

'And why didn't you all drop off to fill the space when he won that header. I can't believe that a team with so many internationals in it was caught out like that. Absolutely fucking shocking.'

Probably Ferguson realised there and then that we were struggling, failing to create chances, and when we got sloppy at the back it sent him over the edge. He was livid.

He couldn't say it in public, but the domestic title race was over. We'd pretty much won it by Christmas and it was just a matter of when we would take the crown. With that in mind, Ferguson decided to concentrate solely on turning around the 1–0 deficit and saving our European season. We arrived at training the day after the Bayern game and he called us into the Carrington dressing room and hatched his plan.

'We've got two games before we meet Bayern again and everything we do from now on will be tailored towards how we're going to play in Munich,' he announced. 'I want us to be far more direct and create chances. We haven't done enough of that in recent weeks and that's got to change.

'We need two goals in Germany and although it's not going to be easy breaking them down, on the law of averages the more opportunities we get the better chance there is we'll score. From now on I don't want to see square passes. Everything has to go forward and quickly; we have to catch teams on the break.'

The new system worked a treat against Charlton, whom we beat 2–0, and Coventry also suffered as our pressure play wore them down so that they conceded late goals in our 4–2 victory. That win took its time coming as Gordon Strachan's men made us work harder for the points than any side in the previous couple of months.

They chased everything, closed us down, and pressured the man on the ball. It paid off. John Hartson scored two as Wes struggled to keep him away from goal and we had to come from behind to win. It was a case of using our heads and being patient.

Because of the vast amount of energy they were consuming in harassing us on the ball, we knew that Coventry would eventually tire and then we could take control. But at half-time, with the scores level, we had to do some reshuffling in the dressing room.

'I think it'd be better if Jaap took Hartson,' Ferguson said.

'It's tricky, Boss, because he's sticking on the right side of the pitch and that's Wes' area,' I replied.

'Well you and Wes swap over. Let Wes play on the left for a while and then he'll be in your area of the pitch.'

We swapped and so did John. It was an obvious chalkboard tactic from Strachan, who wanted Hartson to use his height and physical power to barge in front of a younger player. It was a tough afternoon for Brown but something he'll learn from after a look at Steve McClaren's videotapes from the match.

The game was a morning kick-off and winning had given us an outside chance of lifting the title that day. Arsenal were playing Middlesbrough in the afternoon and a win for Terry Venables' side would hand us the Premiership. Boro had struggled all season and were only just above the relegation zone, so no-one really expected them to win at Fortress Highbury. I drove home to my wife expecting the title race to go on for one more week at least.

But watching the scores come in on teletext, I realised suddenly that a shock was on the cards as Boro went two up through own-goals. Dutch television was showing the match live so I switched on my satellite service and tuned in. I couldn't believe my eyes as Arsenal not only failed to launch a comeback, but conceded another goal.

To everyone's surprise, the title race was over. Even the TV presenters seemed embarrassed by the lack of pomp and circumstance. Ellis had been watching the match and she turned and hugged me before heading to the fridge to hook out a bottle of champagne we had on ice. The cork popped and we drank to another medal in the Stam cabinet.

'Well done,' she said. 'I always knew that coming here would be a good idea.'

'Yeah, but it feels like an anti-climax,' I confided to her. 'Last season we were on the pitch at Southampton and had a party. All the lads were there and we celebrated in style. This year just look at us! A glass of champagne each and then it's time to cook tea for the kids. We haven't even got a babysitter!'

The short-sighted television coverage of English football had ruined it for us. I can't understand why they would change the schedules and miss out on the chance to show us winning the title live.

They had us playing at odd hours all year to satisfy their need to keep United on screen and the policy caught them out when it mattered most. It seems like madness and I bet they don't do it again.

We did party as a team the next day in training – for all of five minutes while the cameras took pictures of us opening champagne as the chants of 'Champions' rang out. But a wet and windy training field on a Sunday is hardly the way a title as important as the Premiership should be celebrated. Sky, take note.

With the title tucked away we headed to Germany, and despite it being a daunting place to win, we were full of confidence. Ferguson's plan looked to be paying off. We'd had 48 shots in our two previous matches and we couldn't believe that kind of pressure wouldn't pay off. Despite the absence of the suspended David Beckham, I felt our direct system of play would cause too many problems for the Germans.

'Whatever you do, don't lose an early goal. Keep it tight,' was Ferguson's last wish as we walked out of the dressing room.

What do we go and do? Four minutes on the clock and we're one down after a cross from Michael Tarnat on the left skidded across our penalty area and Elber got in front of Wes to fire home. It was another goal we could and should have avoided. Our organisation was all at sea with too much space on our right before the ball was played into the box.

That strike was a major blow but it was not the killer one. With away goals counting double we would have to score twice to go through anyway, so nothing had changed.

It did five minutes before half-time, though, when Jens Jeremies surged into our box and centred for Elber to touch the ball into Mehmet Scholl's path for the midfielder to strike the winner. Then we knew it would be difficult.

'We've made it hard for ourselves but we can still do it,' Roy Keane urged at the interval. 'Remember Juventus, we were two down there and won the game. You can't tell me this lot are any better than them. Let's get our fingers out and do something about it. There's 45 minutes to go and plenty can change.'

Within minutes of the restart Ryan Giggs popped up on a late run into the box and lifted the ball into the net past Oliver Kahn. We were back in it, but the expected cavalry charge never came. We couldn't break down their back-line and although Teddy Sheringham had a late chance I sensed there was not going to be a repeat of 1999 this time.

There was silence in the dressing room. No rows, no tearing strips off each other, just silence. No-one talked because there was nothing to say. Our season was over. There was the same sick feeling which had depressed me when Real had knocked us out at the same stage the year before.

I wanted to rip the door off its hinges, run out on to the pitch and play the game again. It's hard to accept defeat when the stakes are so high and you've already sampled the taste of winning.

To make it worse the defeat ruined the high we were on after winning the Premiership. The way we were forced to celebrate that without any real fanfare rankled with me and any remaining feelings of championship joy had been wiped away by going out of Europe.

The whole season had felt flat for me and it ended on a similar note. That was never more evident than during my first Manchester derby. I had missed the clash at Maine Road because of injury, but I had been looking forward to sampling the atmosphere at Old Trafford. Ever since I'd joined United, people had talked about this game and how much it meant to both sides.

I'd missed Denis Irwin's testimonial between the two sides in pre-season, which had been quite a tasty affair with Danny Tiatto diving into several tackles on David Beckham and Gary Neville catching Mark Kennedy before George Weah's tackle forced Irwin to limp off.

I was looking forward to a battle but I was to be disappointed. We were still down after losing to Bayern and City were relieved that, although they were still in deep trouble at the foot of the table, at least they didn't have to worry about being relegated if we beat them on the day. If that had happened, United would have been returning a compliment after 27 years. Denis Law, a former Red and one of the greatest players in United history, had backheeled the winner for City at Old Trafford in 1974 on the day United had tumbled into the Second Division.

Blues fans had lived off that moment for a long time and it would have been nice to give our supporters something to throw back at them, other than all the medals we've picked up in the past few seasons, that is.

Old Trafford was lifeless that day, though, and maybe because it was yet another of those ridiculous morning kick-offs, the supercharged atmosphere I was expecting didn't materialise. It didn't help, either, that City played with no real passion or desire to take us on. They went man for man all over the pitch and let Gary Neville and myself have the ball at will at the back.

At times when they cleared a corner they didn't even have a player outside their own penalty area. We were sucked into their sluggish style and once again we didn't produce. Indeed, we nearly went behind in the opening minutes as a deflected shot hit the bar and I cleared off the line as the tricky Paulo Wanchope burst past Fabien.

But slowly we picked up our pace and after Scholes missed one penalty, Sheringham took command and scored from a second – that is once he'd fought off a determined challenge from Barthez to nick the ball and place it on the spot. We were coasting when, uncharacteristically, we let a corner bounce in the box and Steve Howey touched home a late equaliser. That summed up our day.

Even that strike failed to enliven the sedate atmosphere, although Keane's thigh-high tackle on Alfie Haaland certainly did. Our skipper was shown the eighth red card of his United career and the media went to town on him. His foot was high and it's hard to defend Roy over it, but I think it was all down to his determination to win and frustration at not seeing off a City side we all knew were nowhere near as good as us.

The incident happened during a spell when Keane was in the headlines on a daily basis over his views on why United hadn't succeeded in Europe that season. In his captain's role, Roy spoke to the cameras after the Bayern Munich defeat and let his depression at losing the game get the better of him. He claimed that United weren't good enough in Europe and that the team should be rebuilt.

A week or so later he was plastered over the back pages again under the headline 'Why it's all gone wrong at United'. He said: 'I have seen United players getting complacent, thinking they've done it all and getting carried away by a bit of success. All you have to do is drop your standards by five or ten per cent and it's obvious, especially in Europe, that you can carry maybe one player, but no more than that.

'You can see it in training when players just go through the motions. You can't do that, you always have to give your best. It's up to the manager to spot it. Maybe I'll help him, but ultimately the only person who can sort it out is the player himself. Real desire has to come from within.

'We really have to be careful not to think that our success, and us as a team, is going to go on and on. We really have to start dominating Europe as well as the Premiership. Sometimes you don't realise it; maybe it's already coming to the end. I'm not being over-dramatic.'

Certainly they were hard-hitting words but, dangerous as it is,

I have to disagree with Keane. In 1999 we were the best in Europe, and although we didn't reach the same heights during 2000/2001, we did not become a poor side all of a sudden.

We won the Premiership in record time, for Christ's sake. It's a league which no less a figure than Marcel Desailly claims is the hardest in Europe to win, and he should know. The French international has played in Italy and is well placed to talk about the toughest of title races.

I would claim that we are still one of the top three sides in Europe at the moment. It's just that we haven't been at our best on a consistent basis and that has cost us. I would challenge any outfit in Europe to stand up to us on the day we put six past Arsenal. Unfortunately there haven't been enough performances like that.

Why? Well it's partly down to players being off-key on the occasional day and partly down to teams coming to United and shutting up shop. Some of the best tactical minds in Europe have analysed our play, and we noticed in the early stages of the Champions League that we weren't getting the space we did in the previous couple of seasons.

David Beckham was being marked heavily and he was forced to drop deeper to pick up the ball. In contrast, during our treble-winning campaign, he was producing brilliant crosses from the right, like the two he supplied for Dwight Yorke to score twice against Inter Milan at Old Trafford. More recently, that zone of the pitch has been packed with bodies.

When Liverpool beat us at Old Trafford they played their wide midfielders, Danny Murphy and Nick Barmby, just in front of the full-backs to block any attempts from Beckham and Giggs to exploit the space. It wasn't just a case of a team hauling ten men behind the ball; obviously the position of players had been worked on in training as the system was carried out with military precision.

The stalling tactics didn't always come off and the large majority of visitors to Old Trafford left without a point, despite having a similar game-plan. But the better teams, with players boasting stronger technical skills, could put the strategy into action and often they frustrated us.

Of course, we talked about it; we aren't dumb. We knew what teams were doing and that the only way to break through was to employ a more direct style. We needed to deliver the ball into dangerous areas just in front of their full-backs and then get in behind their defenders more quickly. Then teams wouldn't have time to return to the rigid shape which was denying us space.

But we weren't running like the well-oiled machine of the previous seasons. In the past, things just happened. The ball reached Beckham or Giggs or Scholes, and then someone was in on goal in the blink of an eye. We didn't have to think about it. In 2000/2001, with so many opponents behind the ball, there was always a spanner in the works.

Roy Keane talked about complacency seeping into our game, and I don't know who he's pointing the finger at, but I've definitely not noticed a slackening off in training. No-one's pulling out of tackles, playing the superstar on the pitch, or hiding at the back when it comes to lung-busting runs.

This United team is as committed as ever to winning another European Cup and is just as hungry, if not more so, as when I first joined. Back then the magical feeling of winning the top club prize was just a mystery, a fantasy in our heads. Now we've felt it we know there is nothing better. It is like a drug and we want more of it.

Losing at the quarter-final stage in two successive seasons has made me even more determined to win it again. We know that if we don't get to the final every year we're going to be considered failures, and that's one of the fears driving us on at United. We don't want to be seen as failures.

The players in our team are not past it. It's not as though we've got a bunch of guys hoping for one last shot at the Champions League before hanging up their boots. At the time of writing, during the summer of 2001, the likes of David Beckham, Paul Scholes and Gary Neville are all 26 while I am only 29.

There's been no talk in the dressing room of people wanting to leave. I can't remember one player saying that he fancied getting out and trying his luck at another club. The quality of the guys we have here means they could walk into most other sides in Europe, but we're not quitters at Old Trafford.

This is not a team ready to be broken up, but a side needing a couple of additions to help freshen the squad. We did that the summer I was brought in along with Dwight Yorke and Jesper Blomqvist, as United spent nearly £28 million and went on to win the treble.

Ferguson has admitted that he needs three players and, as I write, two of those have arrived, Juan Sebastien Veron, and my former PSV team-mate Ruud van Nistelrooy. He nearly joined the club a year earlier, but a knee problem was spotted in his medical and, unfortunately for him, he suffered a nasty ligament tear soon afterwards.

Obviously I know all about Ruud from playing alongside him in the PSV team. He's proved himself in Holland and I believe he can repeat his success at a top club like United, although he might find it harder to maintain his Dutch League form as the opposition in England is so much stronger.

However, he is a striker who could reach the same high standard as Cole or Yorke if given the chance. In fact, he's probably as near a combination of all the strikers at United as anyone could wish to find in one man. His finishing is like Solskjaer's, that is straightforward, with no fancy stuff. He blasts the ball at goal and watches it smash into the back of the net. In addition, Ruud can hold up play like Sheringham and is brilliant at losing his marker and finding the net like Cole and Yorke.

I am certain that Van Nistelrooy's arrival will help us, but claims that we must have new players to stop the current crop slacking on the pitch are unbelievable. The idea that if we have a big name sat on the bench then Keane or Beckham will look at the dugout and increase their work rate is a joke. Just look at Roy on the pitch; he's a man possessed in every game. And then watch David work up and down the flank; he never gives less than 100 per cent.

We've got cover in nearly every position anyway, and the guys most frequently on the bench, like Ole Gunnar Solskjaer and Nicky Butt, would walk into most teams in Europe.

Having new faces does freshen up a side, though, and I think that factor, rather than the need to put pressure on the starting line-up, is more important when considering whether we need more signings. Certainly new arrivals offer the fans a bit more excitement, and discussions about who might come have started, even in our dressing room. But it's merely a bit of fun and only the manager knows which guys he's after.

I wonder how many new team-mates I'll have when I get back from my holidays. Enough, I hope, to start another attack on the Champions League. I must win that trophy again. It's the biggest club prize and is now the goal I set for myself every season.

Winning the Premiership is never going to be enough for me now. I want to prove I'm part of the best team in the world. We don't want to be second best here at United and in 2001/2002 I have no intention of letting that happen.

The feeling in the dressing room is that we want that treble again!

Statistics

Born:	Kampen Holland	
Date of Birth:	17 July 1972	
Height:	6ft 3in	
Weight:	14.0st	

Previous clubs

Season	*Team*	*appearances/goals*
1992/1993	FC Zwolle	32/1
1993/1994	Cambuur	33/1
1994/1995	Cambuur	33/2
1995/1996	Willen II	19/1

PSV Eindhoven

1995/1996	Eredivisie (Premiership)	14(1)/1
	Amstel Cup (FA Cup)	4
	Champions League	0
	Total	18(1)/1
1996/1997	Eredivisie	33(2)/6
	Amstel Cup	2
	Champions League	4
	Total	39(2)/6
1997/1998	Eredivisie	29(2)/4
	Amstel Cup	6
	UEFA Champions League	5
	Total	40(2)/4

Manchester United

1998/1999	Premiership	30/1
	FA Cup	6(1)
	Champions League	13
	Charity Shield	1
	Total	50(1)/1
1999/2000	Premiership	33
	Champions League	13
	Charity Shield	1
	European Super Cup	1
	Inter-Continental Cup	1
	Club World Championship	2
	Total	51(0)/0
2000/2001	Premiership	15
	FA Cup	1
	Champions League	6
	Charity Shield	0(1)
	Total	22(1)/0

Total appearances/goals by competition

Premiership	78(0)/1
FA Cup	7(1)
Champions League	32
Charity Shield	2(1)
European Super Cup	1
Inter-Continental Cup	1
Club World Championship	2
Total	123(2)/1

Holland
Debut: 1996
Appearances: 39
Goals: 3

Bracketed figures refer to substitute appearances
All statistics correct to end of season 2000/2001

Index